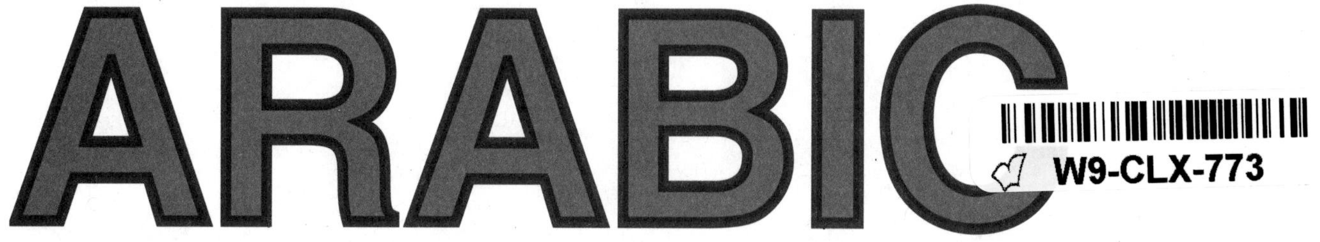

ARABIC

in 10 minutes a day®

Author: Kristine K. Kershul

Consultant: Amina Moujtahid, M.A., Mohamed V University, Rabat, Morocco

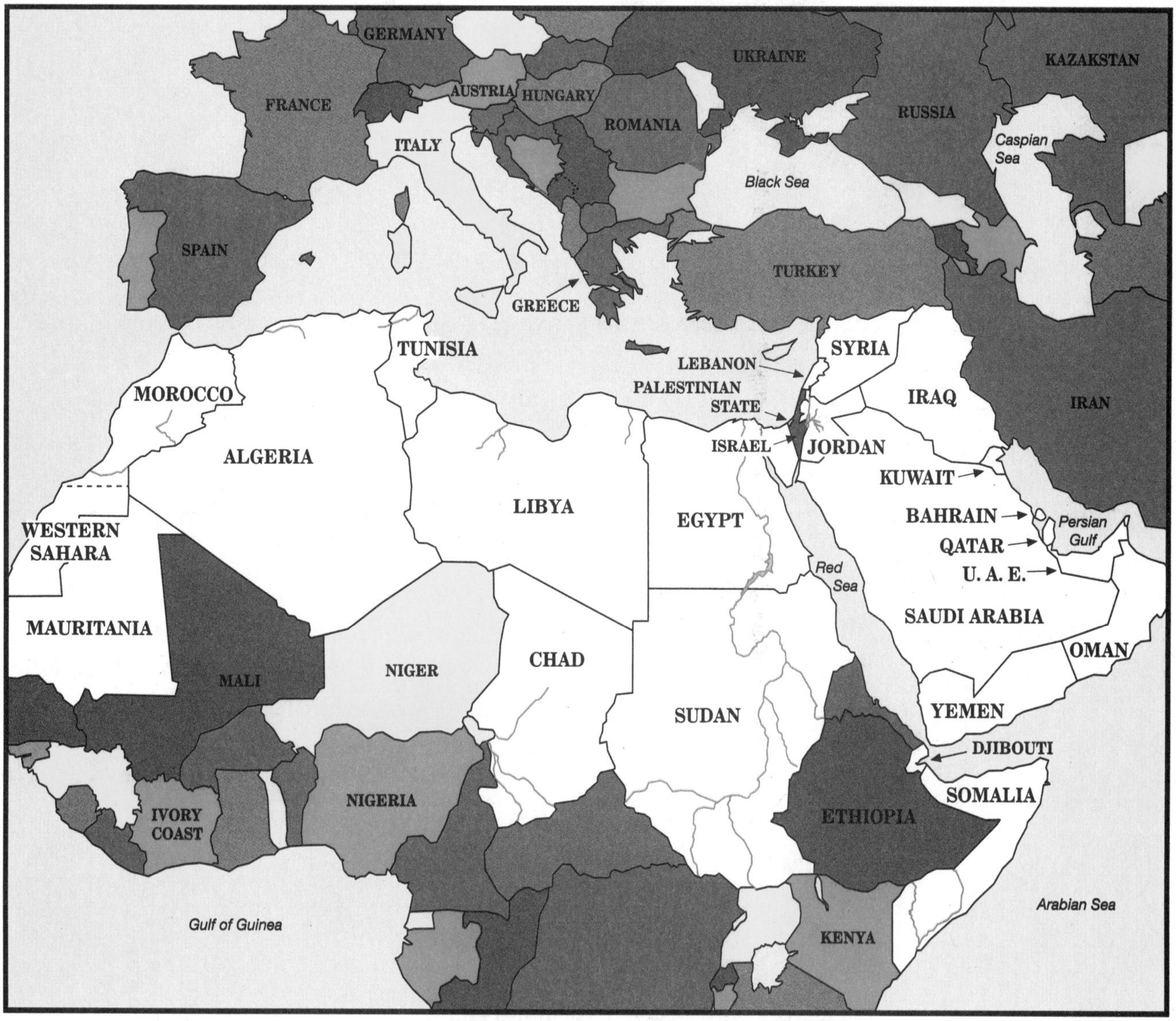

Bilingual Books, Inc.

1719 West Nickerson Street, Seattle, WA 98119

Tel: (206) 284-4211 • Fax: (206) 284-3660

www.10minutesaday.com

ISBN-13: 978-0-944502-40-2 ISBN-10: 0-944502-40-7

Can you say this?

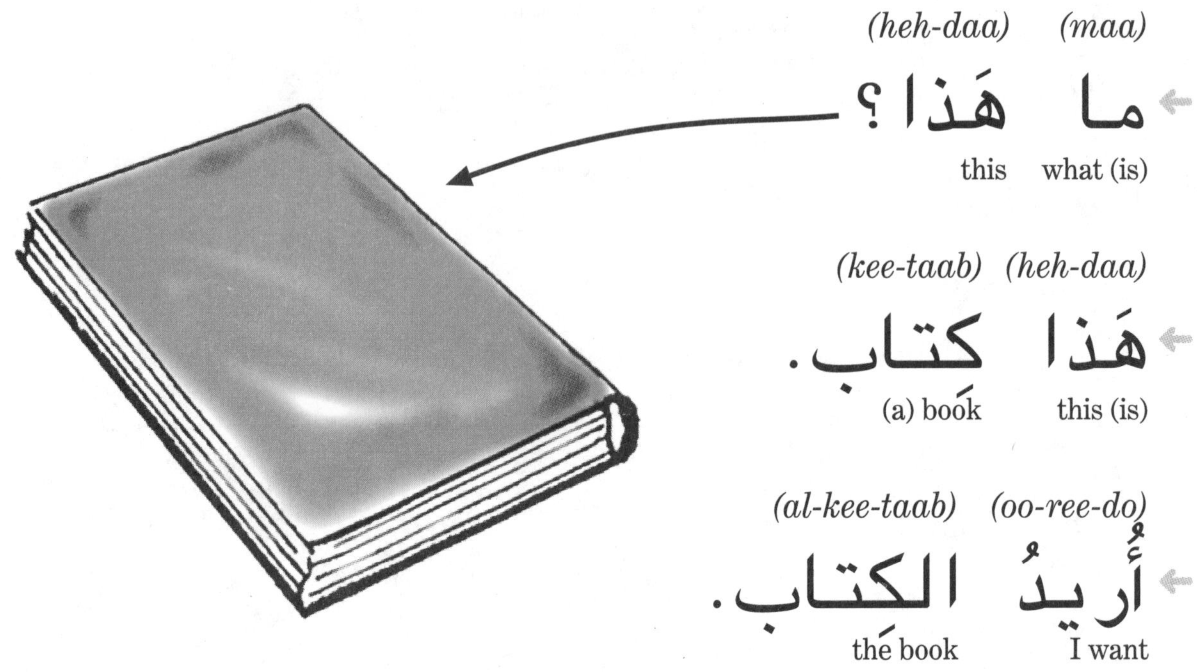

(heh-daa) (maa)
ما هَذا؟
this what (is)
(kee-taab) (heh-daa)
هَذا كتاب.
(a) book this (is)
(al-kee-taab) (oo-ree-do)
أُريدُ الكتاب.
the book I want

If you can say this, you can learn to speak Arabic. You will be able to easily order meals, concert tickets, snacks, or anything else you wish. With your best Arabic accent you simply ask *(heh-daa) (maa)* “ما هَذا؟” and, upon learning what it is, you can order it with *(heh-daa) (oo-ree-do)* “أُريدُ هَذا.” Sounds easy, doesn't it?

The purpose of this book is to give you an **immediate** speaking ability in Arabic. Using the acclaimed “*10 minutes a day®*” methodology, you will acquire a large working vocabulary that will suit your needs, and you will acquire it almost automatically. To aid you, this book offers a unique and easy system of pronunciation above each word which walks you through learning Arabic. Just remember, you read Arabic from right to left. Look for the blue arrows (←) as they will help you develop this habit. Remember to read the English phonetics and the English subscripts from left to right as usual!

If you are planning a trip or moving to where Arabic is spoken, you will be leaps ahead of everyone if you take just a few minutes a day to learn the easy key words and phrases that this book offers. Start with Step 1 and don't skip around. Each day work as far as you can comfortably go in those 10 minutes. Don't overdo it. Some days you might want to just review. If you forget a word, you can always look it up in the glossary. Spend your first 10 minutes studying the map on the previous page. And yes, have fun learning your new language.

As you work through the Steps, always use the special features which only the “*10 minutes a day®*” Series offers. This Series includes sticky labels and flash cards, puzzles and quizzes. Plus, when you have completed the book, cut out the menu guide at the back and take it along on your trip.

١/1 Alphabet

When you first see words like كِتاب and مِصر Arabic can appear forbidding. However, Arabic is a logical language once you learn how to decode these letters and you remember to read from right to left. A wide variety of regional Arabic dialects is spoken. Key is that you learn the standard Arabic presented in this book, and at the same time are prepared for variations in pronunciation depending upon where your travels take you.

In these letters, the dots are the only way to differentiate one letter from another.

(q) (f)	(z) (r)	(sh) (s)	(n) (b)	(varies) (‘)
ق ف	ز ر	ش س	ن ب	غ ع
(Th) (T)	**(D) (ss)**	**(th/d) (d)**	**(ee) (aa/ah)**	**(varies) (H) (zh)**
ظ ط	ض ص	ذ د	ي ى	خ ح ج

Vowels in Arabic look like dashes or symbols above or below the Arabic letters. These vowels make it easier for you to pronounce Arabic. Later when you are more comfortable with the language you will not need them anymore.

	(kee-taab)	(ee/ih)		(foon-dooq)	(oo)		(bahnk)	(ah/eh)
________	كِتاب ← book	ِ	________	فُندُق ← hotel	ُ	________	بَنك ← bank	َ

Hints, Tips and Guidance:

- Sometimes we will include two sets of words as both are commonly used. It doesn't hurt to learn both!
- You will encounter masculine and feminine words indicated by (♂) and (♀).
- Some Arabic letters do not connect with the following letter. Don't let it surprise you.
- When you see the letter "r" or "L" or "n" in the phonetics, pronounce the letter just as you would if you were spelling out a word in English.
- You will see some English words in parentheses underneath the Arabic. This indicates there isn't a corresponding Arabic word for the English.

ّ	a marker doubling (lengthening) the sound of the letter
ة / ـة	pronounced *"ah"* except when linked to the next word and pronounced *"t"*
ً	a special ending with the pronunciation *"ahn"*
(la) لا	the combination of لا = ا + ل ←

Certain combinations of letters and vowels will create completely different sounds than you might anticipate. Just try to learn the words as you see them and eventually these patterns will emerge.

On the next page you will find a listing of all Arabic letters in Arabic alphabetical order. Many Arabic letters change their appearance depending upon whether they are at the beginning of a word, the middle or the end. Practice, practice, practice and then practice some more!

Carefully designed phonetics appear above each word to help you learn to pronounce the Arabic. Sometimes the phonetics may seem to contradict this pronunciation guide. Don't panic. The easiest and best possible phonetics have been chosen for each individual word. Pronounce the phonetics just as you seen them. Don't over-analyze them. Speak with an Arabic accent and, above all, enjoy yourself.

English Sound	Arabic Final	Arabic Medial	Arabic Initial	Arabic Letter
ah / eh / aa	ـا	ـا	ا	ا
b	ـب	ـبـ	بـ	ب
t	ـت	ـتـ	تـ	ت
th (as in *think*)	ـث	ـثـ	ثـ	ث
zh / j	ـج	ـجـ	جـ	ج
H ①	ـح	ـحـ	حـ	ح
h / hk / kh ②	ـخ	ـخـ	خـ	خ
d	ـد	ـد	د	د
th (as in *this*) / d	ـذ	ـذ	ذ	ذ
r (rolled)	ـر	ـر	ر	ر
z	ـز	ـز	ز	ز
s	ـس	ـسـ	سـ	س
sh	ـش	ـشـ	شـ	ش
ss (strong)	ـص	ـصـ	صـ	ص
D (emphatic d)	ـض	ـضـ	ضـ	ض
T (emphatic t)	ـط	ـطـ	طـ	ط
Th (emphatic th)	ـظ	ـظـ	ظـ	ظ
' ③ / almost an "r" sound	ـع	ـعـ	عـ	ع
gh / gr / r ④	ـغ	ـغـ	غـ	غ
f	ـف	ـفـ	فـ	ف
q / k ⑤	ـق	ـقـ	قـ	ق
k	ـك	ـكـ	كـ	ك
l	ـل	ـلـ	لـ	ل
m	ـم	ـمـ	مـ	م
n	ـن	ـنـ	نـ	ن
h	ـه	ـهـ	هـ	ه
w / oo (as in *boot*)	ـو	ـو	و	و
ee / y (as in *yes*)	ـي	ـيـ	يـ	ي
varies ⑥				ء

① strongly aspirated as if you were blowing out a candle from the back of your throat
② breathe hard, almost like gargling, or think of the *ch* in the Scottish word *loch*
③ glottal stop, like the pause in *uh-oh*
④ sound you make when you gargle
⑤ *kaw* at the back of your throat
⑥ may be a short pause like a silent musical beat

Key Question Words

When you arrive in an Arabic-speaking country such as الأردُن (al-oor-doon) Jordan, مِصر (meess-ur) Egypt, المَغرِب (al-ma-greb) Morocco or لُبنان (loob-naan) Lebanon the very first thing you will need to do is ask questions — "Where is the bus stop?" "Where can I exchange money?" "Where (أينَ) (eye-na) where is the lavatory?" "أينَ (eye-na) where is a restaurant?" "أينَ (eye-na) where is a taxi?" "أينَ (eye-na) where is a good hotel?" "أينَ (eye-na) where is my luggage?" and the list will go on and on for the entire length of your visit. In Arabic, there are many question words, but let's focus on these EIGHT KEY QUESTION WORDS. For example, the eight key question words will help you find out exactly what you are ordering in a restaurant before you order it — and not after the surprise (or shock!) arrives. Take a few minutes to study and practice saying the eight key question words listed below. Then cover العَرَبِيّة (al-r-ra-be-ya) the Arabic and fill in each of the blanks with the matching Arabic كَلمة (ka-lee-ma) word.

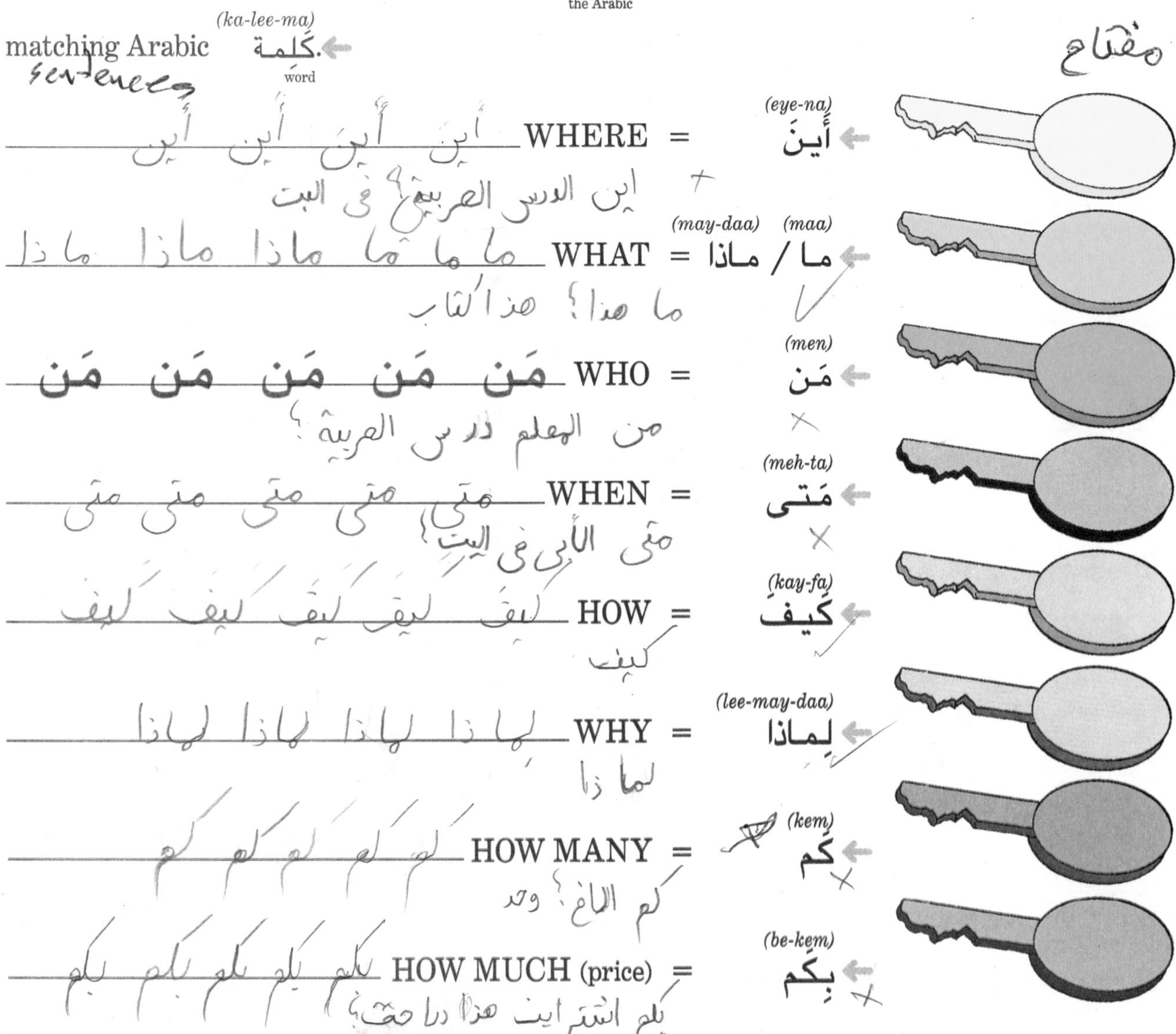

_______ WHERE = أينَ (eye-na)

_______ WHAT = ما / ماذا (maa) (may-daa)

_______ WHO = مَن (men)

_______ WHEN = مَتى (meh-ta)

_______ HOW = كَيف (kay-fa)

_______ WHY = لِماذا (lee-may-daa)

_______ HOW MANY = كَم (kem)

_______ HOW MUCH (price) = بِكَم (be-kem)

Now test yourself to see if you really can keep these (ka-lee-maat) كَلمات (words) straight in your mind. Draw lines between (al-r-ra-be-ya) العَرَبِيّة (the Arabic) and the English equivalents below.

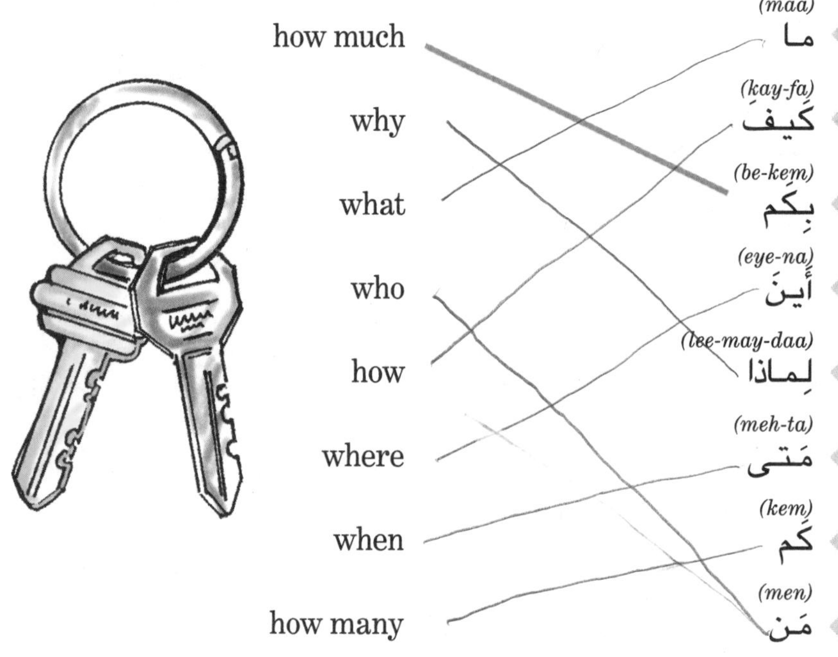

how much	(maa) ما
why	(kay-fa) كَيفَ
what	(be-kem) بِكَم
who	(eye-na) أينَ
how	(lee-may-daa) لِماذا
where	(meh-ta) مَتى
when	(kem) كَم
how many	(men) مَن

Examine the following questions containing these (ka-lee-maat) كَلمات (words). Practice the sentences out loud (wa) وَ (and) then practice by copying (al-r-ra-be-ya) العَرَبِيّة (the Arabic) in the blanks underneath each question.

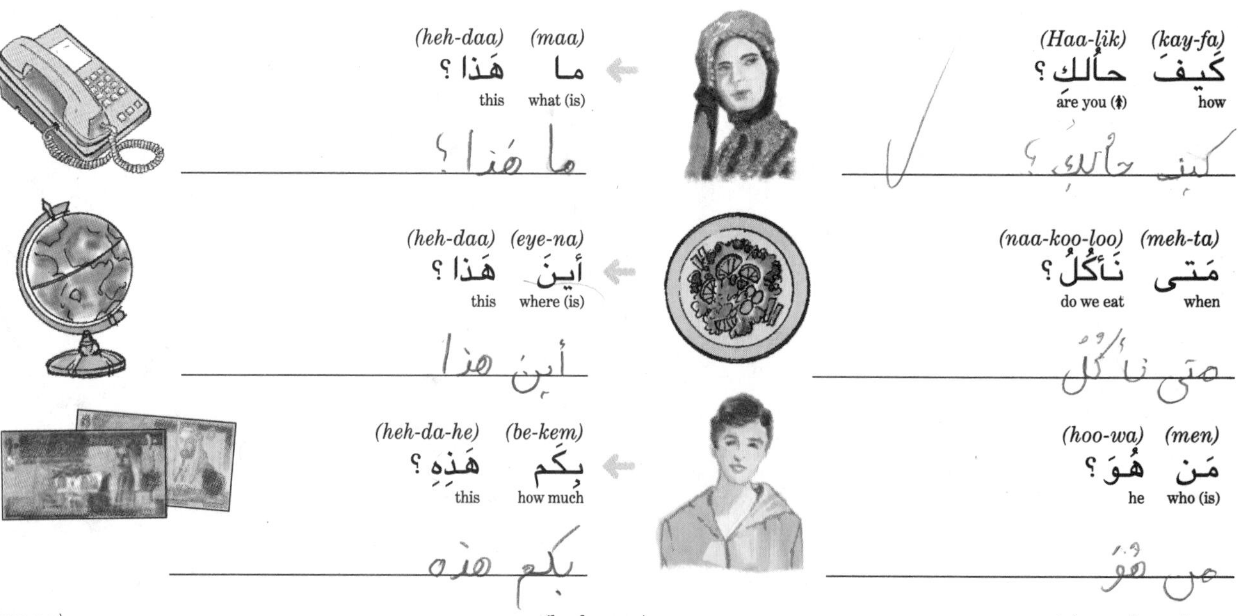

(heh-daa) (maa)
ما هَذا ؟
this what (is)

(Haa-lik) (kay-fa)
كَيفَ حالُك ؟
are you (♂) how

(heh-daa) (eye-na)
أينَ هَذا ؟
this where (is)

(naa-koo-loo) (meh-ta)
مَتى نَأكُل ؟
do we eat when

(heh-da-he) (be-kem)
بِكَم هَذِهِ ؟
this how much

(hoo-wa) (men)
مَن هُوَ ؟
he who (is)

"(eye-na) أينَ؟ (where)" will be your most used question (ka-lee-ma) كَلمة (word). Say each of the following (al-r-ra-be-ya) العَرَبِيّة (Arabic) sentences aloud. Then write out each sentence many times . This is a great way to practice your Arabic handwriting! Repeat each sentence until you are comfortable with it. The blue arrows are there to remind you to read and write from right to left!

(eye-na) أيـنَ where (is) — (al-Hahm-maam) الحَمّام ؟ the toilet / (al-meer-HaaD) المِرحاض the lavatory

(eye-na) أيـنَ where (is) — (ah-taak-see) التّاكسي؟ the taxi

(eye-na) أيـنَ where (is) — (al-Haa-fee-la) الحافِلة ؟ the bus / (al-oo-too-bees) الأوتوبيس؟ the bus

أينَ الحافلة

أينَ التّاكسي ؟

(eye-na) أيـنَ where — (al-ma-Tahm) المَطعَم ؟ the restaurant

(eye-na) أيـنَ where — (al-bahnk) البَنك ؟ the bank

(eye-na) أيـنَ where — (al-foon-dooq) الفُندُق ؟ the hotel

(na-ahm) نَعَم (yes) you can hear similarities between (al-r-ra-be-ya) العَرَبيّة (the Arabic) and (al-een-zhlee-zee-yah) الإنجليزيّة (the English). Don't let the Arabic alphabet confuse you. Just work through each word, letter by letter. Listed below are three related words built around three core letters called the root. Letters are added around the root, but the common core remains. Can you find the root in each of these words? Be sure to say each (ka-lee-ma) كَلِمة (word) aloud (wa) وَ (and) then write out (al-r-ra-be-ya) العَرَبيّة (the Arabic) in the blank to the left.

دَرَس

to study........... (da-ra-sa) .... دَرَسَ	❐
school.......... (ma-dra-sa) .... مَدرَسة	❐
lesson............. (dars) .... دَرس	❐

Additional fun (ka-lee-maat) كَلِمات (words) like these will appear at the bottom of the following pages in a yellow color band. They are easy to learn because they are related to each other–enjoy them!

٣/3 Odds 'n Ends

Arabic does not have words for "a" or "an," which makes things easier for you. The letters "ال" *(al)* in front of an Arabic word (on the right) means "the." If you do not see "ال" *(al)* in front of an Arabic word, "a" or "an" is assumed. Here are some examples.

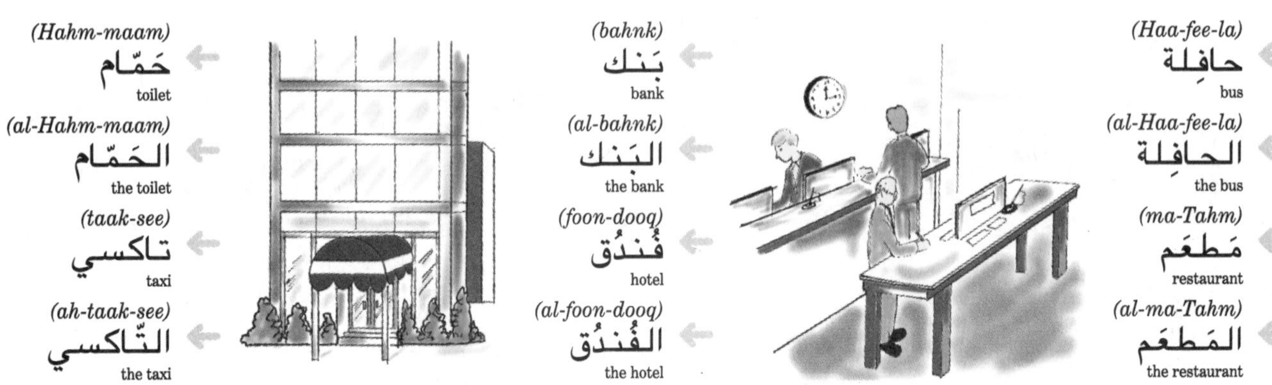

Don't be surprised – "ال" is pronounced both as *"al"* and *"ah."* Just remember the core of الكَلمة *(al-ka-lee-ma)* the word doesn't change, so you should always be able to recognize it. You will be understood whether you say بَنك *(bahnk)* bank or البَنك *(al-bahnk)* the bank. Learn to look and listen for the core of the word, and remember to read from right to left — the blue arrows (←) are there to help you.

In Step 2 you were introduced to the Eight Key Question Words. These eight words are the basics, the most essential building blocks for learning Arabic. Throughout this book you will come across keys asking you to fill in the missing question كَلمة *(ka-lee-ma)* word. Use this opportunity not only to fill in the blank on that key, but to review all your question كَلمات *(ka-lee-maat)* words. Play with the new sounds, speak slowly وَ *(wa)* and have fun.

دَرَس

☐	مُدَرِّس	teacher (♂) ....*(moo-dar-rees)*........
☐	مُدَرِّسة	teacher (♀) ....*(moo-dar-ree-sa)*.......
☐	دِراسة	studying ....*(dee-raa-sa)*...........

Look Around You

Before you proceed مَعَ (mar) with this Step, situate yourself comfortably in your living room. Now look around you. Can you name the things that you see in this غُرفة (roor-fa) room in العَرَبِيّة (al-r-ra-be-ya) Arabic? After practicing these كَلِمات (ka-lee-maat) words out loud, write them in the blanks below وَ (wa) and on the next page.

مِصباح (miss-baaH) lamp ____________

أريكة / كَنَبة (ah-ree-ka) (ka-na-ba) sofa / sofa ____________

كُرسي (koor-see) chair ____________

سَجّادة (sahzh-zheh-da) carpet ____________

طاوِلة (Taa-we-la) table ____________

باب (baab) door ____________

ساعة (saa-ra) clock ____________

سِتارة (see-taa-ra) curtain ____________

تِليفون / هاتِف (teh-lee-foon) (haa-tif) telephone ____________

نافِذة (neh-fee-da) window ____________

صورة (ssoo-ra) picture ____________

Now open your كِتاب (kee-taab) book to the sticky labels on page 17 and later on page 35. Peel off the first 11 labels وَ (wa) and proceed around your غُرفة (roor-fa) room labeling these items in your home. This will help to increase your العَرَبِيّة (al-r-ra-be-ya) Arabic word power easily. Don't forget to say الكَلِمة (al-ka-lee-ma) the word as you attach each label. Now ask yourself, "أينَ (eye-na) where الصّورة؟ (ah-ssoo-ra) the picture" and point at it while you answer, "الصّورة (ah-ssoo-ra) the picture هُنا. (hoo-naa) here (is)" Continue on down the list above until you feel comfortable مَعَ (mar) with these new الكَلِمات (al-ka-lee-maat) the words.

كَتَب

- [ ] to write ....(ka-ta-ba)............ كَتَبَ ____________
- [ ] office / desk ....(mahk-tahb)............ مَكتَب ____________
- [ ] library .... (mahk-ta-ba)............ مَكتَبة ____________

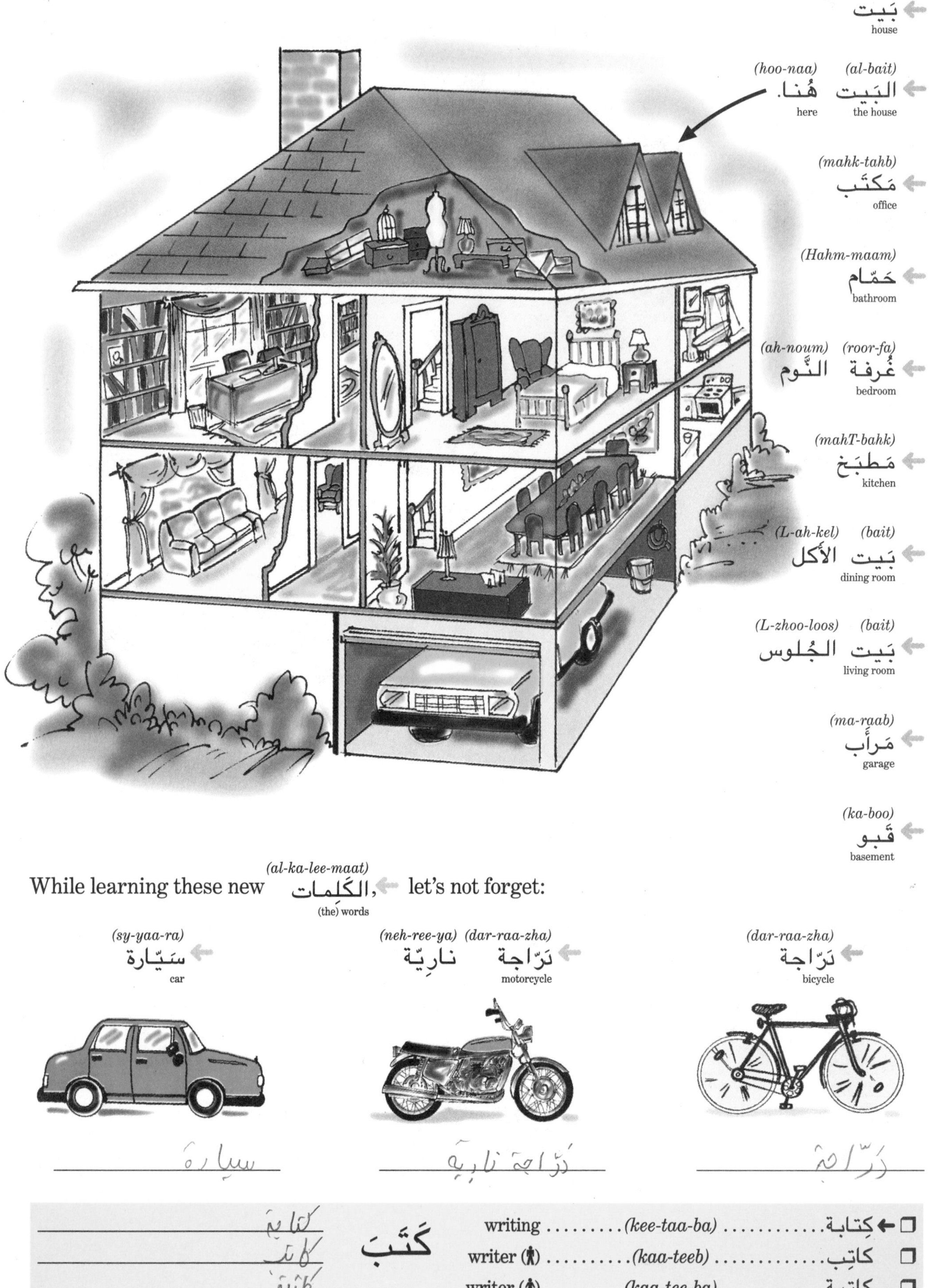

(bait)
بَيت
house

(hoo-naa) (al-bait)
البَيت هُنا.
here the house

(mahk-tahb)
مَكتَب
office

(Hahm-maam)
حَمّام
bathroom

(ah-noum) (roor-fa)
غُرفة النَّوم
bedroom

(mahT-bahk)
مَطبَخ
kitchen

(L-ah-kel) (bait)
بَيت الأكل
dining room

(L-zhoo-loos) (bait)
بَيت الجُلوس
living room

(ma-raab)
مَرأب
garage

(ka-boo)
قَبو
basement

While learning these new (al-ka-lee-maat) الكَلِمات (the) words, let's not forget:

(dar-raa-zha)
دَرّاجة
bicycle

(neh-ree-ya) (dar-raa-zha)
دَرّاجة نارِيّة
motorcycle

(sy-yaa-ra)
سَيّارة
car

كَتَب

- ❒ ➜ كِتابة .... (kee-taa-ba) .... writing
- ❒ كاتِب .... (kaa-teeb) .... writer (♂)
- ❒ كاتِبة .... (kaa-tee-ba) .... writer (♀)

(keT-Ta)
قِطّة ←
cat

(Ha-dee-qa)
حَديقة ←
garden

(zoo-hoor)
زُهور ←
flowers

(kelb)
كَلب ←
dog

(al-ba-reed) (ssoon-dooq)
صُندوق البَريد ←
mailbox

(al-ba-reed)
البَريد ←
mail

Peel off the next set of labels وَ (wa) and wander through your بَيت (bait) house learning these new الكَلِمات (al-ka-lee-maat) (the) words.

It will be somewhat difficult to label your كَلب (kelb) dog, قِطّة (keT-Ta) cat or زُهور (zoo-hoor) flowers but be creative.

Practice by asking yourself, "أينَ (eye-na) where الحَديقة؟ (al-Ha-dee-qa) the garden" and reply, "الحَديقة (al-Ha-dee-qa) the garden هُنا. (hoo-naa) here (is)"

"أينَ (eye-na) where البَيت؟ (al-bait) the house" "أينَ (eye-na) where الحَديقة؟ (al-Ha-dee-ga) the garden"

تَرجَم

☐	to translate .... (tar-zha-ma)	تَرجَم ←
☐	translator (🧍) .... (moo-tar-zheem)	مُترجِم
☐	translation .... (tar-zha-ma)	تَرجَمة

0/5

(tha-laa-tha) (ith-nayn) (waa-Hahd)

← واحِد - اِثنَين - ثَلاثة

one / two / three

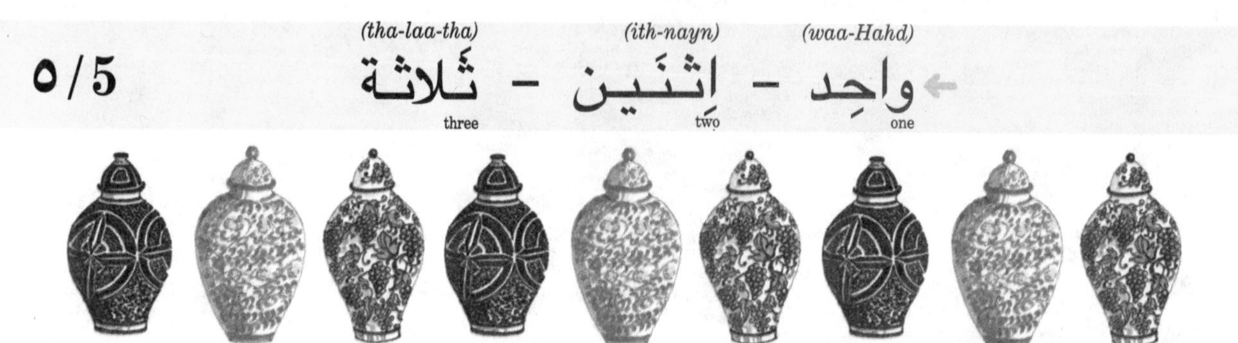

Consider for a minute how important numbers are. How could you tell someone your phone number, your address أو ← (ow) or your hotel غُرفة ← (roor-fa) room if you had no الأرقام ← (al-aar-qaam) (the) numbers? And think of how difficult it would be if you could not understand the time, the price of an apple أو ← (ow) or the correct bus to take. These numbers may look different, لَكِن ← (la-kin) but they are still written from left to right. Notice the similarities between (٤) أربَعة ← (ar-ba-ah) four and (١٤) أربَعة عَشَر ← (ar-ba-ah) ('ah-shar) fourteen, (٦) سِتّة ← (seet-teh) six and (١٦) سِتّة عَشَر ← (seet-teh) ('ah-shar) sixteen and so on.

______ (٠/0)	صِفر	(sif-fur)	← ٠
______ (١/1)	واحِد	(waa-Hahd)	← ١
______ (٢/2)	اِثنَين	(ith-nayn)	← ٢
______ (٣/3)	ثَلاثة	(tha-laa-tha)	← ٣
______ (٤/4)	أربَعة	(ar-ba-ah)	← ٤
______ (٥/5)	خَمسة	(hahm-sa)	← ٥
______ (٦/6)	سِتّة	(seet-teh)	← ٦
______ (٧/7)	سَبعة	(sahb'ah)	← ٧
______ (٨/8)	ثَمانِية	(tha-maa-nee-ya)	← ٨
______ (٩/9)	تِسعة	(tis'ah)	← ٩
______ (١٠/10)	عَشَرة	('ah-sha-ra)	← ١٠

______ (١٠/10)	عَشَرة	('ah-sha-ra)	← ١٠
______ (١١/11)	أحَد عَشَر	('ah-shar) (ah-Hahd)	← ١١
______ (١٢/12)	اِثنا عَشَر	('ah-shar) (ith-naa)	← ١٢
______ (١٣/13)	ثَلاثة عَشَر	('ah-shar) (tha-laa-tha)	← ١٣
______ (١٤/14)	أربَعة عَشَر	('ah-shar) (ar-ba-ah)	← ١٤
______ (١٥/15)	خَمسة عَشَر	('ah-shar) (hahm-sa)	← ١٥
______ (١٦/16)	سِتّة عَشَر	('ah-shar) (seet-teh)	← ١٦
______ (١٧/17)	سَبعة عَشَر	('ah-shar) (sahb'ah)	← ١٧
______ (١٨/18)	ثَمانِية عَشَر	('ah-shar)(tha-maa-nee-ya)	← ١٨
______ (١٩/19)	تِسعة عَشَر	('ah-shar) (tis'ah)	← ١٩
______ (٢٠/20)	عِشرون / عِشرين	(aysh-reen) (aysh-roon)	← ٢٠

شَفى

- ☐ شَفى ← .... (sheh-fa) .... to cure
- ☐ مُستَشفى ...... (moos-tesh-fa) .... hospital
- ☐ شِفاء .... (she-feh') .... cure

يشفي الطفل من المرض
ذهب الطفل الى المستشفى
شفاء الطفل

Use الأرقام *(al-aar-qaam)* (numbers) هَذِهِ *(heh-da-he)* (these) on a daily basis. Count to yourself بِالعَرَبِيّة *(bil-r-ra-be-ya)* (in Arabic) when you brush your teeth, exercise أَو *(ow)* (or) commute to work. Fill in the blanks below according to الأَرقام *(al-aar-qaam)* (the numbers) given in parentheses. Now is also a good time to learn هَذِهِ *(heh-da-he)* (these) two very important phrases.

أُريدُ *(oo-ree-do)* (I want) . . . مِن *(min)* فَضلِك *(fahD-lahk)* ((f) please) . . . ______________________

نُريدُ *(noo-ree-do)* (we want) . . . مِن *(min)* فَضلِك *(fahD-lahk)* ((f) please) . . . ______________________

أُريدُ *(oo-ree-do)* (I want) ______ (٥) مِن *(min)* (please) فَضلِك. *(fahD-lahk)*	كَم؟ *(kem)* (how many) ______ (٥)
أُريدُ *(oo-ree-do)* (I want) ______ (٩) مِن *(min)* (please) فَضلِك. *(fahD-lahk)*	كَم؟ *(kem)* (how many) تِسعة تِسعة (٩)
أُريدُ *(oo-ree-do)* (I want) ______ (٢) مِن *(min)* (please) فَضلِك. *(fahD-lahk)*	كَم؟ *(kem)* (how many) ______ (٢)
أُريدُ *(oo-ree-do)* ______ (٤) مِن *(min)* (please) فَضلِك. *(fahD-lahk)*	كَم؟ *(kem)* (how many) ______ (٤)
أُريدُ *(oo-ree-do)* ______ (٧) مِن *(min)* (please) فَضلِك. *(fahD-lahk)*	كَم؟ *(kem)* ______ (٧)
نُريدُ *(noo-ree-do)* (we want) ______ (١٠) مِن (please) فَضلِك. *(fahD-lahk)*	كَم؟ ______ (١٠)
نُريدُ *(noo-ree-do)* (we want) ______ (١) مِن *(min)* فَضلِك.	كَم؟ *(kem)* ______ (١)
نُريدُ *(noo-ree-do)* (we want) ______ (٨) مِن فَضلِك. *(fahD-lahk)*	كَم؟ ______ (٨)
نُريدُ *(noo-ree-do)* ______ (٣) مِن فَضلِك.	كَم؟ ______ (٣)
نُريدُ *(noo-ree-do)* ______ (٦) مِن فَضلِك.	كَم؟ ______ (٦)
نُريدُ *(noo-ree-do)* ______ (٥) مِن فَضلِك.	(how many) ______ (٥)

طَبَّ

- ❒ طَبَّ ← ....*(Tahb-ba)*......... to remedy ______________________
- ❒ طِبّ ....*(Tehb)*.......... medicine ______________________
- ❒ طِبّي ....*(Tehb-be)*......... medical ______________________

Now see if you can translate the following thoughts *(al-r-ra-be-ya)* العَرَبِيّة (Arabic) *(ee-la)* إلى (into). *(al-ezh-we-ba)* الأجوبة (the answers) are provided at the bottom of *(ah-ssahf-Ha)* الصَّفحة (the page).

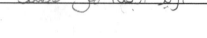

1. I want seven please.

2. I want four please.

3. We want eight please.

4. We want three please.

Review *(al-aar-qaam)* الأرقام (the numbers) 1 through 20. Write out your telephone number, fax number, and cellular number. Then write out a friend's telephone number and then a relative's telephone number. Remember, in Arabic, numbers are written as in English from left to right.

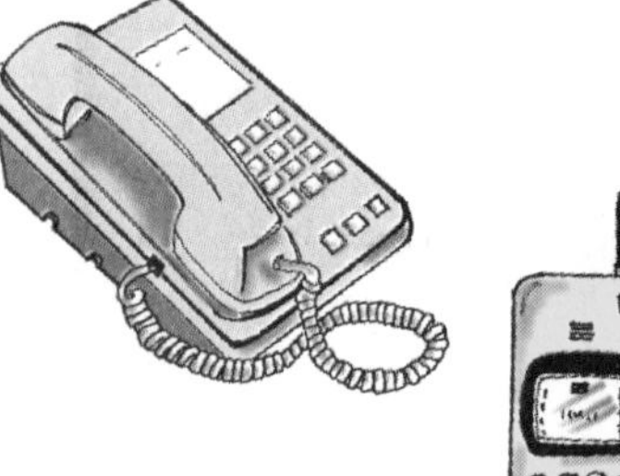

(٢٠٦) ٢٨٤ - ٤٢١١

الأجوبة
the answers

1. ← أُريدُ سَبعة مِن فَضلِك.
2. ← أُريدُ أربَعة مِن فَضلِك.
3. ← نُريدُ ثَمانِية مِن فَضلِك.
4. ← نُريدُ ثَلاثة مِن فَضلِك.

٦ / 6

(ahl-wen)
الأَلـوان
the colors

(ahl-wen) الأَلوان (the colors) are the same in Jordan (ow) أَو (or) Kuwait as they are in (ahm-ree-kaa) أَمـريـكا (America) — they just have different (al-ahs-maa') الأَسـماء (the names).

(aH-mar) أَحمَـر — red

(zeh-ree) زَهـري — pink

(boor-too-qaa-lee) بُـرتُـقـالي — orange

(ah-be-yahD) أَبـيَـض — white

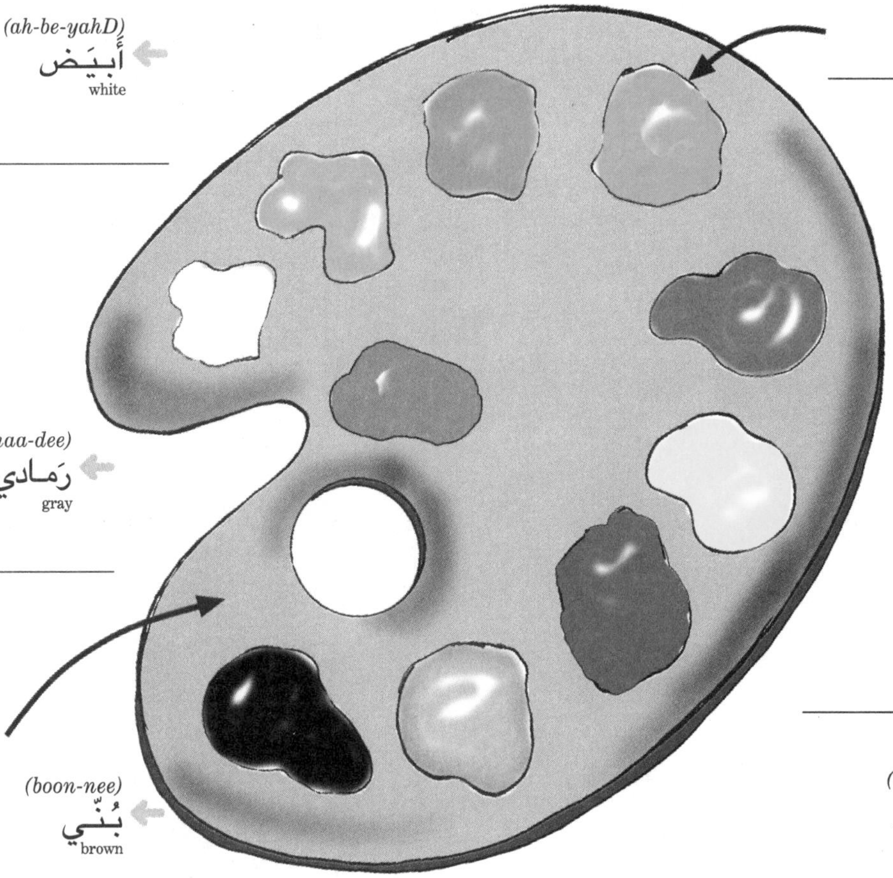

(ahz-rahq) أَزرَق — blue

(reh-maa-dee) رَمـادي — gray

(ahss-far) أَصفَـر — yellow

(boon-nee) بُـنّـي — brown

(ahk-Dar) أَخضَـر — green

(ahs-wed) أَسـوَد — black

(moo-la-wen) مُـلَـوَّن — colorful

Peel off the next group of labels (wa) وَ proceed to label (ahl-wen) الأَلوان (the colors) in your (bait) بَـيت (home).

طَبَّ

- doctor (♂) .... (Ta-beeb) .... طَبيب
- doctor (♀) .... (Ta-bee-ba) .... طَبيبة
- medical practice .... (tahT-beeb) .... تَطبيب

الطبيب في المستشفى
الطبيبة تشفي الطفل
الطبيب والطبيبة يعمل تطبيب

Identify the two or three dominant colors in the flags below.

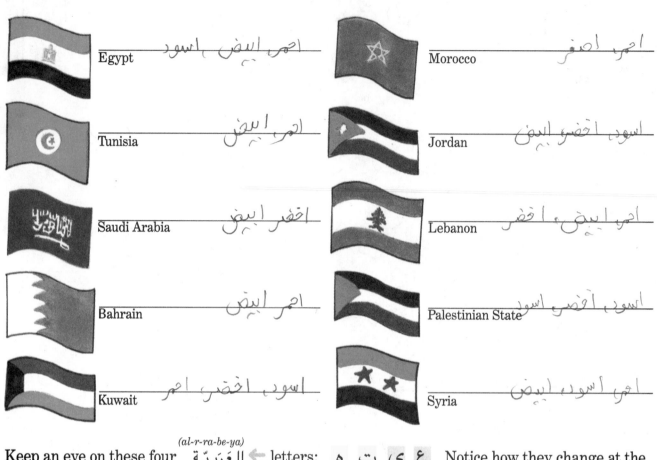

Egypt	احمر ابيض اسود	 Morocco	احمر اصفر
 Tunisia	احمر ابيض	 Jordan	اسود اخضر ابيض
 Saudi Arabia	اخضر ابيض	 Lebanon	احمر ابيض اخضر
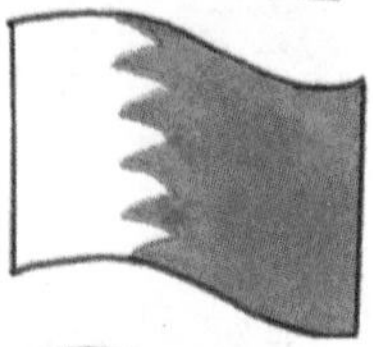 Bahrain	احمر ابيض	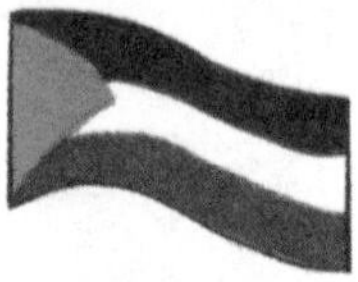 Palestinian State	اسود اخضر اسود
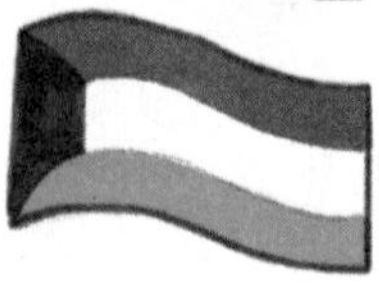 Kuwait	اسود اخضر احمر	 Syria	احمر اسود ابيض

Keep an eye on these four *(al-r-ra-be-ya)* العَرَبِيّة (Arabic) letters: ه ت ي ع Notice how they change at the end of a word as well as internally and at the beginning.

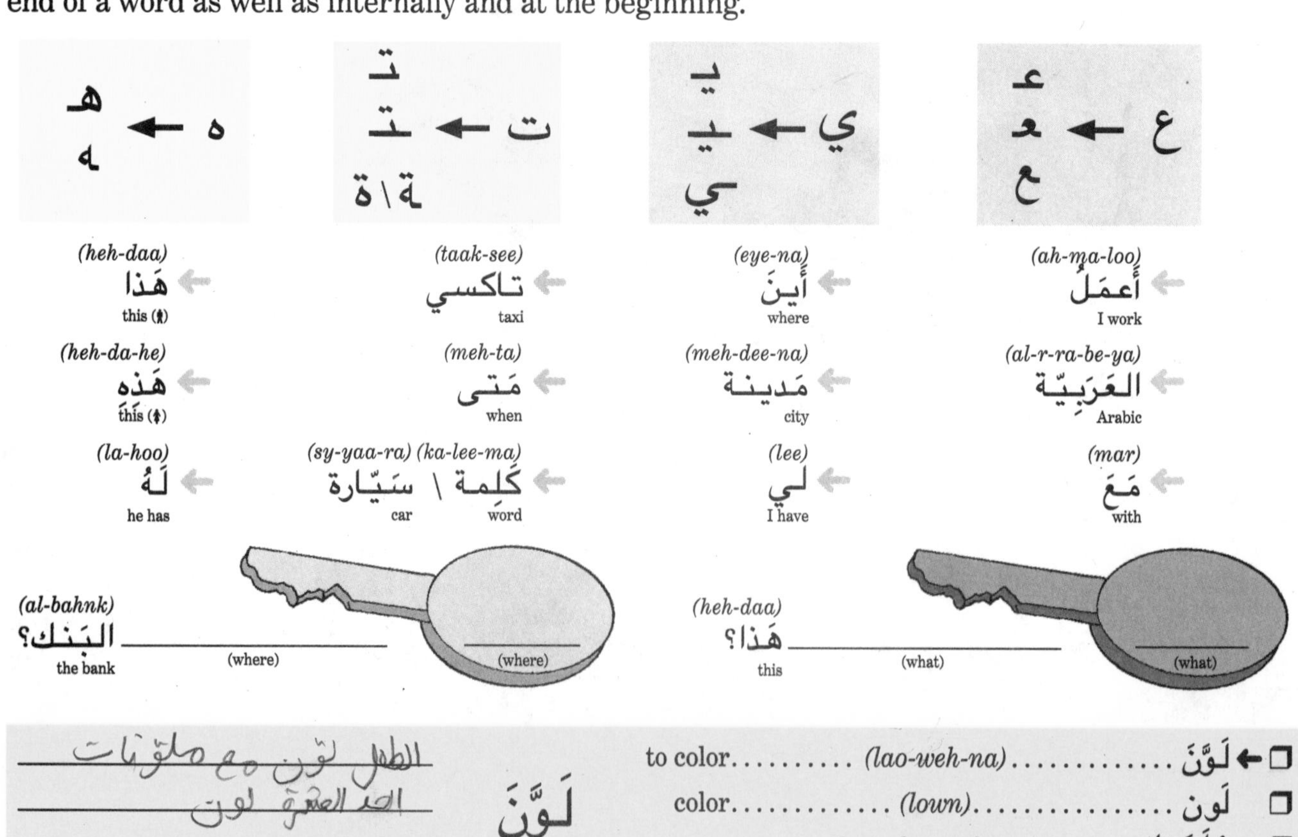

(heh-daa) هَذا this (♂)	*(taak-see)* تاكسي taxi	*(eye-na)* أينَ where	*(ah-ma-loo)* أعمَلُ I work
(heh-da-he) هَذه this (♀)	*(meh-ta)* مَتى when	*(meh-dee-na)* مَدينة city	*(al-r-ra-be-ya)* العَرَبِيّة Arabic
(la-hoo) لَهُ he has	*(sy-yaa-ra)* سَيّارة car \ *(ka-lee-ma)* كَلِمة word	*(lee)* لي I have	*(mar)* مَعَ with

(al-bahnk) البَنك؟ the bank ______ (where) ______ (where)

(heh-daa) هَذا؟ this ______ (what) ______ (what)

الطفل لوّن مع ملوّنات

احد الصفو لون

لَوَّنَ

- ❑ to color.......... *(lao-weh-na)*............ لَوَّنَ
- ❑ color.............. *(lown)*................ لَون
- ❑ crayons........ *(moo-lao-weh-net)* ...... مُلَوَّنات

7/7 فُلوس (foo-loos) money

Before starting this Step, go back وَ (wa) review Step ٥/5. It is important that you can count to عِشرين (aysh-reen) twenty without looking at الكِتاب (al-kee-taab) the book. Let's learn the larger الأرقام (al-aar-qaam) numbers now. After practicing aloud العَرَبيّة (al-r-ra-be-ya) the Arabic numbers ١٠ (10) through ١٠٠٠ (1,000) below, write الأرقام (al-aar-qaam) numbers هَذِهِ (heh-da-he) these in the blanks provided. Again, notice the similarities between الأرقام (al-aar-qaam) numbers such as (٤) أربَعة (ar-ba-ah) four and (١٤) أربَعة عَشَر ('ah-shar)(ar-ba-ah) fourteen and (٤٠) أربَعون (ar-ba-oon) forty.

١٠	عَشَرة ('ah-sha-ra)	١٠. / 10	
٢٠	عِشرون / عِشرين (aysh-roon) (aysh-reen)	٢٠. / 20	
٣٠	ثَلاثون (tha-laa-thoon)	٣٠. / 30	
٤٠	أربَعون (ar-ba-oon)	٤٠. / 40	
٥٠	خَمسون (hahm-soon)	٥٠. / 50	
٦٠	سِتّون (seet-toon)	٦٠. / 60	
٧٠	سَبعون (sahb'oon)	٧٠. / 70	
٨٠	ثَمانون (tha-maa-noon)	٨٠. / 80	
٩٠	تِسعون (tis'oon)	٩٠. / 90	
١٠٠	مِئة (me-ya)	١٠٠. / 100	
٥٠٠	خَمسُمِئة (hahm-soo-me-ya)	٥٠٠. / 500	
١٠٠٠	أَلف (alf)	١٠٠٠. / 1,000	

Here are two important phrases to go مَعَ (mar) with all الأرقام (al-aar-qaam) (the) numbers هَذِهِ (heh-da-he) these. Say them out loud over وَ (wa) over وَ (wa) then write them out twice as many times!

عِندي (rin-dee) I have

عِندَنا (rin-da-naa) we have

نَظَر

- to view .....(na-Tha-ra)...... نَظَرَ
- visionary ......(na-Thar)....... نَظَر
- binoculars / microscope .....(min-Thaar).... مِنظار

Depending upon whether your travels take you to (al-ma-greb) الـمَغرِب (Morocco) or (meess-ur) مِصر (Egypt) or (al-oor-doon) الأُردُن (Jordan) you will encounter a variety of currencies. Let's learn the various kinds of (nahq-dee-ya) (qeh-Tar) قِطَع نَقدِيّة (coins) and (foo-loos) فُلوس (bills). Always be sure to practice each (ka-lee-ma) كَلِمة (word) out loud. You might want to exchange some money (al-ann) الآن (now) so that you can familiarize yourself (mar) مَعَ (with) the various (foo-loos) (wa) (nahq-dee-ya) (qeh-Tar) قِطَع نَقدِيّة وَ فُلوس (coins and bills).

(al-oor-doon) (fee)

في الأُردُن

Jordan

(meess-ur) (fee)

في مِصر

Egypt in

(al-ma-greb) (fee)

في المَغرِب

Morocco in

نَظَرَ

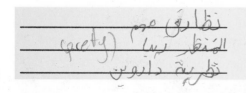

eyeglasses	(naTh-Thaa-ra)	نَظّارة	☐
view	(man-Thar)	مَنظَر	☐
theory	(na-Tha-ree-ya)	نَظَرِيّة	☐

Review عَشَرة (ten, *'ah-sha-ra*) الأرقام (the numbers, *al-aar-qaam*) through أَلف (1,000, *alf*) again. كَيف (how, *kay-fa*) do you say "twenty-two" أَو (or, *ow*) "fifty-three" بِالعَرَبِيّة (in Arabic, *bil-r-ra-be-ya*)? You basically talk backwards – "two and twenty" (اِثنَين وَ عِشرون) أَو (or, *ow*) "three and fifty" (ثَلاثة وَ خَمسون). See if you can say وَ (*wa*) write out الأرقام (the numbers, *al-aar-qaam*) on this صَفحة (page, *ssahf-Ha*). الأجوِبة (the answers, *al-ezh-we-ba*) are at the bottom of الصَّفحة (the page, *ah-ssahf-Ha*).

١ (1) ______ (47 = 7 and 40)

٢ (2) ______ (25 = 5 and 20)

٣ (3) ______ (51 = 1 and 50)

٤ (4) ______ (84 = 4 and 80)

Now, how would you say the following بِالعَرَبِيّة (in Arabic, *bil-r-ra-be-ya*)?

٥ (5) ______ (I have 90 dinars.)

٦ (6) ______ (I have 60 dinars.)

To ask how much something costs بِالعَرَبِيّة (in Arabic, *bil-r-ra-be-ya*), one simply asks — بِكَم؟ (how much, *be-kem*)

Now you try it. ______ (How much?) Again. ______ (How much?)

Answer the following questions based on the numbers in parentheses.

٧ (7) بِكَم؟ (how much, *be-kem*) بِـ (it (costs), *be*) ______ (١٠ / 10) دَراهِم. (dirhams, *deh-raa-him*)

٨ (8) بِكَم؟ (how much, *be-kem*) بِـ (it (costs), *be*) ______ (٨ / 8) دَراهِم. (dirhams, *deh-raa-him*)

٩ (9) بِكَم؟ (*be-kem*) بِـ (*be*) ______ (٩ / 9) دَراهِم. (dirhams, *deh-raa-him*)

١٠ (10) بِكَم؟ بِـ ______ (٥ / 5) دَراهِم.

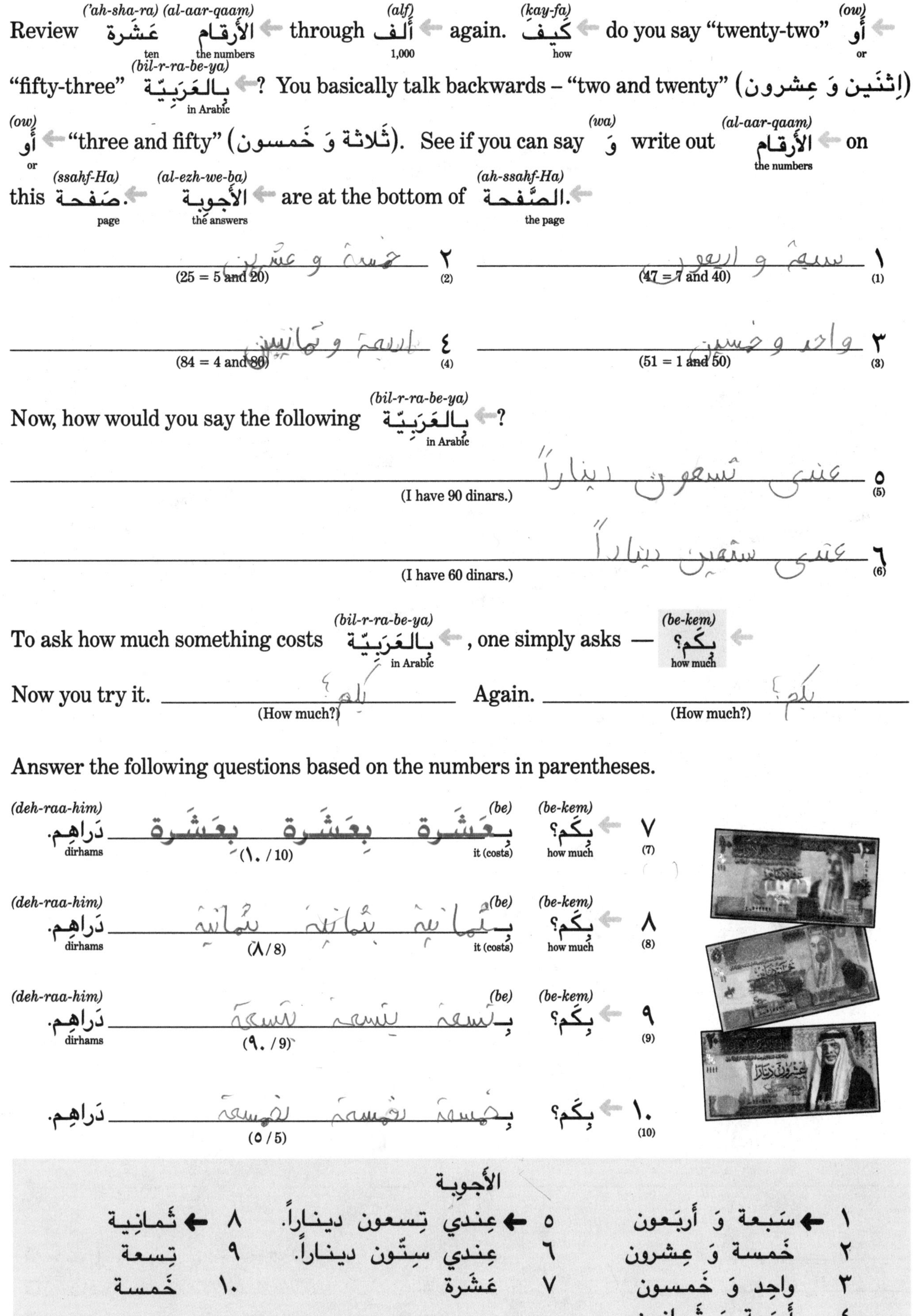

الأجوِبة

١ سَبعة وَ أَربَعون	٥ عِندي تِسعون ديناراً.	٨ ثَمانِية
٢ خَمسة وَ عِشرون	٦ عِندي سِتّون ديناراً.	٩ تِسعة
٣ واحِد وَ خَمسون	٧ عَشَرة	١٠ خَمسة
٤ أَربَعة وَ ثَمانون		

٨/8

(ahms) أَمس ← yesterday – (al-yohm) اليَوم today – (reh-dahn) غَداً tomorrow

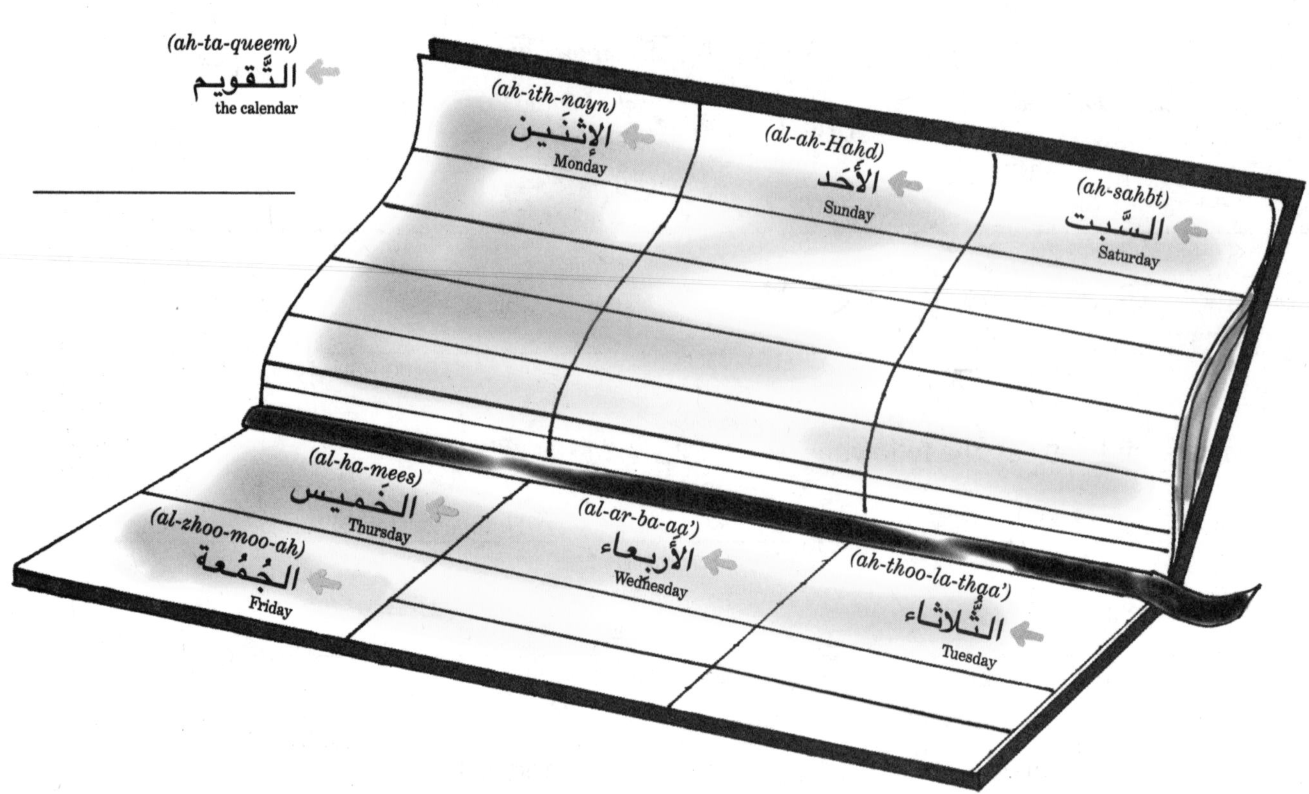

Learn the days of the week by writing them in (ah-ta-queem) التَّقويم ← (the calendar) above and then move on to the (ar-ba-ah) أربَعة ← (four) parts to each (yohm) يَوم ← (day).

(ah-lgil) اللَّيل ← the night

(al-ma-saa') المَساء ← the evening

(ah-Doo-hur) (ba-da) بَعدَ الظُّهر ← the afternoon

(ah-ssa-baaH) الصَّباح ← the morning

طارَ

❐	طارَ ←	(Taa-ra)	to fly
❐	طائِرة	(Taa-ee-ra)	airplane
❐	طَيّار	(Ty-yaar)	pilot

It is very مُهِمّ (moo-him) important to know the days of the week وَ (wa) the various parts of اليَوم (al-yohm) the day. Remember, read from right to left.

غداً (reh-dahn) tomorrow — اليَوم (al-yohm) today — أمس (ahms) yesterday

(al-zhoo-moo-ah) الجُمُعة Friday	(ah-sahbt) السَّبت Saturday
(al-ha-mees) الخَميس Thursday	(al-ah-Hahd) الأحَد Sunday
(al-ar-ba-aa') الأربعاء Wednesday	(ah-ith-nayn) الإثنَين Monday
(ah-thoo-la-thaa') الثُّلاثاء Tuesday	

اليَوم (al-yohm) today ______________________ غداً (reh-dahn) tomorrow ______________________

أمس (ahms) yesterday ______________________ الأسبوع (al-oos-boo') the week ______________________

To say "in the morning," you simply say "في (fee) الصَّباح (ah-ssa-baaH)" or "صَباحاً (ssa-baa-Hahn)." The same applies to "in the evening:" "في (fee) المَساء (al-ma-saa')" or "مَساءً (ma-saa-ahn)." Fill in the following blanks وَ then check your answers at the bottom of الصَّفحة (ah-ssahf-Ha) the page.

a. Sunday = ______________________

b. in the evening = ______________________

c. Thursday afternoon = ______________________

d. tomorrow morning = ______________________

e. tomorrow afternoon = ______________________

f. tomorrow evening = ______________________

هَذا؟ (heh-daa) this ______________ (when) ______________ (when)

هُوَ؟ (hoo-wa) it ______________ (who) ______________ (who)

الأجوِبة

a. الأحَد

b. في المَساء

c. الخَميس بَعدَ الظُّهر

d. غداً صَباحاً (في الصَّباح)

e. غداً بَعدَ الظُّهر

f. غداً مَساءً (في المَساء)

Knowing the parts of اليَوم (al-yohm) (the day) will help you to learn the various العَرَبِيّة (al-r-ra-be-ya) (Arabic) greetings below. Practice these every day until your trip.

صَباح الخَير (ssa-baaH) (al-hair) — good morning ________________

مَساء الخَير (ma-saa') (al-hair) — good evening ________________

تُصبِحونَ عَلى خَير (tooss-beh-Hoo-na) (ah-la) (hair) — good night ________________

مَرحَبا (mar-Ha-baa) — hello ________________

Take the next أربَعة (ar-ba-ah) (four) labels وَ stick them on the appropriate things in your بَيت (bait) (house). Make sure you attach them to the correct items, as they are only بِالعَرَبِيّة (bil-r-ra-be-ya) (in Arabic). How about the bathroom mirror for "تُصبِحونَ عَلى خَير" (tooss-beh-Hoo-na) (ah-la) (hair) (good night)? أو (ow) (or) your alarm clock for "صَباح الخَير" (sah-baaH) (al-hair) (good morning)? Let's not forget,

كَيفَ حالُكَ؟ (kay-fa) (Haa-lahk) — (♂) how are you ________________

كَيفَ حالُكِ؟ (kay-fa) (Haa-lik) — (♀) how are you ________________

Now for some "نَعَم" (na-ahm) (yes) or "لا" (la) (no) questions –

Is your house أزرَق (ahz-rahq) (blue)? ________

Is your desk أسوَد (ahs-wed) (black)? ________

Is your favorite color أصفَر (ahss-far)? ________

Is today الإثنَين (ah-ith-nayn)? ________

Do you own a دَرّاجة (dar-raa-zha) (bicycle)? ________

Do you like الزُّهور (ah-zoo-hoor) (the flowers)? ________

You are about one-fourth of your way through this book وَ it is good time to review الكَلِمات (al-ka-lee-maat) (the words) you have learned قَبلَ (qahb-la) (before) doing the crossword puzzle on the next صَفحة (ssahf-Ha) (page).

الأجوِبة TO THE CROSSWORD PUZZLE

ACROSS

1. غرفة النوم
4. الصباح
7. مئة
11. فندق
12. هنا
14. أريكة
16. ساعة
17. ما
18. صفر
19. كلمات
23. ثمانون
25. بيت الجلوس
28. بني
29. حافلة
30. بكم
31. التقويم
33. سجادة
35. الكتاب
36. حديقة
38. عندنا
42. بيت الأكل
43. سبعة
45. قبو
46. عندي
49. مطبخ
50. برتقالي
52. متى
54. بعد الظهر
56. مدرسة

DOWN

3. من فضلك
5. خمسة
8. من
9. كيف حالك
10. أخضر
13. العربية
15. ثلاثون
18. صندوق البريد
20. مطعم
21. تصبحون على خير
22. أو
24. غرفة
26. سيارة
27. يوم
28. باب
32. في
37. دراجة
39. درس
44. عشرون / عشرين
45. قبل
48. لماذا
51. الحمام
53. مع
54. بنك

(al-moo-ta-qaa-Teh-ah) (al-ka-lee-maat)

الكَلِمات المُتَقاطِعة

crossword puzzle

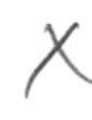

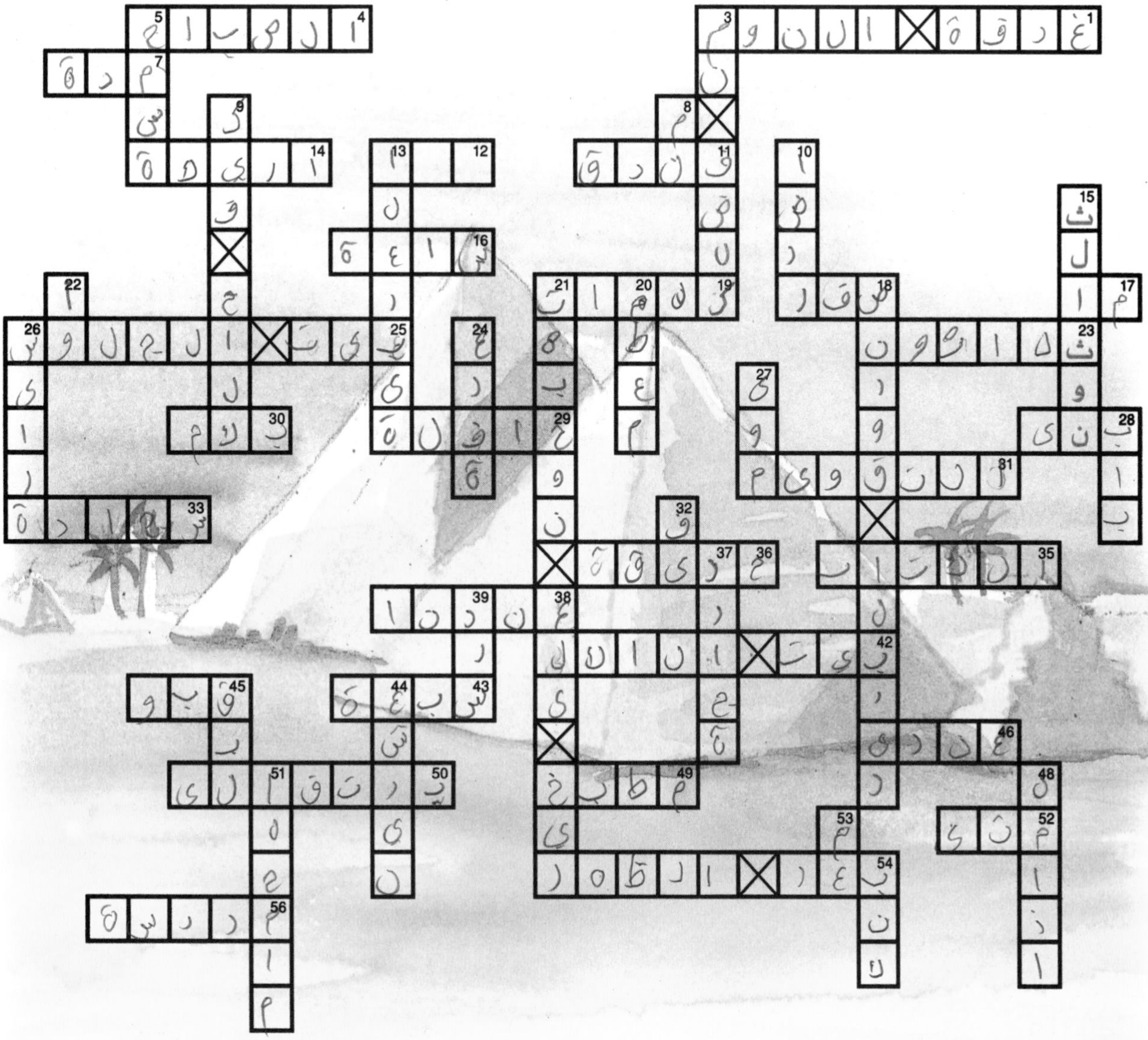

ACROSS

1. bedroom
4. the morning
7. one hundred
11. hotel
12. here is
14. sofa
16. clock
17. what
18. zero
19. words
23. eighty
25. living room
28. brown
29. bus
30. how much
31. the calendar
33. carpet
35. the book
36. garden
38. we have
42. dining room
43. seven
45. basement
46. I have
49. kitchen
50. orange (color)
52. when
54. afternoon
56. school

DOWN

3. please
5. five
8. who
9. how are you (🚹)
10. green
13. Arabic
15. thirty
18. mailbox
20. restaurant
21. good night
22. or
24. room
26. car
27. day
28. door
32. in
37. bicycle
39. to study / he studied
44. twenty
45. before
48. why
51. the toilet
53. with
54. bank

Tip: When you do your crossword puzzles, you do not need to use any of the vowels.

٩/9 (fee) في ← in - (ah-maa-ma) أَمامَ in front of - (be-zhaa-nee-be) بِجانِبِ next to . . .

(al-r-ra-be-ya) العَرَبِيّة ← Arabic prepositions (words like "in," "on," "through" and "next to") are easy to learn وَ they allow you to be precise (mar) مَعَ ← with a minimum of effort. Let's learn some of these little (ka-lee-maat) كَلِمات ← words.

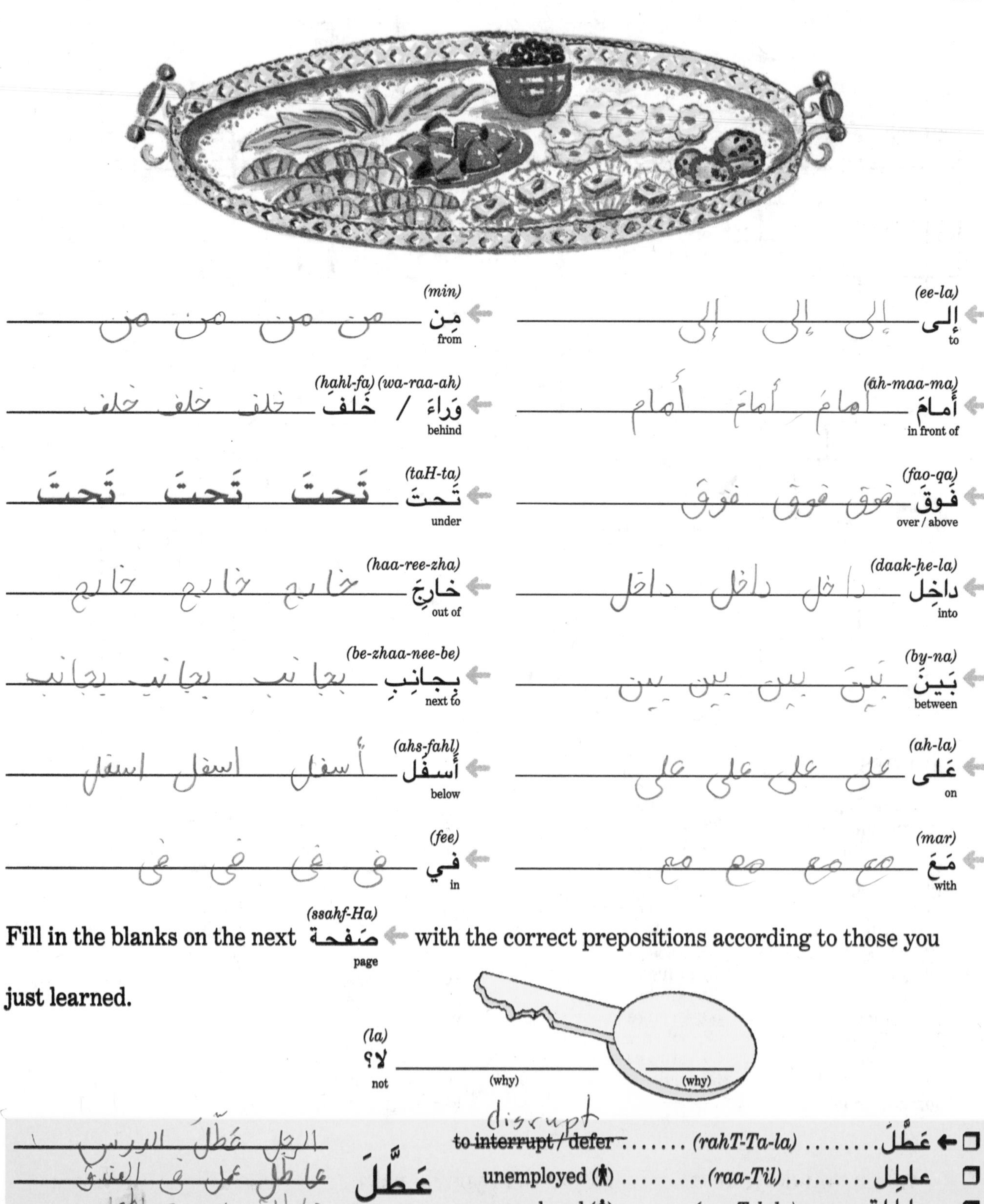

← (ee-la) إلى to	← (min) مِن from
← (ah-maa-ma) أَمامَ in front of	← (hahl-fa) (wa-raa-ah) وَراءَ / خَلفَ behind
← (fao-qa) فَوقَ over / above	← (taH-ta) تَحتَ under
← (daak-he-la) داخِلَ into	← (haa-ree-zha) خارِجَ out of
← (by-na) بَينَ between	← (be-zhaa-nee-be) بِجانِبِ next to
← (ah-la) عَلى on	← (ahs-fahl) أَسفَل below
← (mar) مَعَ with	← (fee) في in

Fill in the blanks on the next (ssahf-Ha) صَفحة ← page with the correct prepositions according to those you just learned.

(la) لا؟ not ______________ (why) ______________ (why)

عَطَّلَ

- ☐ ← عَطَّلَ .... (rahT-Ta-la) .... to interrupt / defer
- ☐ عاطِل .... (raa-Til) .... unemployed (♂)
- ☐ عاطِلة .... (raa-Teh-la) .... unemployed (♀)

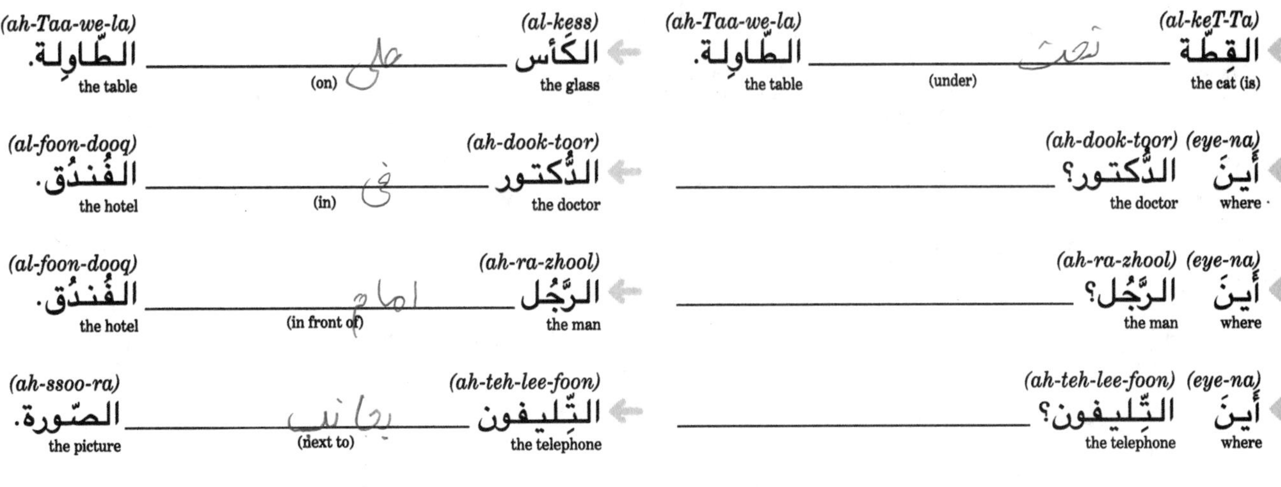

(al-keT-Ta) القِطّة ← the cat (is) ______ (under) الطّاوِلة. (ah-Taa-we-la) the table

(al-kess) الكَأس ← the glass ______ (on) الطّاوِلة. (ah-Taa-we-la) the table

(eye-na) أينَ ← where (ah-dook-toor) الدُّكتور؟ the doctor ______

(ah-dook-toor) الدُّكتور ← the doctor ______ (in) الفُندُق. (al-foon-dooq) the hotel

(eye-na) أينَ ← where (ah-ra-zhool) الرَّجُل؟ the man ______

(ah-ra-zhool) الرَّجُل ← the man ______ (in front of) الفُندُق. (al-foon-dooq) the hotel

(eye-na) أينَ ← where (ah-teh-lee-foon) التِّليفون؟ the telephone ______

(ah-teh-lee-foon) التِّليفون ← the telephone ______ (next to) الصّورة. (ah-ssoo-ra) the picture

Do you recognize قُبّة الصَّخرة (qoob-baht) (ah-ssahk-ra) ← the Dome of the Rock in the picture below? الآن (al-ann) ← now fill in each blank on the picture below مَعَ (mar) ← with the best possible one of these little كَلِمات (ka-lee-maat) ← words.

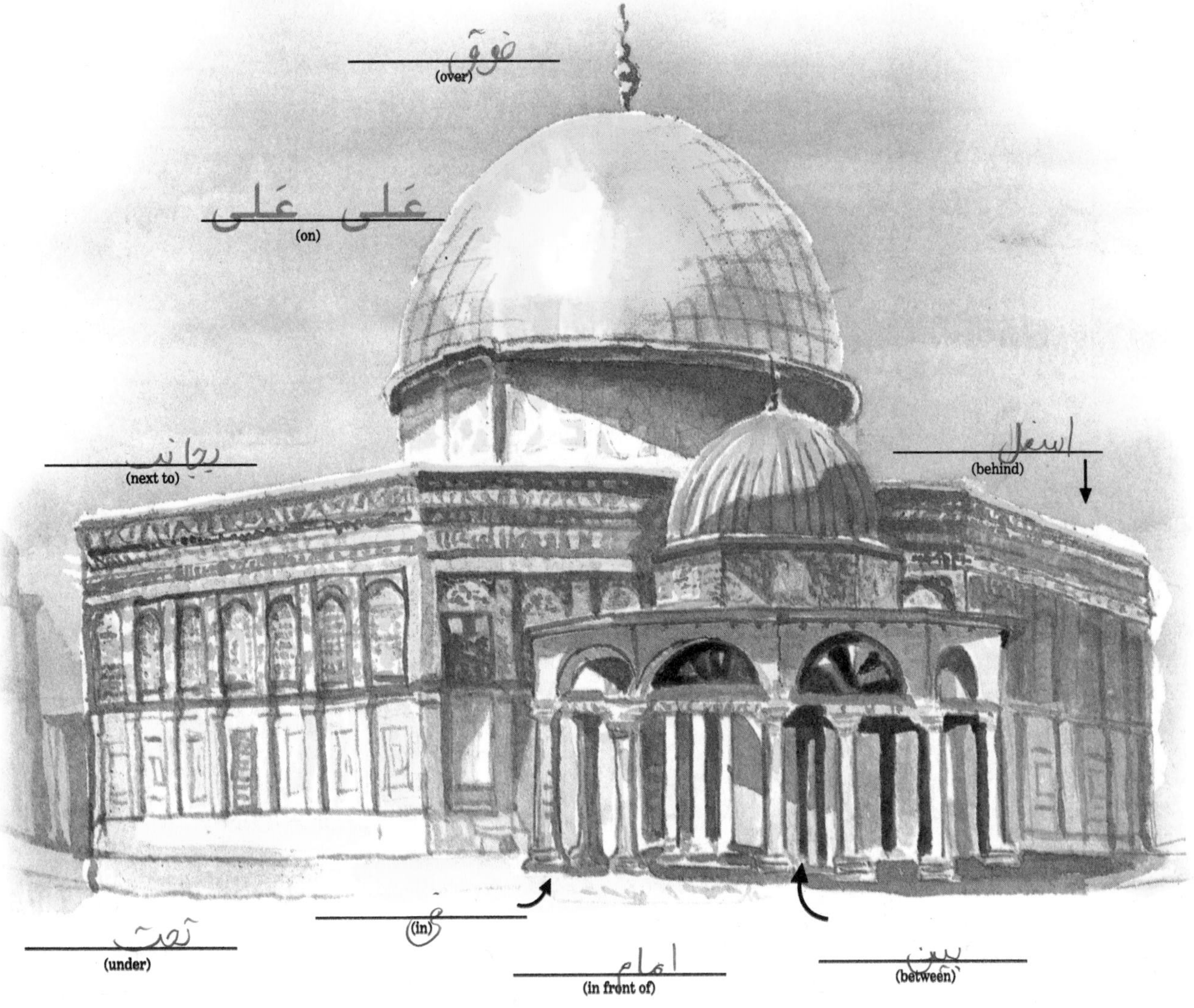

______ (over)

______ (on)

______ (next to)

______ (behind)

______ (in)

______ (under)

______ (in front of)

______ (between)

عَطَّلَ

- ☐ vacation / sabbatical . . . . (rooT-la). . . . . عُطلة ←
- ☐ congestion / tardiness . . . . (ta-Teel). . . . . تَعطيل
- ☐ broken down car . (moo-rahT-Ta-la)(sy-yaa-ra). سَيّارة مُعَطَّلة

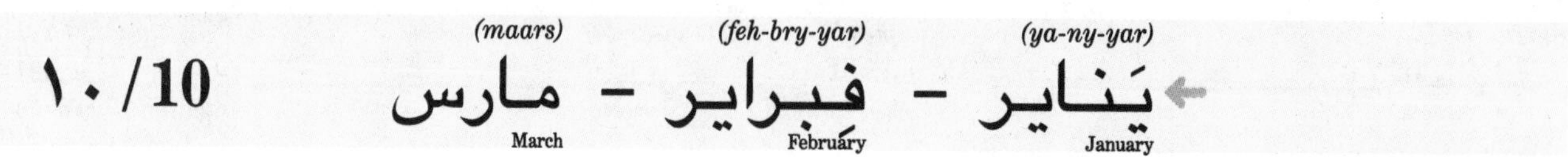

١٠ / 10
(maars) (feh-bry-yar) (ya-ny-yar)
يَنـايـر - فـبـرايـر - مـارس
March February January

You have learned the days of the week, so now it is time to learn الشّهور (ah-shoo-hoor) (the months) of the year and all the different kinds of الجَوّ (al-zhao) (weather). In Arabic there are two names for each month. One set of names sounds very similar to English and is given below. You will find the second set in the yellow color blocks at the bottom of these pages. Try to learn them both.

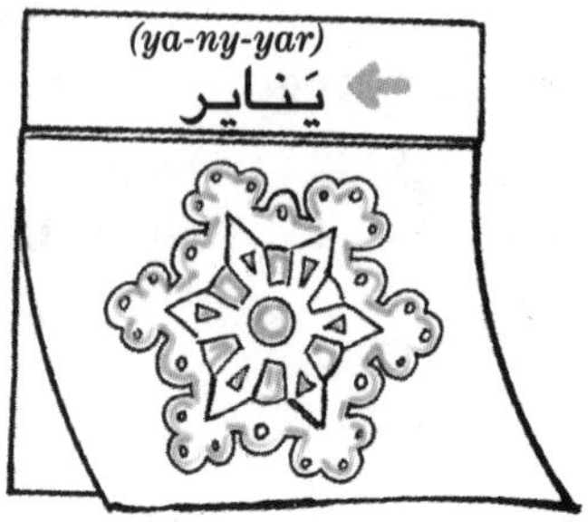

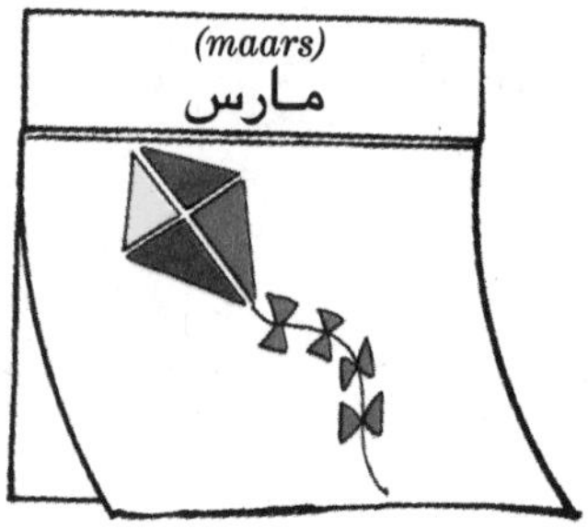

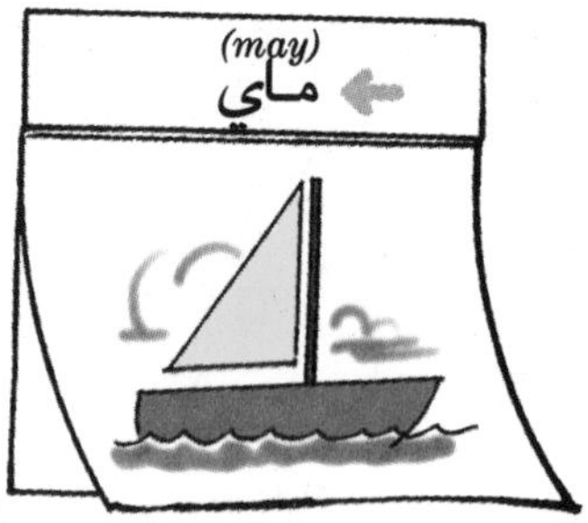

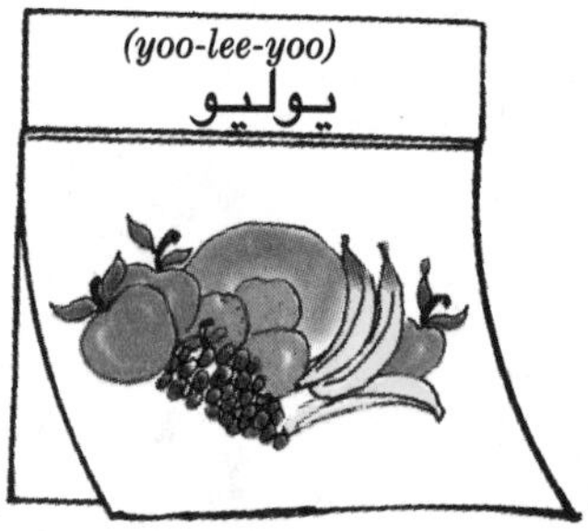

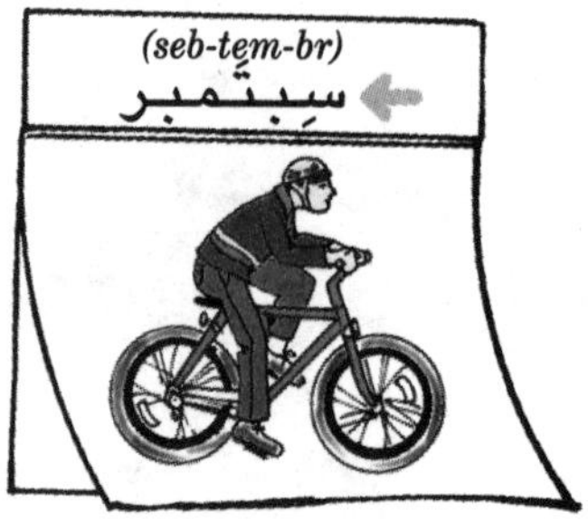

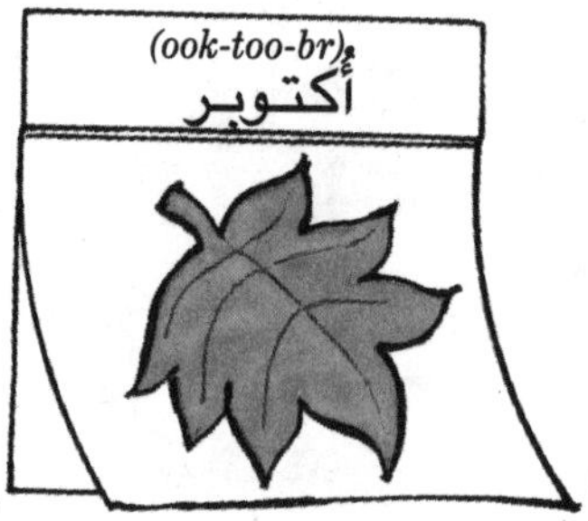

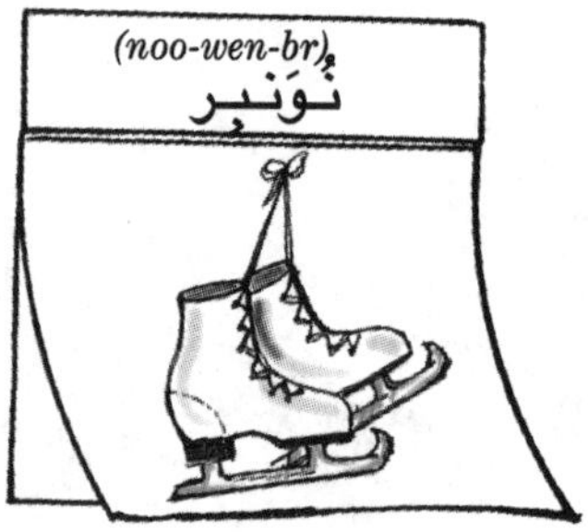

(ah-breel) أبـريـل	(maars) مـارس	(feh-bry-yar) فِـبـرايـر	(ya-ny-yar) يَنـايـر
(rohsht) غُشت	(yoo-lee-yoo) يـولـيـو	(yoo-nee-yoo) يـونـيـو	(may) مـاي
(dee-sem-br) ديـسَمـبـر	(noo-wen-br) نُـوَنـبِـر	(ook-too-br) أكـتـوبـر	(seb-tem-br) سِـبـتـمـبـر

When someone asks, "كَيفَ الجَوّ اليَوم؟" (kay-fa = how (is)) (al-zhao = the weather) (al-yohm = today) you have a variety of answers. Practice all the possible answers to this question on the next صَفحة (ssahf-Ha). Practice using both sets of names so that you master both.

________________	❑ January.... (ah-thaa-nee)(kaa-noon)... كانون الثّاني
________________	❑ February......... (shoo-baaT) .... شُباط
________________	❑ March...........(aa-daar) .... آذار
________________	❑ April.......... (nee-saan) .... نيسان

(kay-fa) (al-zhao) (al-yohm)

كَيفَ الجَوّ اليَوم؟ ____________

how (is) the weather today

(al-zhao) (mooth-leezh) (fee) (ya-ny-yar)

الجَوّ مُثلِج في يَناير. ____________

the weather (is) snowy in January

(al-zhao) (moom-Tair) (fee) (feh-bry-yar)

الجَوّ مُمطِر في فِبراير. ____________

the weather (is) rainy February

(al-zhao) (moom-Tair) (fee) (maars)

الجَوّ مُمطِر في مارس. ____________

the weather (is) rainy March

(al-zhao) (la-Teef) (fee) (ah-breel)

الجَوّ لَطيف في أبريل. ____________

pleasant April

(hoo-naa-ka) (ree-yaaH) (fee) (may)

هُناكَ رياح في ماي. ____________

there is wind

(al-zhao) (la-Teef) (yoo-nee-yoo)

الجَوّ لَطيف في يونيو. ____________

the weather pleasant June

(Haar) (zhid-dahn) (yoo-lee-yoo)

الجَوّ حارّ جِدّاً في يوليو. ____________

hot very July

(Haar) (zhid-dahn) (rohsht)

الجَوّ حارّ جِدّاً في غُشت. ____________

hot very August

(al-zhao) (la-Teef) (seb-tem-br)

الجَوّ لَطيف في سِبتَمبر. ____________

(raa-im) (ook-too-br)

الجَوّ غائِم في أُكتوبر. ____________

cloudy

(bear-id) (noo-wen-br)

الجَوّ بارِد في نُوَنبِر. ____________

cold

(ra-dee') (dee-sem-br)

الجَوّ رَديء في ديسَمبر. ____________

bad

(kay-fa) (al-zhao) (feh-bry-yar)

كَيفَ الجَوّ في فِبراير؟ الجوّ مثلج في فبراير

how the weather

(kay-fa) (ah-breel)

كَيفَ الجَوّ في أبريل؟ الجَوّ لَطيف في أبريل.

(kay-fa) (may)

كَيفَ الجَوّ في ماي؟ الجوّ ممطر في ماي

(kay-fa) (rohsht)

كَيفَ الجَوّ في غُشت؟ الجوّ حارّ جداً في غشت

❒ ← أيّار	(ay-yaar)	May ____________
❒ حَزيران	(Ha-zee-raan)	June ____________
❒ تَمّوز	(tahm-mooz)	July ____________
❒ آب	(aab)	August ____________

(al-ann)
الآن now
for the seasons of
(ah-seh-na)
السَّنة the year . . .

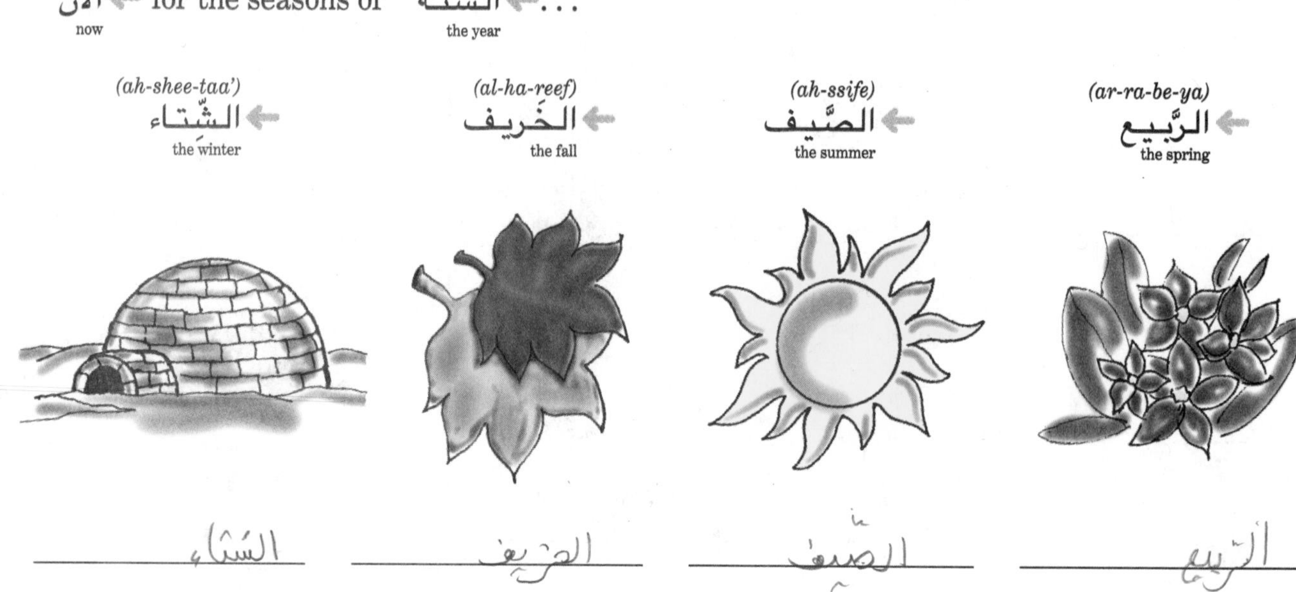

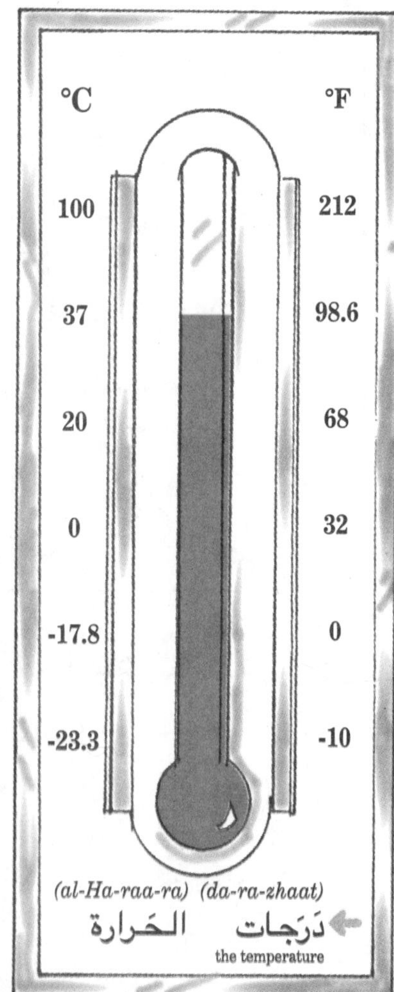

At this point, it is (zhy-yee-da) جَيِّدة (a) good idea to familiarize yourself (mar) مَعَ with temperatures. Carefully study the thermometer because (da-ra-zhaat) (al-Ha-raa-ra) دَرَجات الحَرارة the temperature in (qa-Tar) قَطَر Qatar (wa) وَ (al-baH-rain) البَحرَين Bahrain (wa) وَ (loob-naan) لُبنان Lebanon is calculated on the basis of Celsius (not Fahrenheit).

To convert °C to °F, multiply by 1.8 and add 32.

37 °C x 1.8 = 66.6 + 32 = 98.6 °F

To convert °F to °C, subtract 32 and multiply by 0.55.

98.6 °F - 32 = 66.6 x 0.55 = 37 °C

September.......... (eye-lool)....................	أيلول
October.... (al-ow-wahl)(tish-reen).....	تِشرين الأوَّل
November.... (ah-thaa-nee)(tish-reen) ..	تِشرين الثّاني
December.... (al-ow-wahl)(kaa-noon)	كانون الأوَّل

١١/11 العائِلة وَ الأُسرة وَ البَيت

(al-raa-ee-la) (wa) (al-oos-ra) (wa) (al-bait)

the extended family · and · the family · and · the house

الأُسرة (al-oos-ra, the family) usually eats together في (fee, in) الصَّباح (ah-ssa-baaH, the morning) وَ (wa) on holidays. Our family tree introduces you to some family members starting مَعَ (mar, with) the grandfather Karim وَ the grandmother Mezhda. Arabic does not have الكَلِمة (al-ka-lee-ma, the word) for "cousin" so extended family members are referred to as the "son of the maternal uncle" أو (ow, or) the "son of the paternal aunt." You'll find these names in the yellow boxes. Study the family tree then practice these new words and names on the next صَفحة (ssahf-Ha, page).

ماجدة (mehzh-da)
جَدّة — grandmother

كَريم (ka-reem)
جَدّ — grandfather

عادِل ('aa-dil)
والِد / أَب — father

فاطِمة (faa-Tee-ma)
والِدة / أُمّ — mother

أَيمَن (ay-men)
عَمّ — uncle

جَميلة (zha-me-la)
خالة — aunt

نَبيل (na-beel)
إبن — son

أَمينة (ah-me-na)
إبنة / بِنت — daughter

❐ ←	إبن عَمّ	(ahm)(ibn)	son of paternal uncle ________
❐	إبن عَمّة	(ahm-ma)(ibn)	son of paternal aunt ________
❐	إبن خال	(khaal)(ibn)	son of maternal uncle ________
❐	إبن خالة	(khaa-la)(ibn)	son of maternal aunt ________

Let's learn how to identify (al-oos-ra) الأُسـرة (the family) by name. Study the following examples carefully.

(ees-me) إسـمي (my name is) ____ (fill in your name) — (ees-mook) (maa) ما إسـمُك؟ (what (is) your name) ____

(al-weh-lee-dane) الـوالِدَيـن — the parents

(weh-lid) والِد (father) / (ahb) أب (dad) ____ — (al-weh-lid) (eesm) (maa) ما إسم الوالِد؟ (what name the father) ____

(weh-lee-da) والِدة (mother) / (oom) أمّ (mom) ____ — (al-weh-lee-da) (eesm) (maa) ما إسم الوالِدة؟ (what name the mother) ____

(al-ahT-faal) الأطـفال — the children

(ahk) أخ (brother) — (ohkt) أُخت (sister) = (ibn) إبن (son) — (ib-na) إبنة (daughter) / (bint) بِنت

(ibn) إبن (son) ____ — (al-ibn) (eesm)(maa) ما إسم الإبن؟ (what name the son) ____

(ib-na) إبنة (daughter) / (bint) بِنت ____ — (al-ib-na) (eesm)(maa) ما إسم الإبنة؟ (name the daughter) ____

(al-ah-qaa-rib) الأقـارب — the relatives

(zhed) جَدّ (grandfather) ____ — (al-zhed) (eesm)(maa) ما إسم الجَدّ؟ (name the grandfather) ____

(zhed-da) جَدّة (grandmother) ____ — (al-zhed-da) (eesm) ما إسم الجَدّة؟ (the grandmother) ____

Now you ask — ____ (What is your name?)

And answer — ____ (My name is . . .)

☐ إبنة عَمّ	daughter of paternal uncle ...... (ahm)(ib-na)........	____
☐ إبنة عَمّة	daugther of paternal aunt .....(ahm-ma)(ib-na)....	____
☐ إبنة خال	daughter of maternal uncle ......(khaal)(ib-na).....	____
☐ إبنة خالة	daughter of maternal aunt .....(khaa-la)(ib-na)....	____

(tha-laa-zha)
ثَلاّجة
refrigerator

(foorn)
فُرن
stove

(maa')
ماء
water

(zoob-da)
زُبدة
butter

(Ha-leeb)
حَليب
milk

(ra-sseer)
عَصير
juice

Answer these questions aloud.

(eye-na) (al-ra-sseer) أَينَ العَصير؟ (where) (the juice) . . . . (al-ra-sseer) (fee) (ah-tha-laa-zha) العَصير في الثَّلاّجة. (the juice) (in) (the refrigerator)

(eye-na) (ah-zoob-da) أَينَ الزُّبدة؟ (where) (the butter)

(al-maa') أَينَ الماء؟ (where) (the water)

(al-Ha-leeb) أَينَ الحَليب؟ (the milk)

(al-ann) الآن (now) open your book to (ah-ssahf-Ha) الصَّفحة (the page) with the labels وَ remove the next group of labels وَ proceed to label all these things in your (mahT-bahk) مَطبَخ (kitchen).

- ❑ إبن أَخ . . . .(ahk)(ibn) . . . . son of brother ______________________
- ❑ إبن أُخت . . . .(ohkt)(ibn) . . . . son of sister ______________________
- ❑ إبنة أَخ . . . .(ahk)(ib-na) . . . . daughter of brother ______________________
- ❑ إبنة أُخت . . . .(ohkt)(ib-na) . . . . daughter of sister ______________________

(melH) ملح ← salt ______

(ahs-wed) (fool-fool) فُلفُل أسوَد ← pepper ______

(kess) كَأس ← glass ______

(ssa-He-fa) (zha-ree-da) جَريدة / صَحيفة ← newspaper ______

(feen-zhaan) فِنجان ← cup ______

(zah-ra) زَهرة ← flower ______

(mil'a-qa) مِلعَقة ← spoon ______

(min-deel) منديل ← napkin ______

(shoo-ka) شوكة ← fork ______

(Ta-bahq) طَبَق ← plate ______

(sik-keen) سِكّين ← knife ______

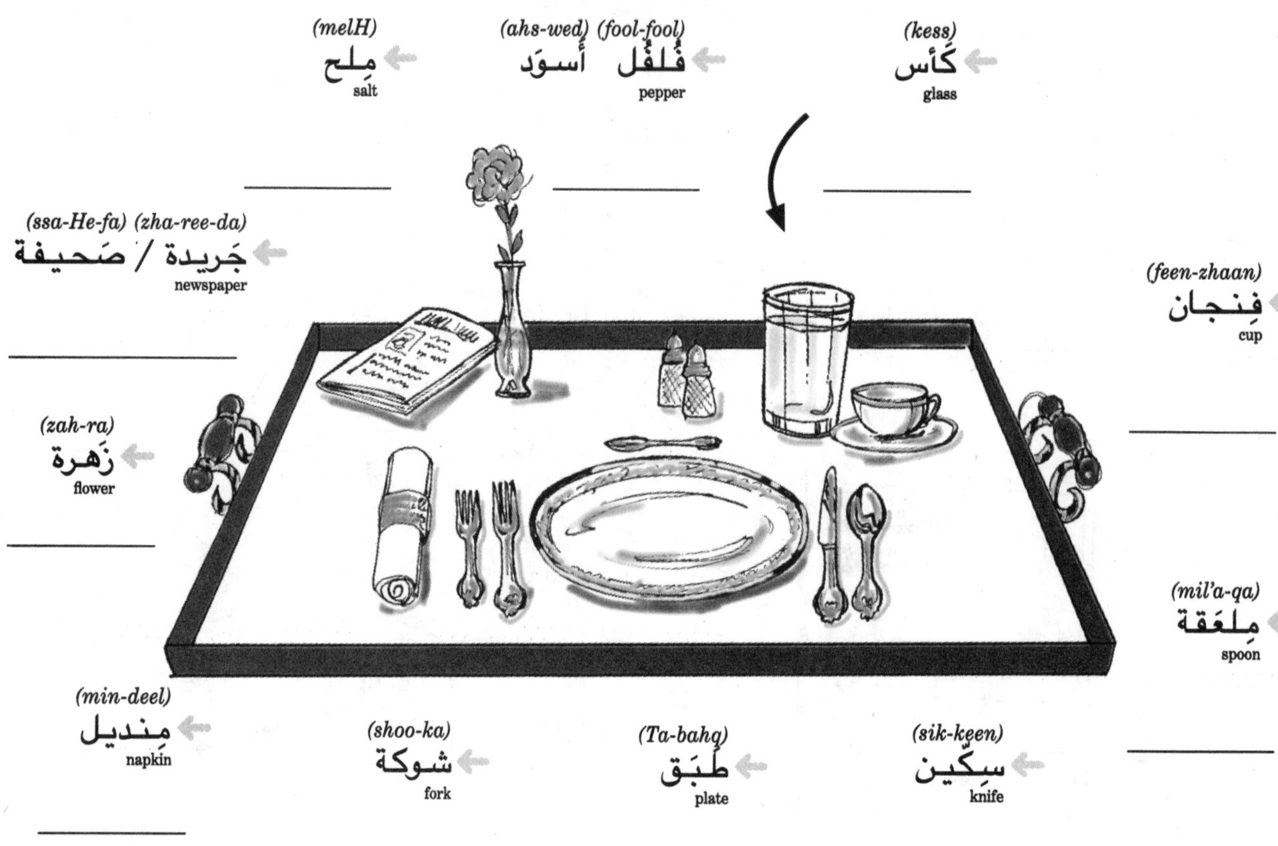

Don't forget to label all these things in your home وَ office.

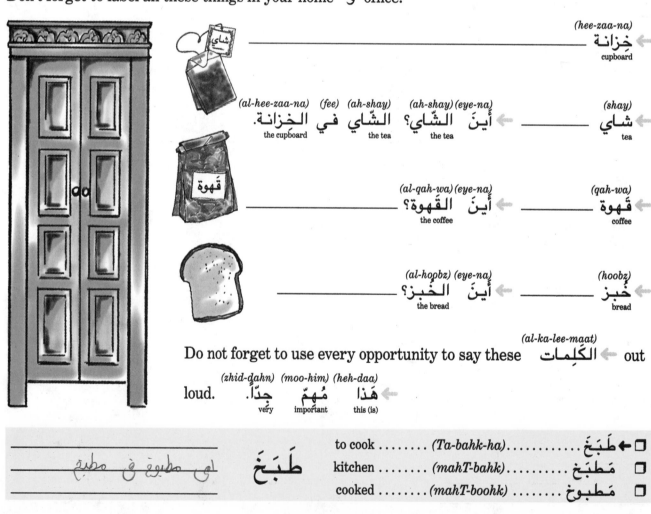

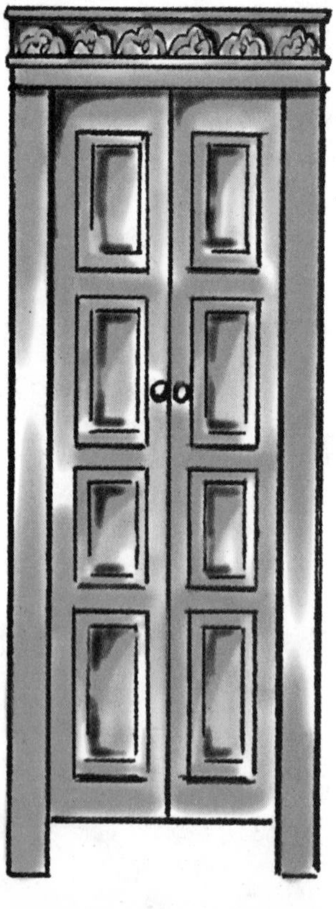

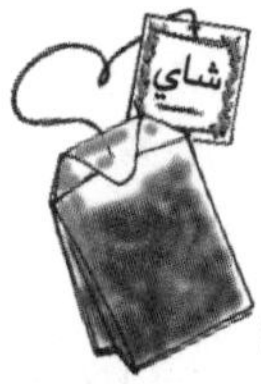

(hee-zaa-na) خِزانة ← cupboard ______

(shay) شاي ← tea ______ (eye-na) (ah-shay) أينَ الشّاي؟ ← the tea (ah-shay) (fee) (al-hee-zaa-na) الشّاي في الخزانة. the tea the cupboard

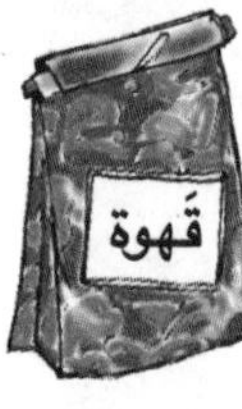

(qah-wa) قَهوة ← coffee ______ (eye-na) (al-qah-wa) أينَ القَهوة؟ ← the coffee ______

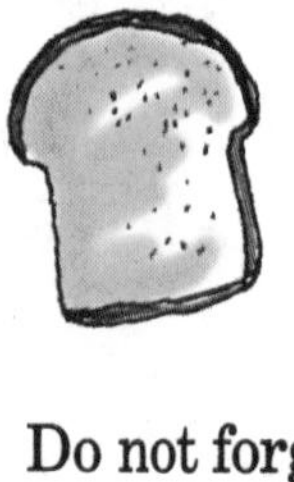

(hoobz) خُبز ← bread ______ (eye-na) (al-hoobz) أينَ الخُبز؟ ← the bread ______

Do not forget to use every opportunity to say these (al-ka-lee-maat) الكَلِمات ← out loud. (heh-daa) (moo-him) (zhid-dahn) هَذا ← this (is) مُهِمّ important جِدّاً. very

طَبَخ

اى مطبوخ فى مطبخ

- ☐ to cook .... (Ta-bahk-ha)............ طَبَخ ←
- ☐ kitchen .... (mahT-bahk).......... مَطبَخ
- ☐ cooked .... (mahT-boohk) .... مَطبوخ

(deen)
ديـن
religion

Whether you are in (al-zheh-zair-ir) الـجَـزائِـر (Algeria), (al-yeh-men) الـيَـمَـن (Yemen) or (loob-naan) لُـبـنـان (Lebanon) religion is very important in everyday life. A person's (deen) ديـن (religion) is usually one of the following:

(moos-lim) مُـسـلِـم — Muslim (♂) ______________________________

(moos-lee-ma) مُـسـلِـمة — Muslim (♀) ______________________________

(meh-see-He) مَـسـيـحـي — Christian (♂) ______________________________

(meh-see-He-ya) مَـسـيـحـيّـة — Christian (♀) ______________________________

(mahs-zhid) (zhaa-mehh) مَـسـجِـد \ جـامِـع — mosque ______________________________

(ka-nee-sa) كَـنـيـسـة — church ______________________________

(hel) (heh-daa) (mahs-zhid) (na-ahm)
هَـل هَـذا مَـسـجِـد؟ نَـعَـم.
(is) this (a) mosque yes

(hel) (heh-daa) (mahs-zhid) (zha-deed)
هَـل هَـذا مَـسـجِـد جَـديـد؟
(is) mosque new

(hel) (mahs-zhid) (qa-deem)
هَـل هَـذا مَـسـجِـد قَـديـم؟
(is) old

مَـسـجِـد الـحَـسَـن الـثّـانـي - الـدّار الـبَـيـضـاء
Hasan II Mosque — Casablanca

Let's learn how to say "I" and "we" (bil-r-ra-be-ya) بِـالـعَـرَبِـيّـة (in Arabic):

(ah-naa) أنـا — I ______________________________

(naH-noo) نَـحـنُ — we ______________________________

Test yourself - write each sentence on the next page for more practice. Add your own personal variations as well.

(al-be-Taa-ga) الـبـطـاقـة؟ (the postcard) ______________ (how much) ______________ (how much)

طَـبَـخ

☐ ← طَـبّـاخ .... (Tahb-baahk) .... chef (♂)
☐ طَـبّـاخـة .... (Tahb-baa-kha) .... chef (♀)
☐ طَـبـيـخ .... (Ta-beehk) .... cooked food

الطباخ مطبوخ في مطبخ
الطباخة مطبوخ طبيخ
____

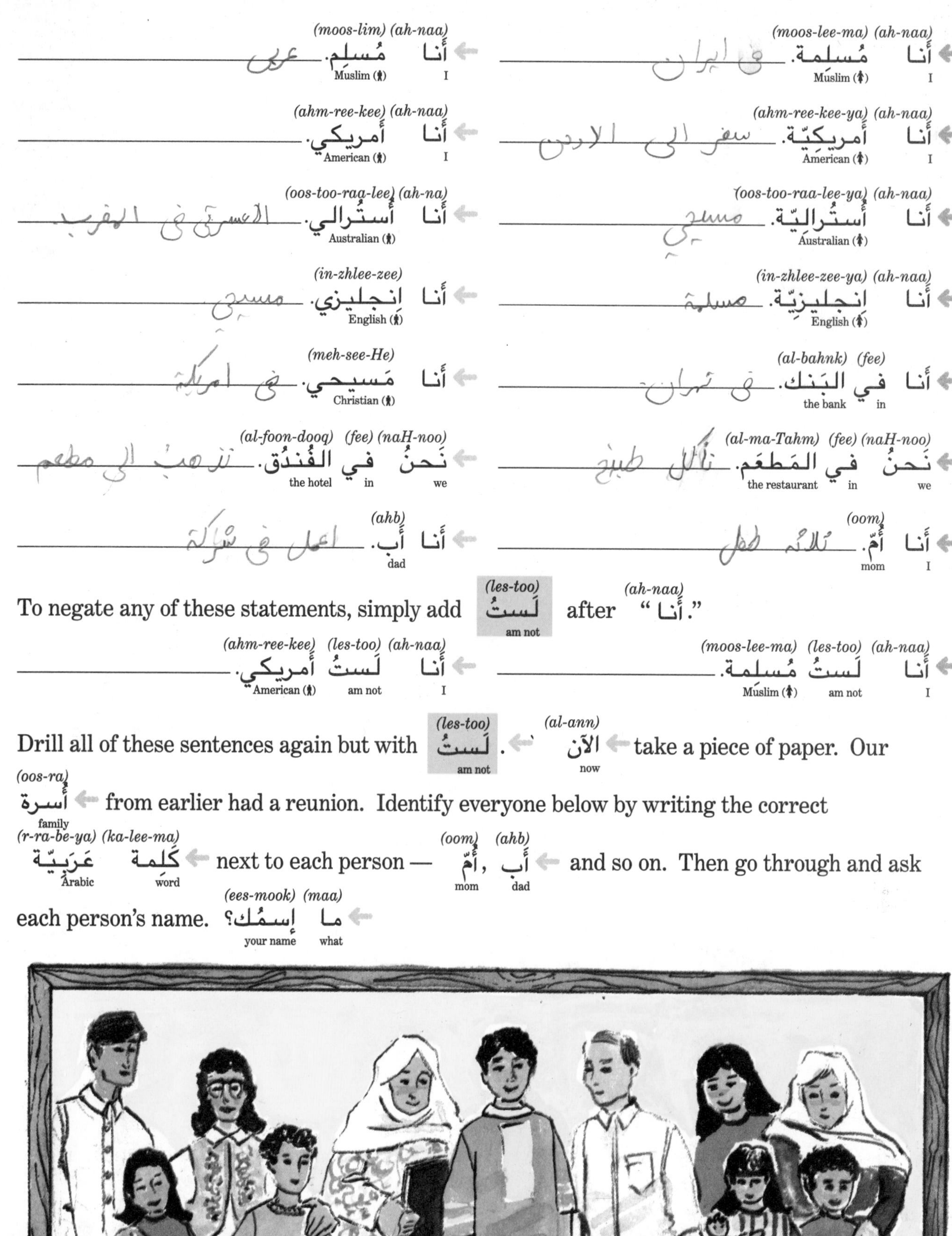

(moos-lim) (ah-naa)
← أنا مُسلِم. ______________________
Muslim (♂) I

(moos-lee-ma) (ah-naa)
← أنا مُسلمة. ______________________
Muslim (♀) I

(ahm-ree-kee) (ah-naa)
← أنا أمريكي. ______________________
American (♂) I

(ahm-ree-kee-ya) (ah-naa)
← أنا أمريكِيّة. ______________________
American (♀) I

(oos-too-raa-lee) (ah-na)
← أنا أُستُرالي. ______________________
Australian (♂)

(oos-too-raa-lee-ya) (ah-naa)
← أنا أُستُرالِيّة. ______________________
Australian (♀)

(in-zhlee-zee)
← أنا انجليزي. ______________________
English (♂)

(in-zhlee-zee-ya) (ah-naa)
← أنا انجليزيّة. ______________________
English (♀)

(meh-see-He)
← أنا مَسيحي. ______________________
Christian (♂)

(al-bahnk) (fee)
← أنا في البَنك. ______________________
the bank in

(al-foon-dooq) (fee) (naH-noo)
← نَحنُ في الفُندُق. ______________________
the hotel in we

(al-ma-Tahm) (fee) (naH-noo)
← نَحنُ في المَطعَم. ______________________
the restaurant in we

(ahb)
← أنا أب. ______________________
dad

(oom)
← أنا أمّ. ______________________
mom I

To negate any of these statements, simply add (les-too) لَستُ (am not) after (ah-naa) "أنا."

(ahm-ree-kee) (les-too) (ah-naa)
← أنا لَستُ أمريكي. ______________________
American (♂) am not I

(moos-lee-ma) (les-too) (ah-naa)
← أنا لَستُ مُسلمة. ______________________
Muslim (♀) am not I

Drill all of these sentences again but with (les-too) لَستُ (am not). ← (al-ann) الآن (now) ← take a piece of paper. Our (oos-ra) أسرة (family) ← from earlier had a reunion. Identify everyone below by writing the correct (r-ra-be-ya) (ka-lee-ma) كَلِمة عَرَبيّة (Arabic word) ← next to each person — (oom) (ahb) أب, أمّ (dad, mom) ← and so on. Then go through and ask each person's name. (ees-mook) (maa) ← ما إسمُك؟ (what your name)

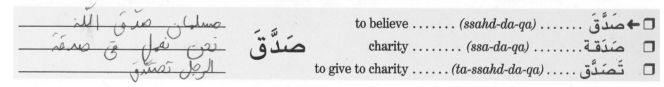

☐	←صَدَّق .... (ssahd-da-qa) .... to believe	صَدَّق
☐	صَدَقة .... (ssa-da-qa) .... charity	
☐	تَصَدَّق ..... (ta-ssahd-da-qa) ..... to give to charity	

١٢ / 12

(ah-ta-rahl-la-moo)
أَتَعَلَّمُ
I learn

You have already used two very important phrases: (oo-ree-do) أُرِيدُ (I want) and (rin-dee) عِندي (I have). Although you might be able to get by (mar) مَعَ (with) only these, let's assume you want to do better. Let's start مَعَ these key words.

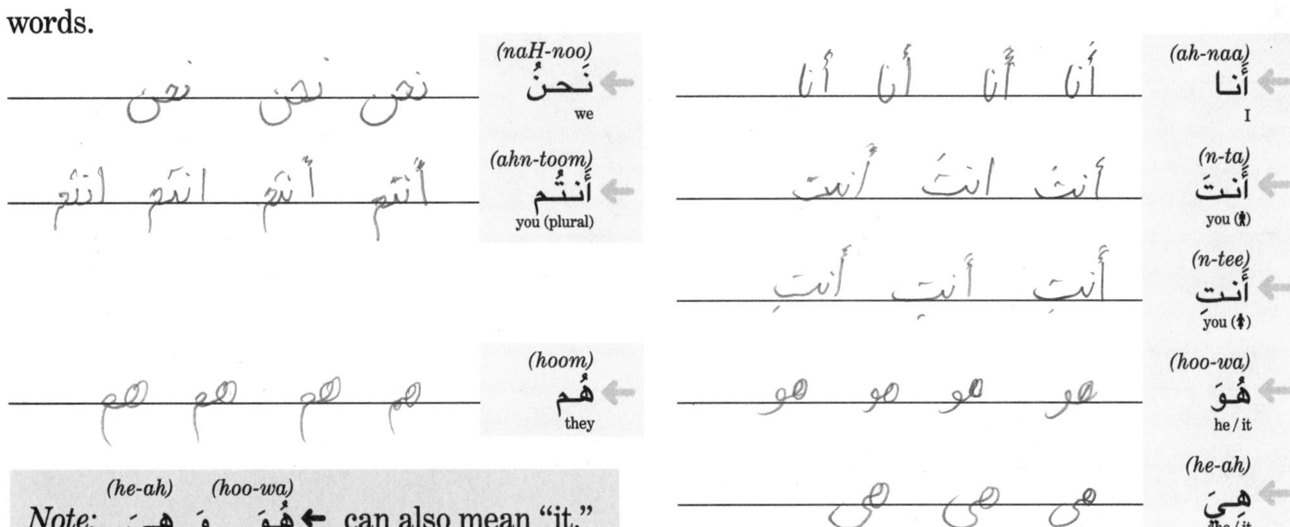

(ah-naa) أنا — I		(naH-noo) نَحنُ — we	
(n-ta) أنتَ — you (♂)		(ahn-toom) أنتُم — you (plural)	
(n-tee) أنتِ — you (♀)			
(hoo-wa) هُوَ — he / it		(hoom) هُم — they	
(he-ah) هِيَ — she / it			

Note: (he-ah) هِيَ و (hoo-wa) هُوَ can also mean "it."

Not too hard, is it? Draw lines between the matching (al-in-zhlee-zee-ya) الإنجليزيّة (English) and (al-r-ra-be-ya) العَرَبيّة (Arabic) words below to see if you can keep (heh-da-he) هَذِهِ (these) (al-ka-lee-maat) الكَلِمات (words) straight in your mind.

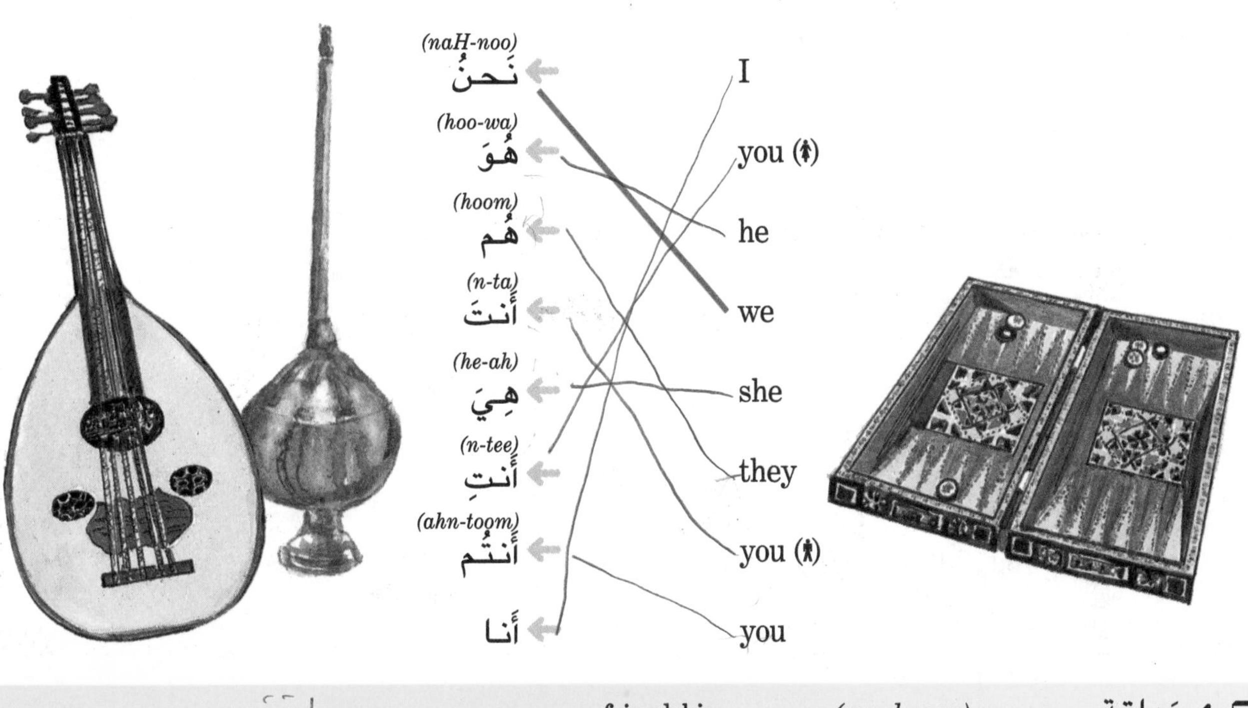

(naH-noo) نَحنُ	I
(hoo-wa) هُوَ	you (♂)
(hoom) هُم	he
(n-ta) أنتَ	we
(he-ah) هِيَ	she
(n-tee) أنتِ	they
(ahn-toom) أنتُم	you (♀)
أنا	you

صَدَّق

- ❒ friendship ....(ssa-daa-qa).......... صَداقة
- ❒ friend (♂).........(ssa-deeq).......... صَديق
- ❒ friend (♀).........(ssa-dee-qa).......... صَديقة

(al-ann) الآنَ now ← close (al-kee-taab) الكِتاب book (heh-daa) هَذا this ← and write out both columns of this practice on (wa-ra-qa) وَرَقة a piece of paper. ← How did (n-ta) أنتَ you (♂) ← do? You can say almost anything (bil-r-ra-be-ya) بِالعَرَبِيّة in Arabic ← with one basic formula: the "plug-in" formula. Let's take (seet-teh) سِتّة six ← basic وَ practical verbs وَ see how the "plug-in" formula works. Write the verbs in the blanks after (n-ta) أنتَ ← have practiced saying them out loud many times.

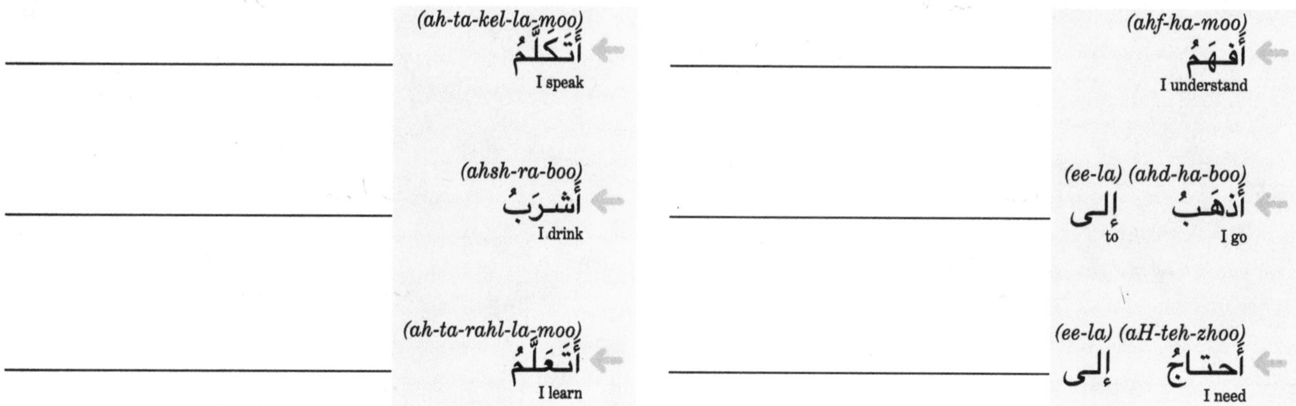

(ah-ta-kel-la-moo) أتَكَلَّمُ I speak
(ahsh-ra-boo) أشرَبُ I drink
(ah-ta-rahl-la-moo) أتَعَلَّمُ I learn
(ahf-ha-moo) أفهَمُ I understand
(ee-la) (ahd-ha-boo) أذهَبُ إلى I go to
(ee-la) (aH-teh-zhoo) أحتاجُ إلى I need

In Arabic, the subject – I, we, you – is contained in the verb as you will see in the following patterns. Associate أ with the "I" form and نـ with the "we" form. Study the following patterns carefully then write out your new verbs in the spaces provided.

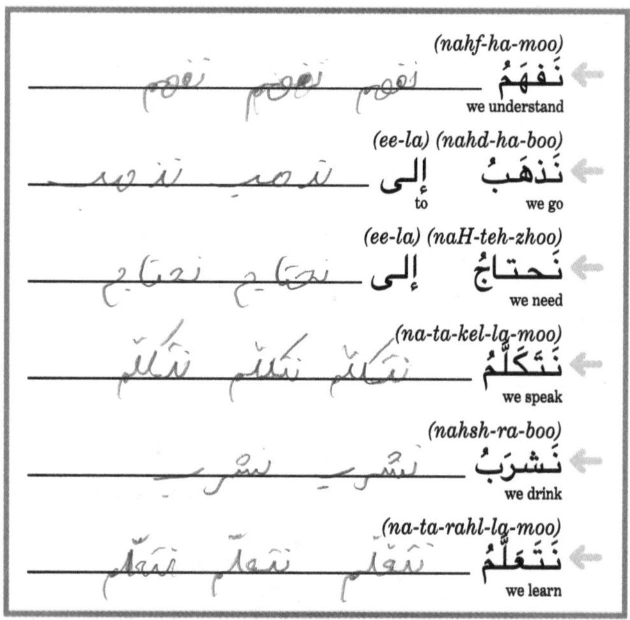

(nahf-ha-moo) نَفهَمُ we understand
(ee-la) (nahd-ha-boo) نَذهَبُ إلى we go to
(ee-la) (naH-teh-zhoo) نَحتاجُ إلى we need
(na-ta-kel-la-moo) نَتَكَلَّمُ we speak
(nahsh-ra-boo) نَشرَبُ we drink
(na-ta-rahl-la-moo) نَتَعَلَّمُ we learn

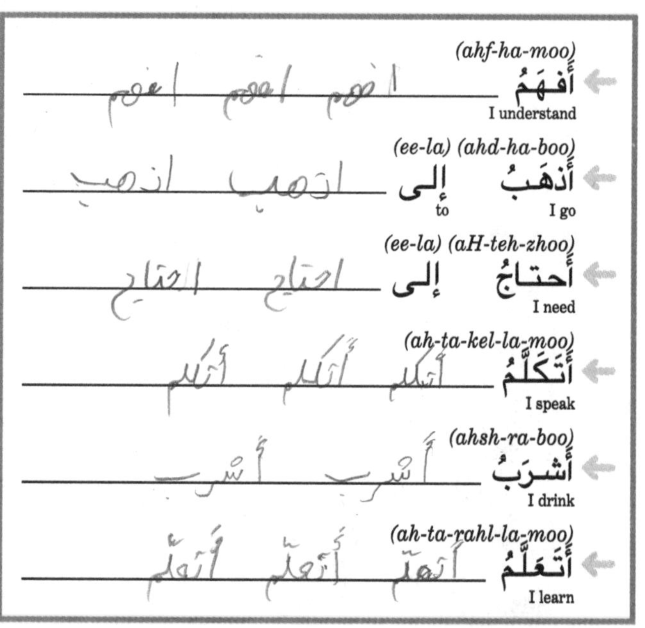

(ahf-ha-moo) أفهَمُ I understand
(ee-la) (ahd-ha-boo) أذهَبُ إلى I go to
(ee-la) (aH-teh-zhoo) أحتاجُ إلى I need
(ah-ta-kel-la-moo) أتَكَلَّمُ I speak
(ahsh-ra-boo) أشرَبُ I drink
(ah-ta-rahl-la-moo) أتَعَلَّمُ I learn

Did you hear the slight difference in pronunciation with these two patterns? Yes! *"na"* for "we" and *"ah"* for "I."

بَدَأ

- ☐ بَدَأ ← to begin ....(*beh-da-aa*)..........
- ☐ بِدائي primitive ....(*be-dair-ee*)........
- ☐ بِداية beginning ....(*be-dair-ya*)........

Next – the patterns for "you" (♂) and "you" (♀).

Note: • Both patterns start with " تـ " (تَـ pronounced *"ta"* or تُـ pronounced *"too"*)

• "You" (♀) ends with " ـينَ" which is pronounced *"ee-na."*

(tahf-ha-me-na)
تَفهَمينَ
you (♀) understand
(ee-la) (tahd-ha-be-na)
تَذهَبينَ إلى
you (♀) go to
(ee-la) (taH-teh-zhee-na)
تَحتاجينَ إلى
you (♀) need
(ta-ta-kel-la-me-na)
تَتَكَلَّمينَ
you (♀) speak
(tahsh-ra-be-na)
تَشرَبينَ
you (♀) drink
(ta-ta-rahl-la-me-na)
تَتَعَلَّمينَ
you (♀) learn

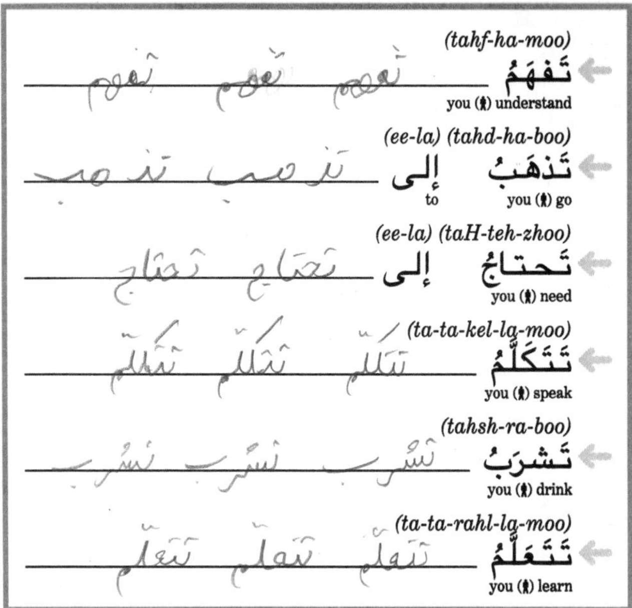

(tahf-ha-moo)
تَفهَمُ
you (♂) understand
(ee-la) (tahd-ha-boo)
تَذهَبُ إلى
you (♂) go to
(ee-la) (taH-teh-zhoo)
تَحتاجُ إلى
you (♂) need
(ta-ta-kel-la-moo)
تَتَكَلَّمُ
you (♂) speak
(tahsh-ra-boo)
تَشرَبُ
you (♂) drink
(ta-ta-rahl-la-moo)
تَتَعَلَّمُ
you (♂) learn

The patterns for "he" and "she" are easy.

Note: • The pattern for "she" is identical to the "you" (♂) form so you can practice these together.

• The "he" pattern starts with " يـ " (يَـ pronounced *"ya"* or يُـ pronounced *"yoo"*)

(tahf-ha-moo)
تَفهَمُ
she understands
(ee-la) (tahd-ha-boo)
تَذهَبُ إلى
she goes to
(ee-la) (taH-teh-zhoo)
تَحتاجُ إلى
she needs
(ta-ta-kel-la-moo)
تَتَكَلَّمُ
she speaks
(tahsh-ra-boo)
تَشرَبُ
she drinks
(ta-ta-rahl-la-moo)
تَتَعَلَّمُ
she learns

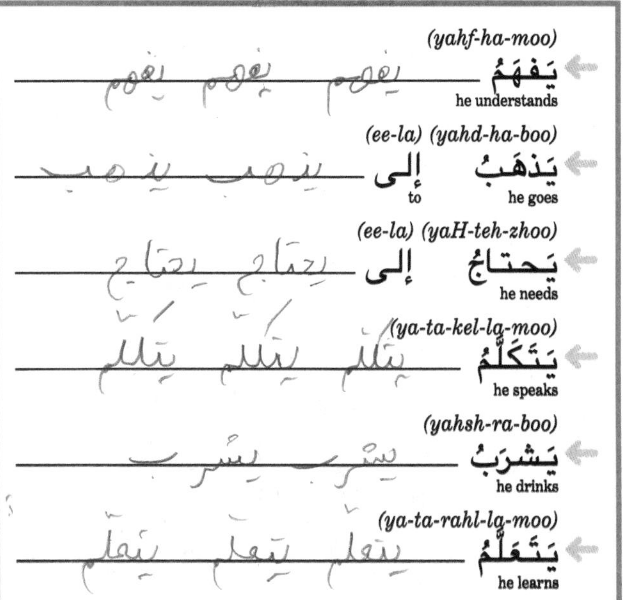

(yahf-ha-moo)
يَفهَمُ
he understands
(ee-la) (yahd-ha-boo)
يَذهَبُ إلى
he goes to
(ee-la) (yaH-teh-zhoo)
يَحتاجُ إلى
he needs
(ya-ta-kel-la-moo)
يَتَكَلَّمُ
he speaks
(yahsh-ra-boo)
يَشرَبُ
he drinks
(ya-ta-rahl-la-moo)
يَتَعَلَّمُ
he learns

بَدَأَ

☐ ← مُبتَدِئ .... (moob-teh-dih') ..... beginner

☐ مَبادِئ .... (ma-baa-dih') ...... principles

☐ مَدرَسة إبتِدائِيّة .. (ib-tee-dair-ee-ya)(ma-dra-sa) . elementary school

Now for أَنْتُمْ (ahn-toom) you all and هُمْ (hoom) they. They are similar. Both end in the sound *"oo-na."* Otherwise the "you all" pattern begins with تـ and the "they" pattern with يـ . That's it.

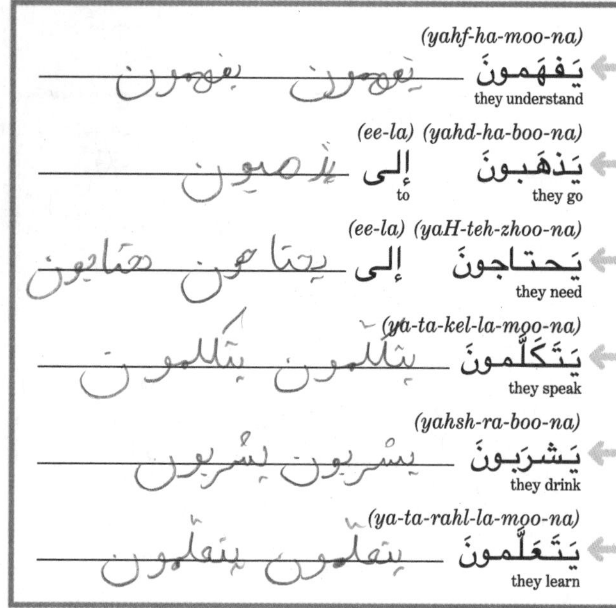

يَفْهَمونَ (yahf-ha-moo-na) they understand
يَذْهَبونَ (yahd-ha-boo-na) they go إلى (ee-la) to
يَحْتاجونَ (yaH-teh-zhoo-na) they need إلى (ee-la)
يَتَكَلَّمونَ (ya-ta-kel-la-moo-na) they speak
يَشْرَبونَ (yahsh-ra-boo-na) they drink
يَتَعَلَّمونَ (ya-ta-rahl-la-moo-na) they learn

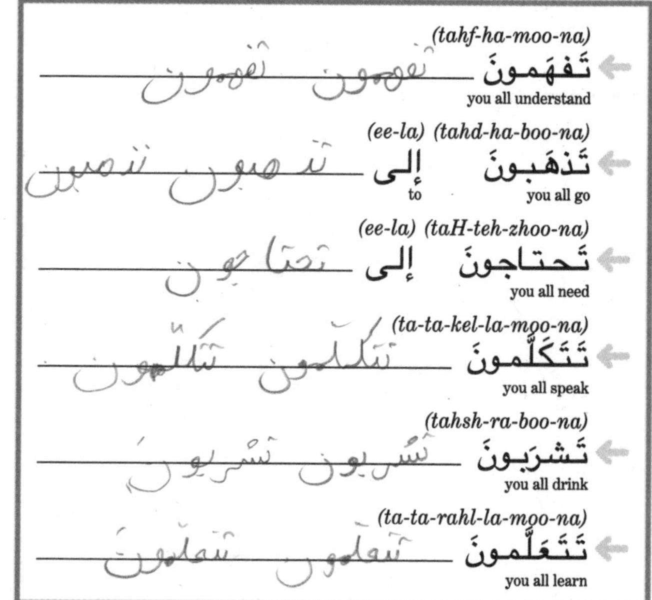

تَفْهَمونَ (tahf-ha-moo-na) you all understand
تَذْهَبونَ (tahd-ha-boo-na) you all go إلى (ee-la) to
تَحْتاجونَ (taH-teh-zhoo-na) you all need إلى (ee-la)
تَتَكَلَّمونَ (ta-ta-kel-la-moo-na) you all speak
تَشْرَبونَ (tahsh-ra-boo-na) you all drink
تَتَعَلَّمونَ (ta-ta-rahl-la-moo-na) you all learn

Initially you won't use the أَنْتُمْ (ahn-toom) you all form a lot so we don't focus on it. Just remember to speak slowly وَ clearly وَ you will be understood. Arabic speakers will be delighted you have taken the time to learn their language. Here are six more verbs.

آكُلُ (aa-koo-loo) I eat	أُسافِرُ (oo-seh-fee-roo) I travel
أَدْرُسُ (ah-droo-soo) I study	أُرسِلُ (oor-see-loo) I send
أَسْكُنُ (es-koo-noo) I live	أعرِفُ (ah-ree-foo) I know

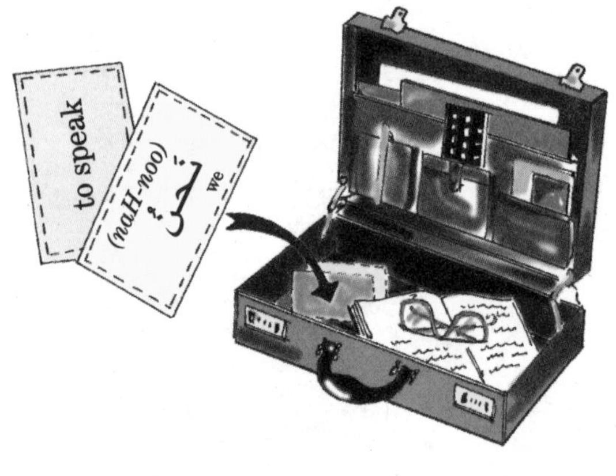

At the back of هَذا (heh-daa) this الكِتاب (al-kee-taab) book أَنْتَ (n-ta) you will find twelve pages of flash cards to help you learn هَذِهِ (heh-da-he) these الكَلِمات (al-ka-lee-maat) words الجَديدة (al-zha-dee-da) new. Cut them out; carry them in your briefcase, purse, pocket أو (ow) or knapsack; وَ review them whenever أَنْتَ (n-ta) you have a free moment.

عادَ	to return .... (reh-da)	عادَ	❏
	return .... (ow-da)	عَودة	❏
	usually .... (raa-da-tahn)	عادةً	❏

Practice what (n-ta) أَنتَ you (♂) have learned by filling in the blanks with the correct form of the verb.

(ah-ta-kel-la-moo) (al-r-ra-be-ya)
→ أَتَكَلَّمُ ______ العَرَبِيّة.
I speak ______ Arabic

(ta-ta-kel-la-moo) (al-r-ra-be-ya)
تَتَكَلَّمُ ______ العَرَبِيّة.
you (♂) speak / she speaks

(ta-ta-kel-la-me-na) (al-in-zhlee-zee-ya)
تَتَكَلَّمينَ ______ الإنجليزيّة.
you (♀) speak ______ English

(ya-ta-kel-la-moo) (al-in-zhlee-zee-ya)
يَتَكَلَّمُ ______ الإنجليزيّة.
he speaks

(na-ta-kel-la-moo) (al-fa-rahn-see-ya)
نَتَكَلَّمُ ______ الفَرَنسِيّة.
we speak ______ French

(ya-ta-kel-la-moo-na) (al-ees-baa-nee-ya)
يَتَكَلَّمونَ ______ الإسبانِيّة.
they speak ______ Spanish

(ahf-ha-moo) (al-r-ra-be-ya)
→ أفهَمُ ______ العَرَبِيّة.
I understand ______ Arabic

(tahf-ha-moo) (al-r-ra-be-ya)
تَفهَمُ ______ العَرَبِيّة.
you (♂) understand / she understands

(tahf-ha-me-na)
تَفهَمينَ ______ العَرَبِيّة.
you (♀) understand

(yahf-ha-moo) (al-in-zhlee-zee-ya)
يَفهَمُ ______ الإنجليزيّة.
he understands ______ English

(nahf-ha-moo) (al-fa-rahn-see-ya)
نَفهَمُ ______ الفَرَنسِيّة.
we understand ______ French

(yahf-ha-moo-na) (al-fa-rahn-see-ya)
يَفهَمونَ ______ الفَرَنسِيّة.
they understand

(ahsh-ra-boo) (al-maa')
→ أشرَبُ ______ الماء.
I drink ______ (the) water

(tahsh-ra-boo) (al-maa')
تَشرَبُ ______ الماء.
you (♂) drink / she drinks

(tahsh-ra-be-na) (al-ra-sseer)
تَشرَبينَ ______ العَصير.
you (♀) drink ______ (the) juice

(yahsh-ra-boo) (al-ra-sseer)
يَشرَبُ ______ العَصير.
he drinks

(nahsh-ra-boo) (ah-shay)
نَشرَبُ ______ الشّاي.
we drink ______ (the) tea

(yahsh-ra-boo-na) (al-qa-wa)
يَشرَبونَ ______ القَهوة.
they drink ______ (the) coffee

(ee-la) (ahd-ha-boo) (al-foon-dooq)
→ أذهَبُ إلى ______ الفُندُق.
I go to ______ the hotel

(ee-la) (tahd-ha-boo) (al-foon-dooq)
تَذهَبُ إلى ______ الفُندُق.
you (♂) go / she goes

(ee-la) (tahd-ha-be-na) (al-bahnk)
تَذهَبينَ إلى ______ البَنك.
you (♀) go ______ the bank

(ee-la) (yahd-ha-boo) (al-ma-Tahm)
يَذهَبُ إلى ______ المَطعَم.
he goes ______ the restaurant

(ee-la) (nahd-ha-boo) (ah-ssahf)
نَذهَبُ إلى ______ الصَّف.
we go ______ the class

(yahd-ha-boo-na) (ah-ssahf)
يَذهَبونَ إلى ______ الصَّف.
they go

(ah-ta-rahl-la-moo) (al-r-ra-be-ya)
→ أَتَعَلَّمُ ______ العَرَبِيّة.
I learn ______ Arabic

(ta-ta-rahl-la-moo) (al-in-zhlee-zee-ya)
تَتَعَلَّمُ ______ الإنجليزيّة.
you (♂) learn / she learns ______ English

(ta-ta-rahl-la-me-na) (rahn)(meess-ur)
تَتَعَلَّمينَ ______ عَن مِصر.
you (♀) learn ______ about Egypt

(ya-ta-rahl-la-moo) (rahn)(meess-ur)
يَتَعَلَّمُ ______ عَن مِصر.
he learns ______ about

(na-ta-rahl-la-moo) (rahn)(al-zheh-zair-ir)
نَتَعَلَّمُ ______ عَن الجَزائِر.
we learn ______ Algeria

(ya-ta-rahl-la-moo-na) (rahn)(leeb-yaa)
يَتَعَلَّمونَ ______ عَن ليبيا.
they learn ______ Libya

(ee-la) (aH-teh-zhoo) (taak-see)
→ أحتاجُ إلى ______ تاكسي.
I need ______ (a) taxi

(ee-la) (taH-teh-zhoo) (bahnk)
تَحتاجُ إلى ______ بَنك.
you (♂) need / she needs ______ (a) bank

(ee-la) (taH-teh-zhee-na) (foon-dooq)
تَحتاجينَ إلى ______ فُندُق.
you (♀) need ______ (a) hotel

(ee-la) (yaH-teh-zhoo) (feen-zhaan)(qa-wa)
يَحتاجُ إلى ______ فِنجان قَهوة.
he needs ______ (a) cup coffee

(ee-la) (naH-teh-zhoo) (feen-zhaan)(shay)
نَحتاجُ إلى ______ فِنجان شاي.
we need ______ (a) cup tea

(ee-la) (yaH-teh-zhoo-na) (feen-zhaan)(shay)
يَحتاجونَ إلى ______ فِنجان شاي.
they need

عادَ

- ❑ عادات ← customs / habits ....(raa-daat)........
- ❑ إعتِيادي habitual ..... (ear-tee-eh-dee) ....
- ❑ إعتادَ to be accustomed to .... (ear-teh-da) ....

Now take a break, walk around the room, take a deep breath and do the next six verbs.

← أَكُلُ (aa-koo-loo) I eat ______ كَثيراً. (ka-thee-rahn) a lot	← أُسافِرُ (oo-seh-fee-roo) I travel ______ إلى مِصر. (ee-la)(meess-ur) to Egypt
تَأكُلُ (taa-koo-loo) you (♂) eat / she eats ______ كَثيراً. (ka-thee-rahn)	تُسافِرُ (too-seh-fee-roo) you (♂) travel / she travels ______ إلى مِصر. (ee-la)(meess-ur)
تَأكُلينَ (taa-koo-lee-na) you (♀) eat ______ قَليلاً. (qa-lee-lahn) a little	تُسافِرينَ (too-seh-fee-ree-na) you (♀) travel ______ إلى المَغرِب. (ee-la)(al-ma-greb) Morocco
يَأكُلُ (yaa-koo-loo) he eats ______ قَليلاً. (qa-lee-lahn)	يُسافِرُ (yoo-seh-fee-roo) he travels ______ إلى المَغرِب. (al-ma-greb)
لا نَأكُلُ (la) (na-koo-loo) we eat ______ أيَّ شَيء. (eye) (shay') nothing	نُسافِرُ (noo-seh-fee-roo) we travel ______ إلى لُبنان. (loob-naan) Lebanon
يَأكُلونَ (ya-koo-loo) they eat ______ كُل شَيء. (kool) (shay') everything	يُسافِرونَ (yoo-seh-fee-roo-na) they travel ______ إلى الأُردُن. (al-oor-doon) Jordan
← أَدرُسُ (ah-droo-soo) I study ______ العَرَبِيّة. (al-r-ra-be-ya)	← أُرسِلُ (oor-see-loo) I send ______ رِسالة. (ree-saa-la) (a) letter
تَدرُسُ (ta-droo-soo) you (♂) study / she studies ______ الفَرَنسِيّة. (al-fa-rahn-see-ya) French	تُرسِلُ (toor-see-loo) you (♂) send / she sends ______ رِسالة. (ree-saa-la)
تَدرُسينَ (ta-droo-see-na) you (♀) study ______ الإسبانِيّة. (al-ees-baa-nee-ya) Spanish	تُرسِلينَ (toor-see-lee-na) you (♀) send ______ بِطاقة. (be-Taa-qa) (a) postcard
يَدرُسُ (ya-droo-soo) he studies ______ العِبرِيّة. (al-ay-bree-ya) Hebrew	يُرسِلُ (yoor-see-loo) he sends ______ بِطاقة. (be-Taa-qa)
نَدرُسُ (na-droo-soo) we study ______ الألمانِيّة. (al-ahl-maa-nee-ya) German	نُرسِلُ (noor-see-loo) we send ______ الكِتاب. (al-kee-taab) the book
يَدرُسونَ (ya-droo-soo-na) they study ______ الإيطالِيّة. (al-ee-Taa-lee-ya) Italian	يُرسِلونَ (yoor-see-loo-na) they send ______ ثَلاث بِطاقات. (tha-laath) three (be-Taa-qaat) postcards
← أَسكُنُ (es-koo-noo) I live ______ في إنجلَترا. (fee) (in-zhla-tair-raa) England	← أَعرِفُ (ah-ree-foo) I know ______ العَرَبِيّة.
تَسكُنُ (tes-koo-noo) you (♂) live / she lives ______ في إنجلَترا. (fee) (in-zhla-tair-raa)	تَعرِفُ (ta-ree-foo) you (♂) know / she knows ______ الإنجليزِيّة. (al-in-zhlee-zee-ya)
تَسكُنينَ (tes-koo-nee-na) you (♀) live ______ في أُستُراليا. (fee) (oos-too-raa-lee-yaa) Australia	تَعرِفينَ (ta-ree-fee-na) you (♀) know ______ العُنوان. (al-roon-wen) the address
يَسكُنُ (yes-koo-noo) he lives ______ في أُستُراليا. (oos-too-raa-lee-yaa)	يَعرِفُ (ya-ree-foo) he knows ______ الإسبانِيّة. (al-ees-baa-nee-ya) Spanish
نَسكُنُ (nes-koo-noo) we live ______ في أمريكا. (ahm-ree-kaa) the United States	نَعرِفُ (na-ree-foo) we know ______ كُل شَيء. (kool) (shay') everything
يَسكُنونَ (yes-koo-noo-na) they live ______ في كَنَدا. (ka-na-daa) Canada	لا يَعرِفونَ (la) (ya-ree-foo-na) they know ______ أيَّ شَيء. (eye) (shay') nothing

فَضَّلَ

☐ ← فَضَّلَ to prefer.......(fahD-Da-la) ....

☐ مِن فَضلِك please (♂).....(fahD-lahk)(min) ..

☐ تَفَضَّل go ahead please (♂)......(ta-fahD-Dahl) ....

______

______

______

نَعَم (na-ahm) yes, it is hard to get used to all those كَلِمات (ka-lee-maat) words جَديدة (zha-dee-da) new. ← But just keep practicing وَ before you know it, أنتَ (n-ta) ← will be using them naturally. الآنَ (al-ann) ← is a perfect time to turn to the back of هَذا (heh-daa) this الكِتاب (al-kee-taab) book, ← clip out your verb flash cards وَ start flashing. See if أنتَ (n-ta) you (♂) ← can fill in the blanks below. The correct الأجوِبة (al-ezh-we-ba) answers ← are at the bottom of هَذِهِ (heh-da-he) this الصَّفحة (ah-ssahf-Ha) page. ←

1. ____
(I speak Arabic.)

2. ____
(We learn Arabic.)

3. ____
(He studies Arabic.)

4. ____
(She lives in the United States / America.)

5. ____
(I travel to Jordan.)

6. ____
(You (♂) send a postcard.)

In the following Steps, أنتَ (n-ta) ← will be introduced to more verbs and أنتَ (n-ta) you (♂) should drill them in exactly the same way as أنتَ (n-ta) did in this section. Look up كَلِمات (ka-lee-maat) words جَديدة (zha-dee-da) new ← in your قاموس (qaa-moos) dictionary ← and make up your own sentences. Try out your new words for that's how you make them yours to use on your holiday. Remember, the more أنتَ (n-ta) practice الآنَ (al-ann) now ← the more enjoyable your trip will be.

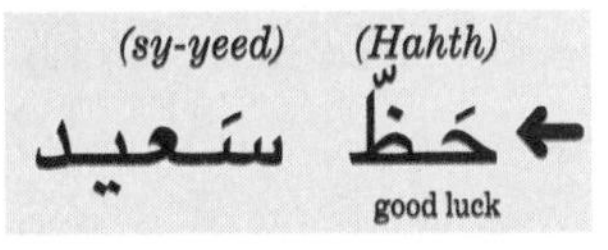

الأجوِبة

١ ← أتَكَلَّمُ العَرَبِيّة. ٣ ← يَدرُسُ العَرَبِيّة. ٥ ← أُسافِرُ إلى الأُردُن.

٢ نَتَعَلَّمُ العَرَبِيّة. ٤ تَسكُنُ في أمريكا. ٦ تُرسِلينَ بِطاقة.

(kem) *(ah-saa-ra)*

←كَم السّاعة؟

what / time is it

(ta-ree-fee-na) *(eye-yaam)* *(ah-shoo-hoor)*

←تَعرفينَ how to tell أيّام ← of the week and الشّهور ← of the year. As a traveler

you (♀) know / days / the months

(soo-ree-yaa) *(fee)* *(ow)* *(loob-naan)* *(fee)*

←في سوريا أو في لبنان, ← you need to be able to tell time in order to make reservations,

Syria / or / Lebanon

(al-Haa-fee-laat)

schedule appointments and to catch الحافلات.← Here are the "basics."

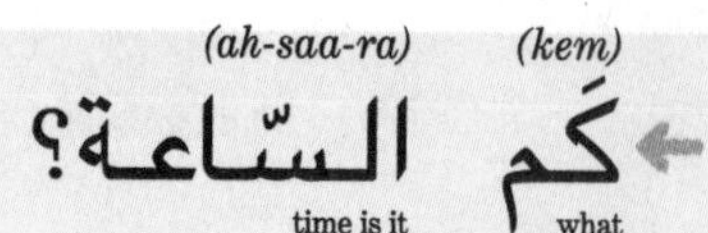

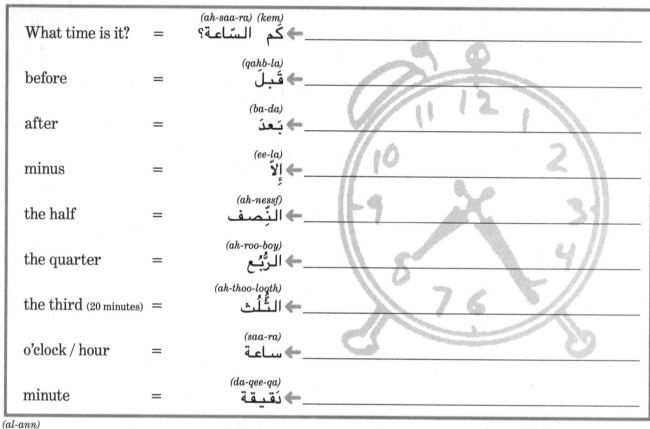

the buses

What time is it?	=	←كَم السّاعة؟ *(kem) (ah-saa-ra)* _____
before	=	←قَبلَ *(qahb-la)* _____
after	=	←بَعدَ *(ba-da)* _____
minus	=	←إلّا *(ee-la)* _____
the half	=	←النِّصف *(ah-nessf)* _____
the quarter	=	←الرُّبُع *(ah-roo-boy)* _____
the third (20 minutes)	=	←الثُّلُث *(ah-thoo-looth)* _____
o'clock / hour	=	←ساعة *(saa-ra)* _____
minute	=	←دَقيقة *(da-qee-qa)* _____

(al-ann)

الآن ←quiz yourself. Fill in the missing letters below.

now

before = | ل | بَ | قَ |

the quarter = | عَ | رُ | لـ | ا |

after = | د | عَ | بَ |

the third = | ثُ | لُ | لـ | ا |

the half = | ف | صّ | نِ | لـ | ا |

o'clock = | ة | ا | سـ |

What time is it? = | ة | عَ | ا | سّـ | لـ | ا | ☒ | مَ | كَ |

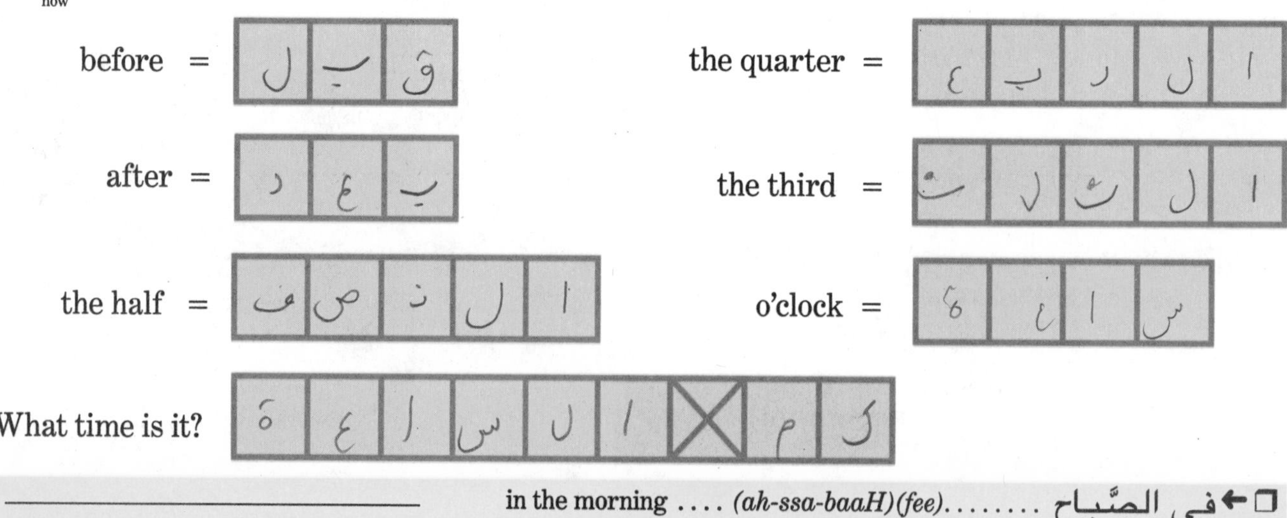

_____	in the morning .... *(ah-ssa-baaH)(fee)*........	←في الصّباح
_____	in the evening ..... *(al-ma-saa')(fee)*.........	في المَساء
_____	noon ....*(ah-Doo-hur)*.............	الظُّهر
_____	midnight ... *(ah-lail)(moon-ta-ssahf)* ..	مُنتَصَف اللَّيل

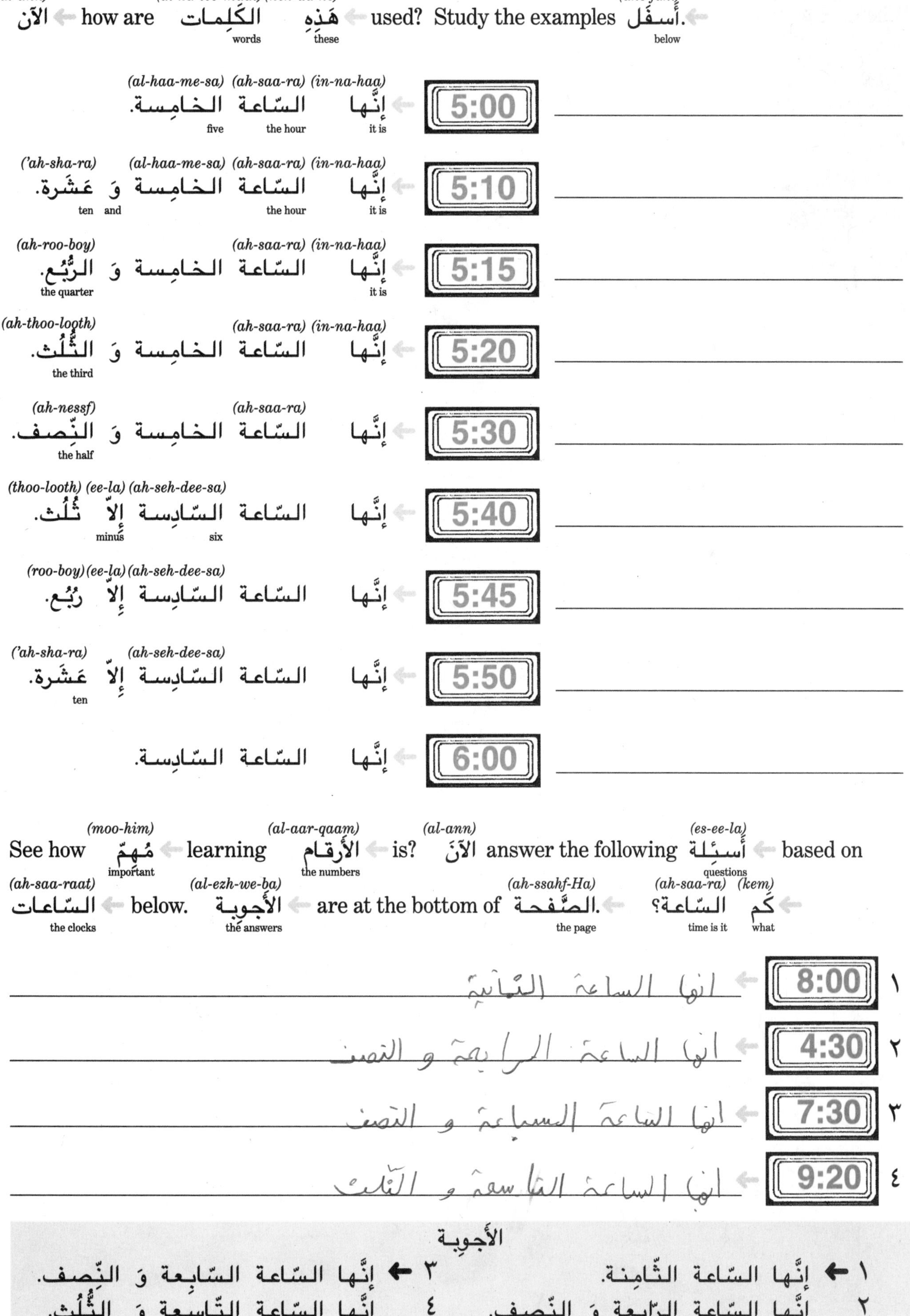

(al-ann) الآن ← how are (al-ka-lee-maat) الكَلِمات (words) (heh-da-he) هَذِهِ (these) ← used? Study the examples (ahs-fahl) أسفَل (below). ←

5:00	← إنَّها (in-na-haa, it is) السّاعة (ah-saa-ra, the hour) الخامِسة (al-haa-me-sa, five).
5:10	← إنَّها (in-na-haa, it is) السّاعة (ah-saa-ra, the hour) الخامِسة (al-haa-me-sa) وَ (and) عَشَرة ('ah-sha-ra, ten).
5:15	← إنَّها (in-na-haa, it is) السّاعة (ah-saa-ra) الخامِسة وَ الرُّبُع (ah-roo-boy, the quarter).
5:20	← إنَّها (in-na-haa) السّاعة (ah-saa-ra) الخامِسة وَ الثُّلُث (ah-thoo-looth, the third).
5:30	← إنَّها السّاعة (ah-saa-ra) الخامِسة وَ النِّصف (ah-nessf, the half).
5:40	← إنَّها السّاعة السّادِسة (ah-seh-dee-sa, six) إلاّ (ee-la, minus) ثُلُث (thoo-looth).
5:45	← إنَّها السّاعة السّادِسة (ah-seh-dee-sa) إلاّ (ee-la) رُبُع (roo-boy).
5:50	← إنَّها السّاعة السّادِسة (ah-seh-dee-sa) إلاّ عَشَرة ('ah-sha-ra, ten).
6:00	← إنَّها السّاعة السّادِسة.

See how (moo-him) مُهِمّ (important) ← learning (al-aar-qaam) الأرقام (the numbers) ← is? (al-ann) الآنَ answer the following (es-ee-la) أسئِلة (questions) ← based on (ah-saa-raat) السّاعات (the clocks) ← below. (al-ezh-we-ba) الأجوِبة (the answers) ← are at the bottom of (ah-ssahf-Ha) الصَّفحة (the page). ← (kem) كَم (what) (ah-saa-ra) السّاعة؟ (time is it) ←

١ 8:00 ← انها الساعة الثامنة

٢ 4:30 ← انها الساعة الرابعة و النصف

٣ 7:30 ← انها الساعة السابعة و النصف

٤ 9:20 ← انها الساعة التاسعة و الثلث

الأجوِبة

١ ← إنَّها السّاعة الثّامِنة.

٢ إنَّها السّاعة الرّابِعة وَ النِّصف.

٣ ← إنَّها السّاعة السّابِعة وَ النِّصف.

٤ إنَّها السّاعة التّاسِعة وَ الثُّلُث.

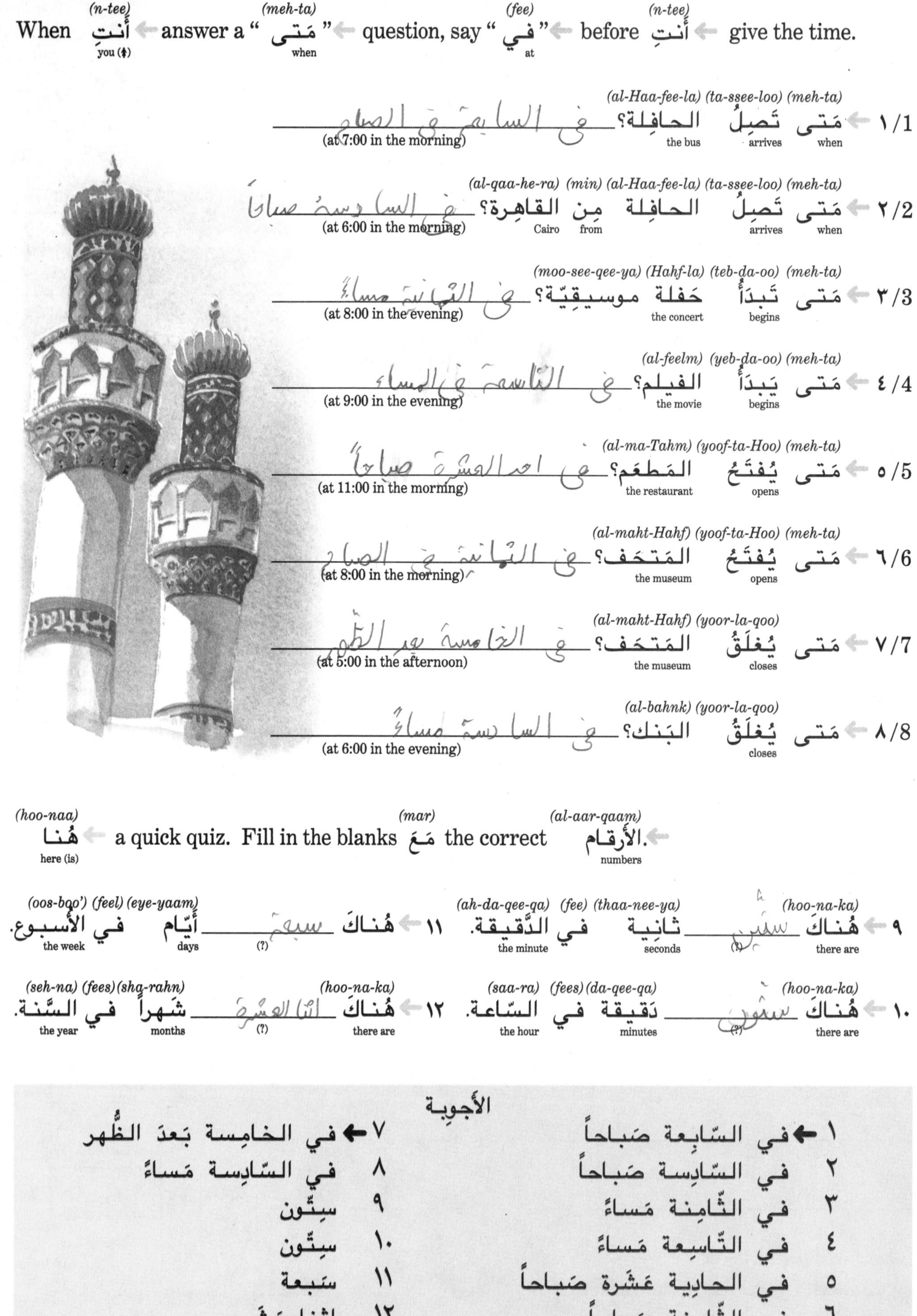

When أنتِ (n-tee) you answer a "مَتى (meh-ta) when" question, say "في (fee) at" before أنتِ (n-tee) give the time.

١/1 مَتى (meh-ta) when تَصِلُ (ta-ssee-loo) arrives الحافِلة؟ (al-Haa-fee-la) the bus ____________ (at 7:00 in the morning)

٢/2 مَتى (meh-ta) when تَصِلُ (ta-ssee-loo) arrives الحافِلة (al-Haa-fee-la) مِن (min) from القاهِرة؟ (al-qaa-he-ra) Cairo ____________ (at 6:00 in the morning)

٣/3 مَتى (meh-ta) تَبدأُ (teb-da-oo) begins حَفلة (Hahf-la) the concert موسيقِيّة؟ (moo-see-qee-ya) ____________ (at 8:00 in the evening)

٤/4 مَتى (meh-ta) يَبدأُ (yeb-da-oo) begins الفيلم؟ (al-feelm) the movie ____________ (at 9:00 in the evening)

٥/5 مَتى (meh-ta) يُفتَحُ (yoof-ta-Hoo) opens المَطعَم؟ (al-ma-Tahm) the restaurant ____________ (at 11:00 in the morning)

٦/6 مَتى (meh-ta) يُفتَحُ (yoof-ta-Hoo) opens المَتحَف؟ (al-maht-Hahf) the museum ____________ (at 8:00 in the morning)

٧/7 مَتى يُغلَقُ (yoor-la-qoo) closes المَتحَف؟ (al-maht-Hahf) the museum ____________ (at 5:00 in the afternoon)

٨/8 مَتى يُغلَقُ (yoor-la-qoo) closes البَنك؟ (al-bahnk) ____________ (at 6:00 in the evening)

هُنا (hoo-naa) here (is) a quick quiz. Fill in the blanks مَعَ (mar) the correct الأرقام (al-aar-qaam) numbers.

٩ هُناكَ (hoo-na-ka) there are ________ (?) ثانِية (thaa-nee-ya) seconds في (fee) الدَّقيقة. (ah-da-qee-qa) the minute

١٠ هُناكَ (hoo-na-ka) there are ________ (?) دَقيقة (da-qee-qa) minutes في (fees) السّاعة. (saa-ra) the hour

١١ هُناكَ ________ (?) أيّام (eye-yaam) days في (feel) الأُسبوع. (oos-boo') the week

١٢ هُناكَ (hoo-na-ka) there are ________ (?) شَهراً (sha-rahn) months في (fees) السَّنة. (seh-na) the year

الأجوِبة

١	في السّابِعة صَباحاً	٧	في الخامِسة بَعدَ الظُّهر
٢	في السّادِسة صَباحاً	٨	في السّادِسة مَساءً
٣	في الثّامِنة مَساءً	٩	سِتّون
٤	في التّاسِعة مَساءً	١٠	سِتّون
٥	في الحادِية عَشرة صَباحاً	١١	سَبعة
٦	في الثّامِنة صَباحاً	١٢	إثنا عَشَر

Do أنتِ (n-tee) [you] remember your greetings from earlier? It is a good time to review them as they will always be جداً (zhid-dahn) [very] important.

ماذا (may-daa) [what] نَقولُ (na-qoo-loo) [do we say] في الصَّباح؟ (ah-ssa-baaH)

"صَباح الخَير سَيِّدة مَبروك." (sa-baaH) (al-hair) (sy-yee-da) (ma-brook) [good morning Mrs. Mabrook]

ماذا (may-daa) [what] نَقولُ؟ (na-qoo-loo) [do we say] ____________________

ماذا (may-daa) نَقولُ (na-qoo-loo) [do we say] بَعدَ الظُّهر؟ (ba-da) (ah-Doo-hur) [(in) the afternoon]

"مَرحَبا مَيمونة." (mar-Ha-baa) (may-moo-na) [hello Maymoona]

ماذا (may-daa) نَقولُ؟ (na-qoo-loo) [do we say] ____________________

ماذا (may-daa) نَقولُ (na-qoo-loo) في [in] المَساء؟ (al-ma-saa') [the evening]

"مَساء الخَير سَيِّد وَليد." (ma-saa') (al-hair) (sy-yeed) (weh-leed) [good evening Mr. Wehlid]

ماذا نَقولُ؟ (na-qoo-loo) ____________________

ماذا نَقولُ في (feel) العاشِرة (aa-she-ra) [ten] مَساءً؟ (ma-saa-ahn)

"تُصبِحُ عَلى خَير نَبيل." (tooss-beh-Hoo) (ah-la) (hair) (na-beel) [good night Nabil]

ماذا نَقولُ؟ ____________________

Just as a bonus, let's add ____________________ تَشَرَّفنا (ta-shar-rahf-naa) [nice to meet you]

If أنتِ (n-tee) are lucky enough to be visiting عُمان (roo-maan) [Oman] or الكُوَيت (al-koo-wait) [Kuwait] or المَغرِب (al-ma-greb) [Morocco] over a holiday or a special occasion, أنتِ (n-tee) may want to use one of the following greetings.

Congratulations! = مَبروك! (ma-brook)	Happy Birthday! = عيد ميلاد سَعيد! (reed) (me-lahd) (sy-yeed)
Good Luck! = حَظ سَعيد! (Hahth) (sy-yeed)	Happy New Year! = سَنة سَعيدة! (seh-na) (sy-yee-da)

Here are a few holidays which you might experience during your visit!

- Ramadan . . . . (ra-ma-Dhahn) . . . . رَمَضان
- Eid Al Fitr (End of Ramadan) . . . . (al-fehtr)(reed) . . . . عيد الفِطر

(hoo-naa) هُنا (here are) the new verbs for Step 13. (n-tee) أنتِ have already used both of these, (la-kin) لَكِن (but) it is time to practice them officially.

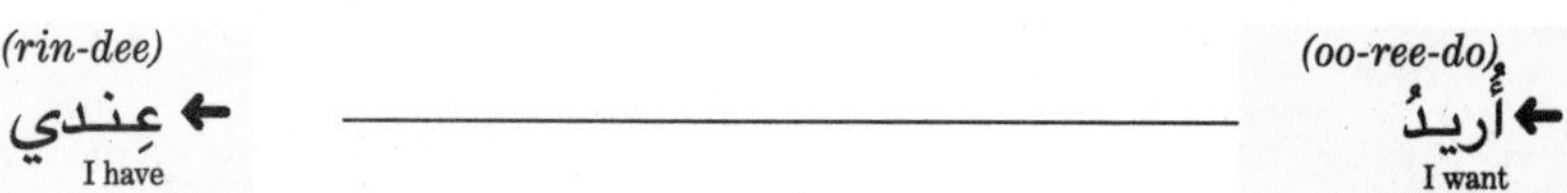

(oo-ree-do) ← أريدُ (I want) ____________________

(rin-dee) ← عِندي (I have) ____________________

(oo-ree-do) ← أريدُ (I want) ____________ (maa'ahn) ماءاً (water) (min) (fahD-lahk) مِن فضلِك. (please)	(rin-dee) ← عِندي (I have) ____________ (tis-oon) تِسعون (90) (dee-naa-rahn) ديناراً. (dinars)
(too-ree-do) تُريدُ (you (♂) want) ____________ (ra-ssee-rahn) عَصيراً. (juice)	(rin-da-ka) عِندَكَ (you (♂) have) ____________ (sy-yaa-ra) سَيّارة. (a car)
(too-ree-dee-na) تُريدينَ (you (♀) want) ____________ (shay-yen) شاياً. (tea)	(rin-da-kee) عِندَكِ (you (♀) have) ____________ (kelb) كَلب. (a dog)
(yoo-ree-do) يُريدُ (he wants) ____________ (qa-wa) قَهوة. (coffee)	(rin-da-hoo) عِندَهُ (he has) ____________ (bait) بَيت. (a house)
(too-ree-do) تُريدُ (she wants) ____________ (shoor-ba) شوربة. (soup)	(rin-da-haa) عِندَها (she has) ____________ (shooq-qa) شُقّة. (an apartment)
(noo-ree-do) نُريدُ (we want) ____________ (sa-la-Ta) سَلَطة. (salad)	(rin-da-naa) عِندَنا (we have) ____________ (ha-ree-Ta) خَريطة. (a map)
(yoo-ree-do-na) يُريدونَ (they want) ____________ (ahk-thar) أكثر. (more)	(rin-da-hoom) عِندَهُم (they have) ____________ (kee-taab) كِتاب. (a book)

Note: There are two expressions for "to have." "(rin-dee) عِندي" is used with things. On page 61 you will be introduced to "(lee) لي" which is used with people such as "I have a friend." Not too difficult, right?

- ❒ ← عيد الأضحى .... (al-ahD-Ha)(reed) .... Eid Al Adha (Abraham's sacrafice)
- ❒ عيد المَولِد النَّبَوي .... (ah-neh-ba-we)(al-mao-lid)(reed) ..... Eid Al Mawlid (Birth of Mohammed)
- ❒ رَأس السَّنة الميلاديّة .... (al-me-la-dee-ya)(ah-seh-na)(rahs) .... New Years

(n-tee)
أَنتِ ← have learned a lot of material in the last few steps وَ that means it is time to quiz yourself. Don't panic, this is just for you وَ no one else needs to know how (n-tee) أَنتِ did. Remember, this is a chance to review, find out (n-tee) أَنتِ (may-daa) ماذا (what) ← remember (n-tee) أَنتِ (may-daa) ماذا (what) (wa) وَ ← need to spend more time on. After (n-tee) أَنتِ have finished, check your (al-ezh-we-ba) الأَجوِبة (answers) ← in the glossary at the back of (al-kee-taab) الكِتاب (book) (heh-daa) هَذا (this). ← Circle the correct (al-ezh-we-ba) الأَجوِبة (answers). ←

(qa-wa) قَهوة	tea	coffee
(na-ahm) نَعَم	yes	no
(ahm) عَمّ	aunt	uncle
(ow) أَو	and	or
(ahsh-ra-boo) أَشرَبُ	I drink	I learn
(ah-ssa-baaH) الصَّباح	morning	night
(al-zhoo-moo-ah) الجُمُعة	Friday	Tuesday
(ah-ta-kel-la-moo) أَتَكَلَّمُ	I speak	I understand
(bear-id) بارِد	cold	hot
(foo-loos) فُلوس	money	page
(tis'ah) تِسعة	nine	ten
(hoobz) خُبز	a lot	bread

(oos-ra) أُسرة	seven	family
(zhed) جَدّ	children	grandfather
(ra-sseer) عَصير	butter	juice
(melH) مِلح	pepper	salt
(taH-ta) تَحت	under	over
(ra-zhool) رَجُل	man	doctor
(yoo-nee-yoo) يونيو	June	July
(deen) دين	kitchen	religion
(rin-dee) عِندي	I want	I have
(ah-ree-foo) أَعرِفُ	I know	I live
(reh-dahn) غَداً	yesterday	tomorrow
(aass-far) أَصفَر	good	yellow

(ah-saa-ra) (kem)
كَم السّاعة؟ ← What time is it? How are you? Well, how are you after this quiz?

جَمَع

- ☐ to collect .... (zha-ma-ahh) .... جَمَعَ ←
- ☐ university .... (zheh-me-ah)........... جامِعة
- ☐ mosque .... (zhaa-mehh)........... جامِع

١٤ / 14 ←الشَّمالْ - الجَنوب الشَّرق - الغَرب

(eh-sheh-mel) north, (al-zha-noob) south, (ah-shark) east, (al-greb) west

If (n-tee) ←أنتِ are looking at (ha-ree-Ta) ←خَريطة (a) map and you see the following (ka-lee-maat) ←كَلِمات words, it should not be too difficult to figure out (may-daa) ←ماذا what they mean. Take an educated guess. (al-ezh-we-ba) ←الأجوبة the answers (ahs-fahl) أسفَل below.

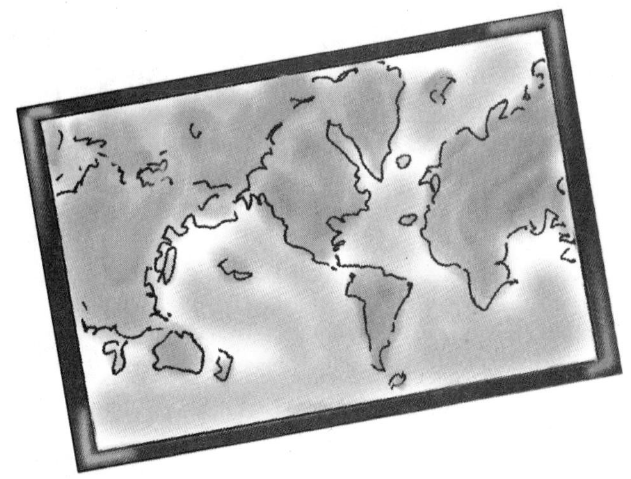

(zha-noob) (ef-ree-qee-yaa) ←جَنوب إفريقيا

(zha-noob)(ahm-ree-kaa) ←جَنوب أمريكا

(ah-saH-raa') (al-grer-be-ya) ←الصَّحراء الغَربِيّة

(sheh-mel)(ahm-ree-kaa) ←شَمال أمريكا

(ah-shark) (al-ow-sahT) ←الشَّرق الأوسَط

(shark) (ef-ree-qee-yaa) ←شَرق إفريقيا

(heh-da-he) (al-ka-lee-maat) ←هَذِهِ الكَلِمات are also essential for understanding directions. Learn them (al-ann) ←الآن.

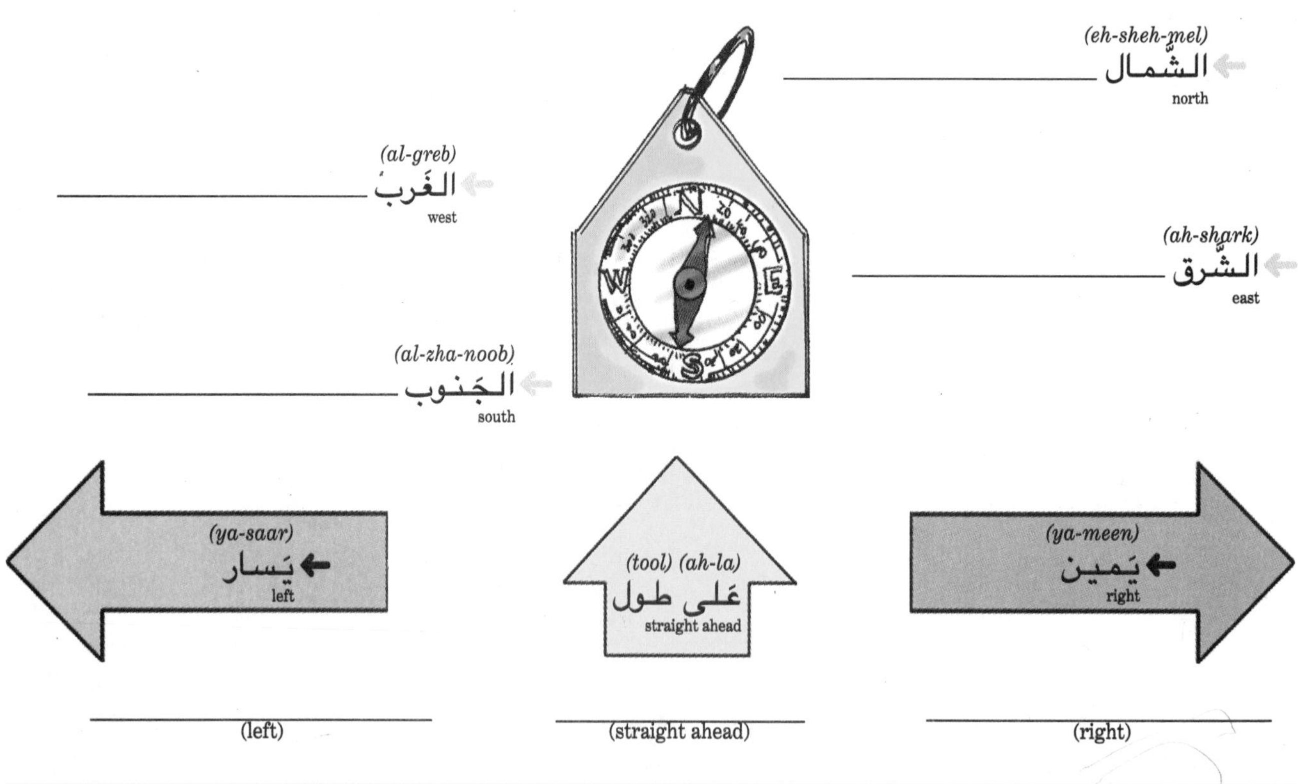

______________ (left)

______________ (straight ahead)

______________ (right)

الأجوبة

South America	South Africa
North America	Western Sahara
East Africa	the Middle East

These الجَديدة (al-zha-dee-da) new الكَلِمات (al-ka-lee-maat) words can go a long way. Say them aloud each time you write them in the blanks below.

مِن فَضلِك (min) (fahD-lahk) please (🚹) / مِن فَضلِك (min) (fahD-lik) please (🚺) ____________________

شُكراً (shook-rahn) thank you ____________________

آسِف (eh-sif) (🚹) / آسِفة (eh-sih-fa) (🚺) excuse me / I'm sorry / pardon ____________________

عَفواً (ahf-wahn) you're welcome ____________________

هُنا (hoo-naa) here (are) two typical conversations for someone who is trying to find something. Write them out.

نَبيل (na-beel) Nabil : مِن (min) please فَضلِك (fahD-lahk)، أينَ (eye-na) فُندُق (foon-dooq) "مَرحَبا" (mar-Ha-baa) Hello ؟

____

أحمَد (aH-med) Ahmed : إذهَب (eed-hahb) go ثَلاثة (tha-laa-tha) شَوارِع (shao-wear-id) streets وَ إذهَب (eed-hahb) go عَلى (ah-la) to اليَسار (al-ya-saar) left إلى (ee-la) at الشّارِع (ah-share-reh) the street الثّالِث (ah-thaa-leeth) third.

____

الفُندُق (al-foon-dooq) عَلى (ah-la) on اليَمين (al-ya-meen) the right.

____

نَبيلة (na-bee-la) Nabila : مِن (min) please فَضلِك (fahD-lik)، أينَ (eye-na) مَتحَف (maht-Hahf) Museum الأهرام (al-ah-raam) Pyramids؟

____

بُشرى (boosh-ra) Bushra : إذهَبي (eed-ha-bee) go عَلى to اليَمين (al-ya-meen) the right وَ إذهَبي (eed-ha-bee) go خَمسين (hahm-seen) 50 مِتراً (meh-trahn) meters.

____

إذهَبي (eed-ha-bee) عَلى اليَسار (al-ya-saar) وَ المَتحَف (al-maht-Hahf) في الزّاوية (al-zair-we-ya) the corner.

____

جَمَع

- ☐ جَميعاً ← all of us together .... (zheh-me-ahn) ....
- ☐ جامِعي ... university student (🚹) .... (zhaa-meh-ee) ....
- ☐ جامِعيّة . university student (🚺) ...(zhaa-meh-ee-ya) .

Are أنتِ (n-tee) you (♀) lost? There is no need to be lost if أنتِ (n-tee) have learned the basic direction كَلِمات (ka-lee-maat).

Do not try to memorize these الحِوارات (al-He-waa-raat) conversations because أنتِ (n-tee) will never be looking for precisely these places. One day, أنتِ (n-tee) might need to ask for directions to مَسجِد (mahs-zhid) Mosque الحَسَن (al-Ha-sahn) Hasan الثّاني (ah-thaa-nee) 2nd or صَومَعة (ssao-maht) Minaret حَسّان (Hahs-saan) Hassan. Learn the key direction كَلِمات (ka-lee-maat) so you can be sure أنتِ (n-tee) can find your destination. أنتِ (n-tee) may want to buy a guidebook to start planning what places أنتِ (n-tee) would like to visit. ماذا (may-daa) what if the person responding to your سُؤال (soo-wel) question answers too quickly for أنتِ (n-tee) to understand the entire reply? Just ask مَرّة (mar-ra) once أُخرى (ook-ra) more مِن فَضلِك saying,

مِن (min) فَضلِك (fahD-lahk) (♀) excuse me. أتَكَلَّمُ (ah-ta-kel-la-moo) I speak قَليلاً (qa-lee-lahn) a little مِنَ (me-na) of العَرَبيّة (al-r-ra-be-ya). أعِد (ah-rid) repeat مِن (min) please فَضلِك (fahD-lahk).

الآنَ (al-ann) say this again وَ then write it out below.

____

(Excuse me. I speak a little Arabic. Please repeat.)

نَعَم (na-ahm) yes it is difficult at first but don't give up! مَتى (meh-ta) when the directions are repeated, أنتِ (n-tee) will be able to understand them if أنتِ (n-tee) have learned the key كَلِمات (ka-lee-maat) for directions.

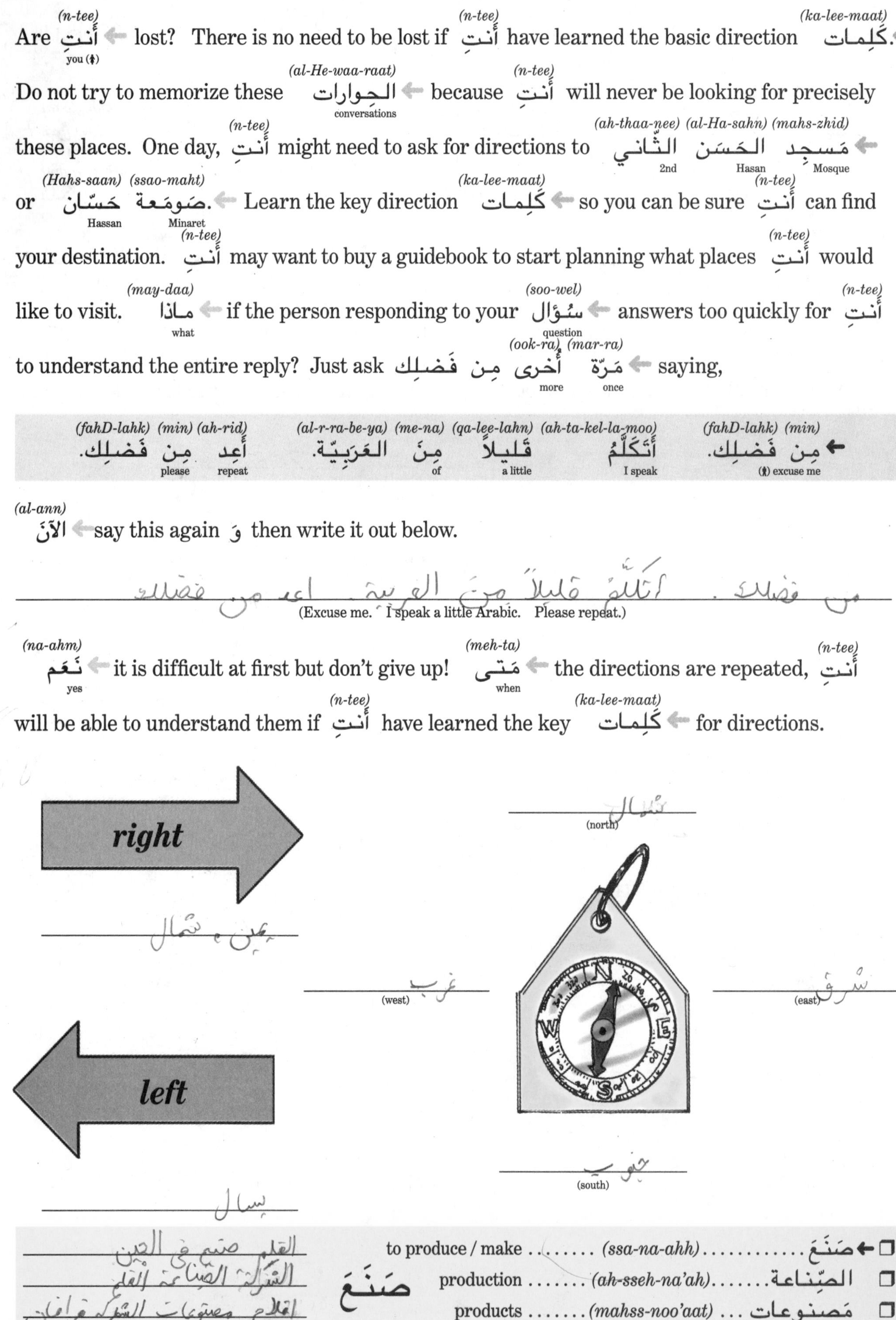

☐	صَنَعَ	(ssa-na-ahh)	to produce / make
☐	الصِّناعة	(ah-sseh-na'ah)	production
☐	مَصنوعات	(mahss-noo'aat)	products

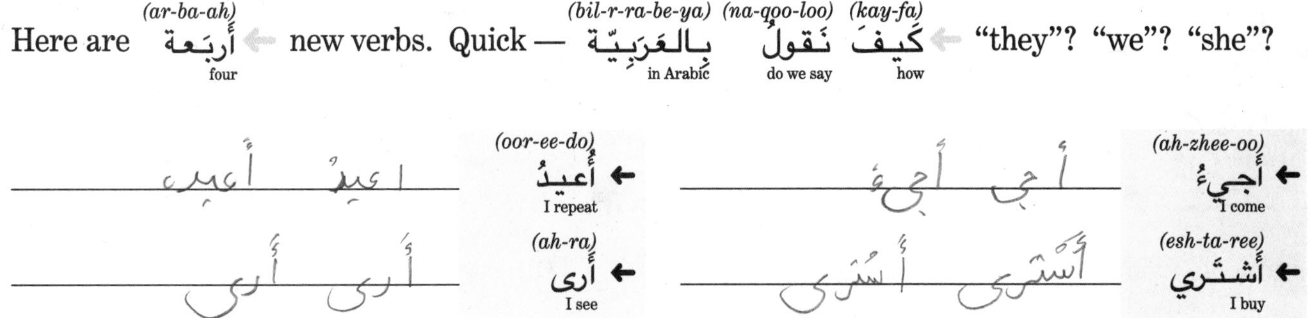

Here are أربعة (ar-ba-ah) four new verbs. Quick — كيف (kay-fa) how نقول (na-qoo-loo) do we say بالعربيّة (bil-r-ra-be-ya) in Arabic — "they"? "we"? "she"?

- أجيءُ (ah-zhee-oo) I come
- أشتري (esh-ta-ree) I buy
- أُعيدُ (oor-ee-do) I repeat
- أرى (ah-ra) I see

As always, say each sentence out loud. Say each كلمة (ka-lee-ma) word carefully, pronouncing each العربيّة (al-r-ra-be-ya) sound as well as أنتِ can. Repeat, repeat, repeat!

- أجيءُ (ah-zhee-oo) I come ______ مِن (min) from مصر (meess-ur) Egypt.
- تجيءُ (ta-zhee-oo) you (♂) come / she comes ______ مِنَ (min) from المغرب (al-ma-greb) Morocco.
- تجيئينَ (ta-zhee-ee-na) you (♀) come ______ مِن أمريكا (ahm-ree-kaa) America.
- يجيءُ (ya-zhee-oo) he comes ______ مِن كندا (ka-na-daa) Canada.
- نجيءُ (na-zhee-oo) we come ______ مِن إنجلترّا (in-zhla-tair-raa) England.
- يجيئونَ (ya-zhee-oo-na) they come ______ مِن فلسطين (fa-les-Teen) Palestine.

- أُعيدُ (oor-ee-do) I repeat ______ الكلمة (al-ka-lee-ma) the word.
- تُعيدُ (toor-ee-do) you (♂) repeat / she repeats ______ الجواب (al-zha-web) the answer.
- تُعيدينَ (toor-ee-dee-na) you (♀) repeat ______ الإسم (al-eesm) the name.
- يُعيدُ (yoor-ee-doo) he repeats ______ الإسم (al-eesm).
- نُعيدُ (noor-ee-do) we repeat ______ العنوان (al-roon-wen) the address.
- يُعيدونَ (yoor-ee-do-na) they repeat ______ الأرقام (al-aar-qaam) the numbers.

- أشتري (esh-ta-ree) I buy ______ الكتاب (al-kee-taab) the book.
- تشتري (tesh-ta-ree) you (♂) buy / she buys ______ تذكرة (teth-kee-ra) (a) ticket.
- تشترينَ (tesh-ta-ree-na) you (♀) buy ______ تذكرة (teth-kee-ra).
- يشتري (yesh-ta-ree) he buys ______ بطاقة (be-Taa-qa) (a) postcard.
- نشتري (nesh-ta-ree) we buy ______ أربعة (ar-ba-ah) four طوابع (Tao-waa-bihh) stamps.
- يشترونَ (yesh-ta-roo-na) they buy ______ ستّة (seet-teh) six طوابع (Tao-waa-bihh) stamps.

- أرى (ah-ra) I see ______ الفندق (al-foon-dooq) the hotel.
- ترى (ta-ra) you (♂) see / she sees ______ البنك (al-bahnk) the bank.
- ترينَ (ta-ra-ee-na) you (♀) see ______ البيت (al-bait) the house.
- يرى (ya-ra) he sees ______ السيّارة (ah-sy-yaa-ra) the car.
- نرى (na-ra) we see ______ المتحف (al-maht-Hahf) the museum.
- يرونَ (ya-ra-oo-na) they see ______ كلّ (kool) شيء (shay') everything.

صنع

- ☐ مصنع factory .... (mahss-nahh)
- ☐ صانِع maker (♂) .... (ssaa-nehh)
- ☐ صانِعة maker (♀) .... (ssaa-nee'ah)

١٥/15 الطّابَق العُلوي - الطّابَق السُّفلي

(ah-Taa-bahq) (al-rool-we) (ah-Taa-bahq) (ah-soo-flee)

الطّابَق العُلوي — the upstairs; الطّابَق السُّفلي — the downstairs

(roor-fa) (ah-noum) غُرفة النَّوم (bedroom) ← Go to your ← هُنا بَيت في البَحرين (Bahrain) *(hoo-naa)(bait) (al-baH-rain)*. ← كَلِمات let's learn more ← الآنَ *(al-ahn)* ← just like ← في *(fee)*, غُرفة النَّوم (the bedroom) *(roor-fa) (ah-noum)* Let's learn the names of the things ← الغُرفة (the room) *(al-roor-fa)*. and look around ← البَيت (the house) *(al-bait)*. learned the various parts of ← نَحنُ (we) *(naH-noo)*

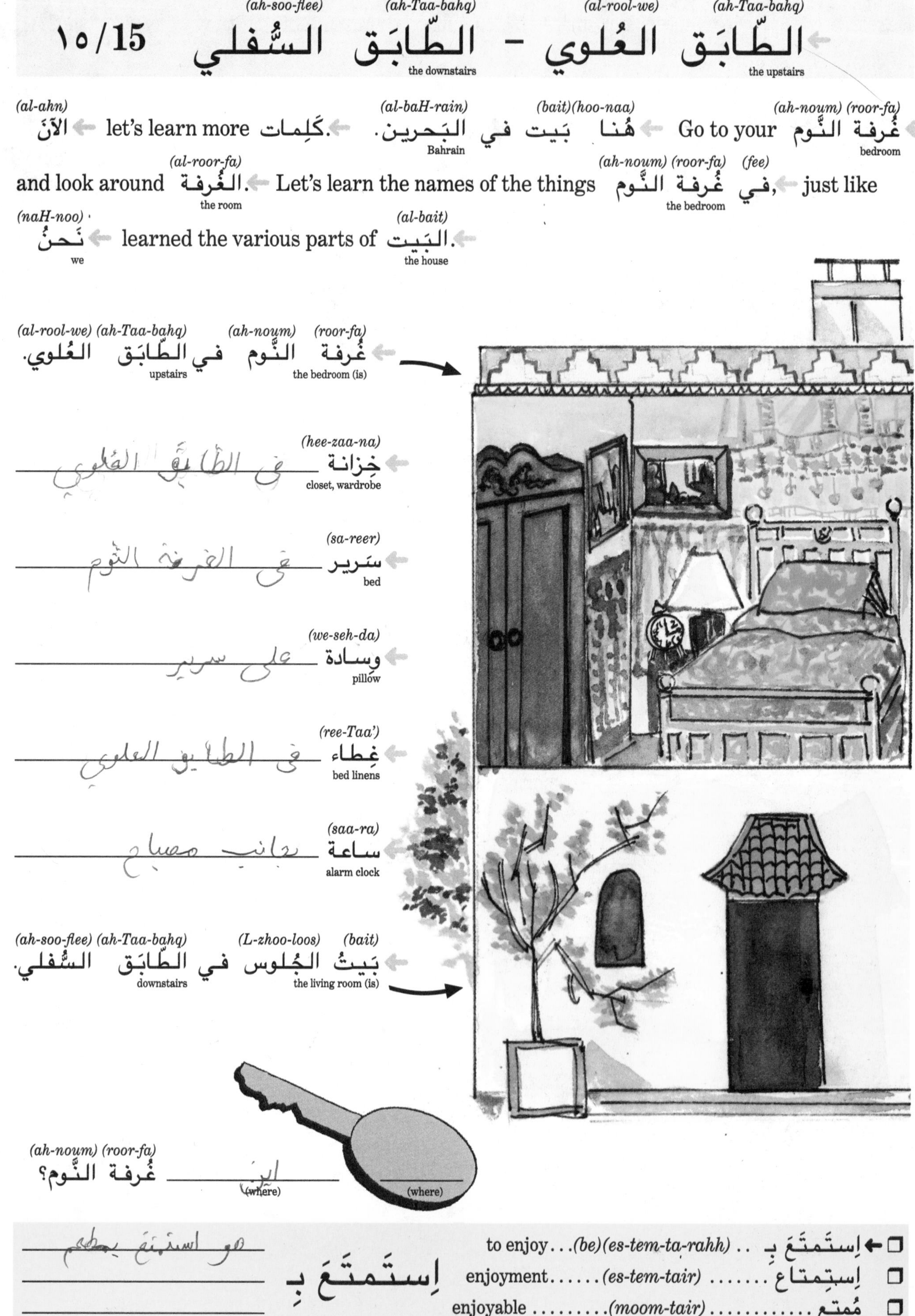

(roor-fa) (ah-noum) (ah-Taa-bahq) (al-rool-we)
← غُرفة النَّوم (the bedroom (is)) في الطّابَق العُلوي (upstairs).

← خِزانة *(hee-zaa-na)* closet, wardrobe ______________

← سَرير *(sa-reer)* bed ______________

← وِسادة *(we-seh-da)* pillow ______________

← غِطاء *(ree-Taa')* bed linens ______________

← ساعة *(saa-ra)* alarm clock ______________

(bait) (L-zhoo-loos) (ah-Taa-bahq) (ah-soo-flee)
← بَيتُ الجُلوس (the living room (is)) في الطّابَق السُّفلي (downstairs).

(roor-fa) (ah-noum)
غُرفة النَّوم؟ ______________ (where) ______________ (where)

إستَمتَعَ بِ

❑ ← إستَمتَعَ بِ	*(be)(es-tem-ta-rahh)*	to enjoy
❑ إستِمتاع	*(es-tem-tair)*	enjoyment
❑ مُمتِع	*(moom-tair)*	enjoyable

____
____
____

(al-ann) الآنَ ← remove the next (hahm-sa) خَمسة ← stickers وَ label these (eh-shee') أشياء ← (things) in your (ah-noum) (roor-fa) غُرفة النَّوم ← (bedroom).

Let's move to (wa) وَ (al-Hahm-maam) الحَمّام ← (the bathroom), do the same thing. Remember, (al-Hahm-maam) الحَمّام ← is generally "the bathroom." In a restaurant or public facility, ask for (al-meer-HaaD) "المِرحاض." ← (the lavatory) Restrooms are marked (ah-nee-seh') النِّساء ← (ladies) and (ah-ree-zhel) الرِّجال ← (gentlemen).

(ah-nee-seh') النِّساء

(ah-ree-zhel) الرِّجال

(al-Hahm-maam) الحَمّام ← (the bathroom (is)) (eye-Dahn) أيضاً (also) في (ah-Taa-bahq) الطّابَق (upstairs) (al-rool-we) العُلوي.

(mir-et) مِرآة ← mirror ______

(meer-sahl) مِغسَل ← sink / washstand ______

(foo-ahT) فُوَط ← towels ______

(Hahm-maam) حَمّام ← bathroom / toilet ______

(rahsh-shair-sha) رَشّاشة ← shower ______

(al-mahk-tahb) المَكتَب ← (the study (is)) (eye-Dahn) أيضاً (also) في (ah-Taa-bahq) الطّابَق (downstairs) (ah-soo-flee) السُّفلي.

☐	سَمِعَ ←	to hear .... (sem-ee-ahh) ......
☐	السَّمع	hearing .... (ah-sem-ahh) ......
☐	المُستَمِعون	the listeners .. (al-moos-teh-mee-roon) ..

سَمِعَ

Do not forget to remove the next group of stickers وَ label الأَشيـاء *(al-eh-shee')* things هَـذِهِ *(heh-da-he)* these ← in your حَمّام *(Hahm-maam)* bathroom ←. Okay, it is time to review. هُـنـا *(hoo-naa)* a quick quiz to see what you remember.

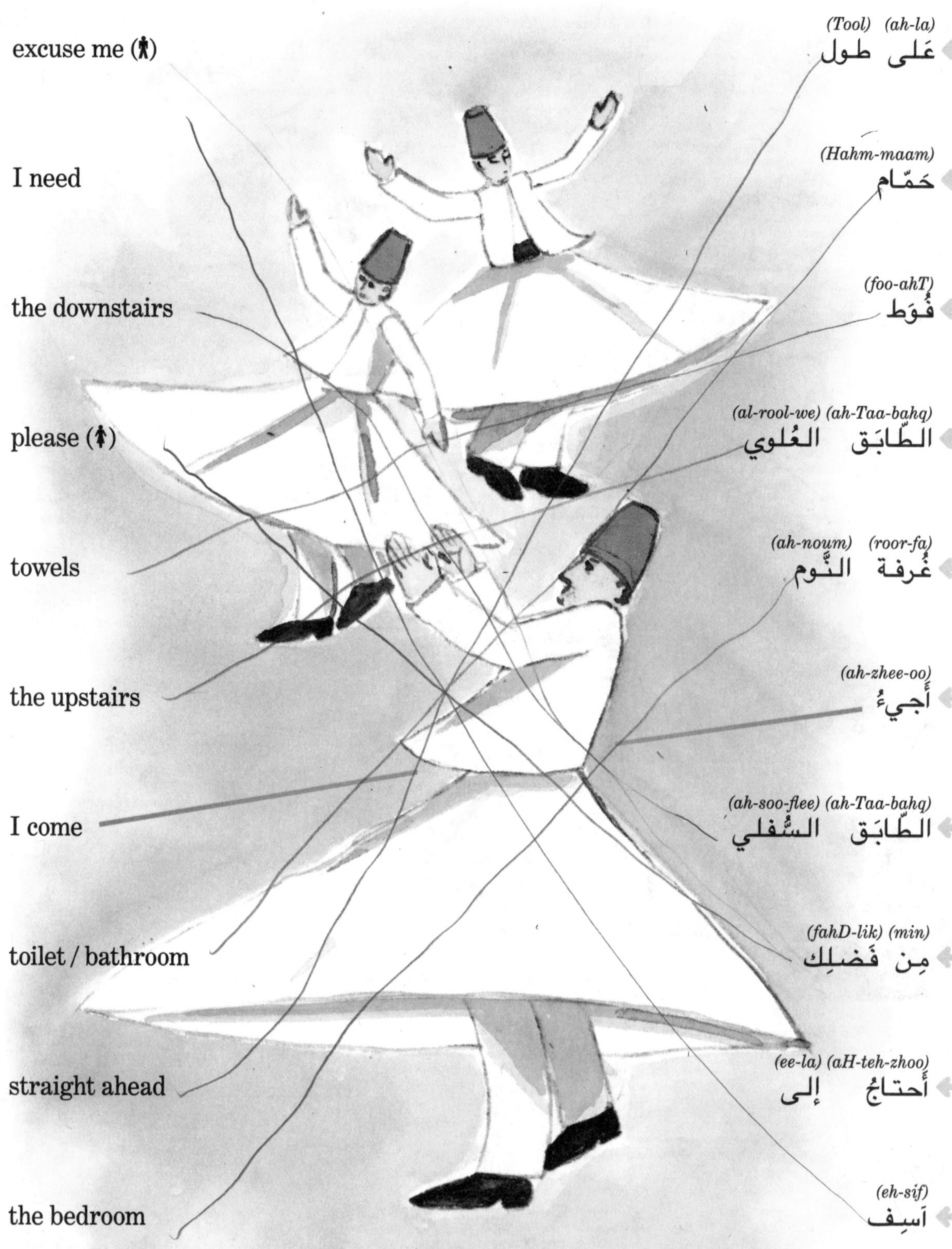

excuse me (🚹)	عَلى طول *(ah-la) (Tool)* ←
I need	حَمّام *(Hahm-maam)* ←
the downstairs	فُوَط *(foo-ahT)* ←
please (🚺)	الطّابَق العُلوي *(ah-Taa-bahq) (al-rool-we)* ←
towels	غُرفة النَّوم *(roor-fa) (ah-noum)* ←
the upstairs	أَجيءُ *(ah-zhee-oo)* ←
I come	الطّابَق السُّفلي *(ah-Taa-bahq) (ah-soo-flee)* ←
toilet / bathroom	مِن فَضلِك *(min) (fahD-lik)* ←
straight ahead	أَحتاجُ إلى *(aH-teh-zhoo) (ee-la)* ←
the bedroom	آسِف *(eh-sif)* ←

كَسَّرَ

- [ ] كَسَّرَ ← to break . . . . . *(kes-sa-ra)* . . . . . .
- [ ] مُكَسَّر something being broken . . . *(moo-kahs-sar)* . .
- [ ] مُكَسِّر someone who breaks things . . . *(moo-kes-seer)*. . .

Next stop — المَكتَب (al-mahk-tahb) the study, specifically المَكتَب (al-mahk-tahb) the desk in this room. ماذا (may-daa) what فَوقَ (fao-qa) on المَكتَب (al-mahk-tahb) the desk؟

Let's identify الأَشياء (al-eh-shee') the things that one normally finds on المَكتَب (al-mahk-tahb) the desk or strewn about البَيت (al-bait) the house.

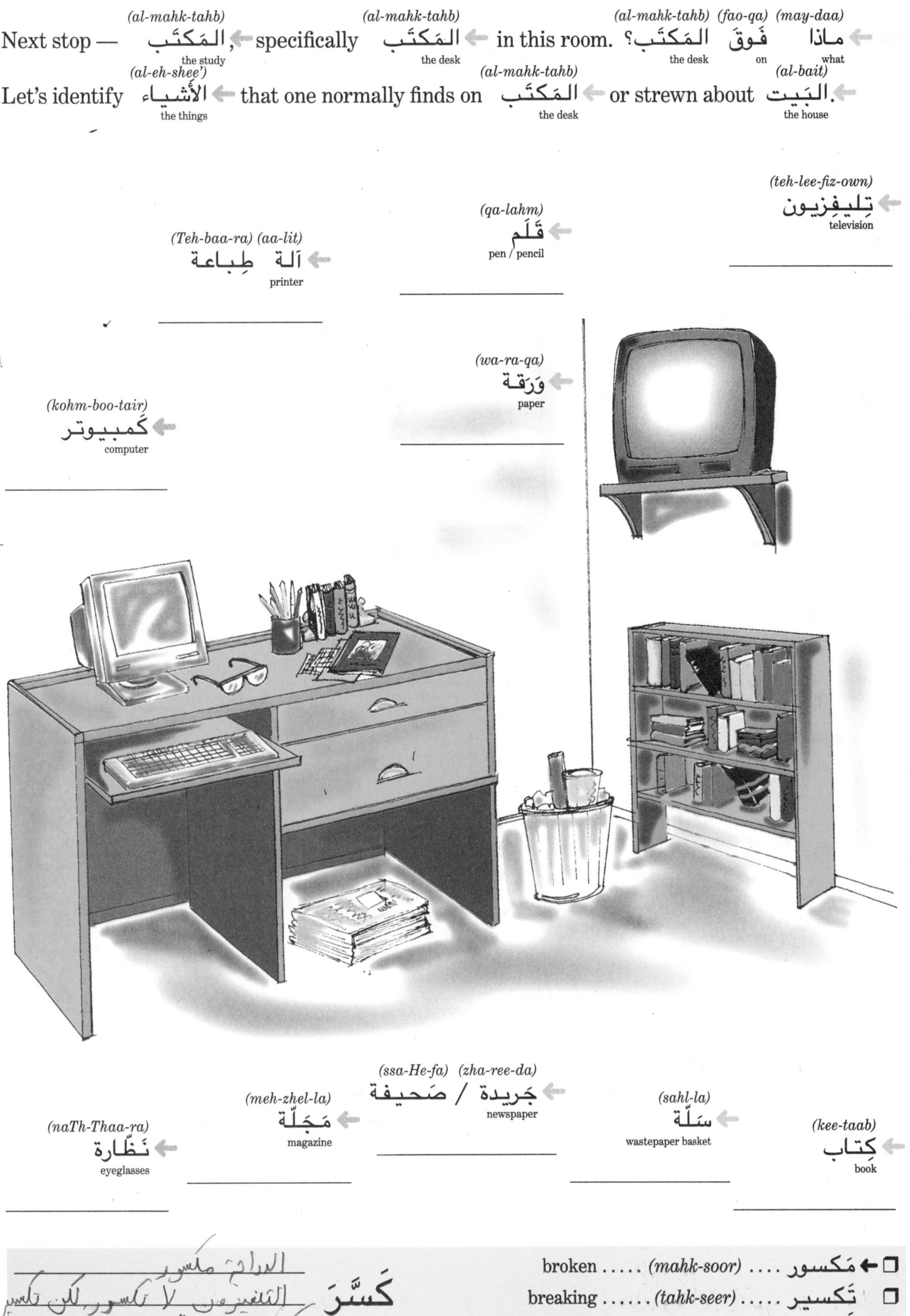

كَسَّرَ

- broken ..... (mahk-soor) .... مَكسور
- breaking ...... (tahk-seer) ..... تَكسير
- kasra (vowel underneath) .... (kes-ra) .... كَسرة

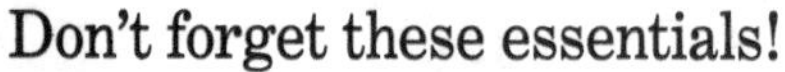

Don't forget these essentials!

(ree-saa-la)	(Taa-bahh)	(be-Taa-qa)
رسالة ←	طابَع ←	بِطاقة ←
letter	stamp	postcard

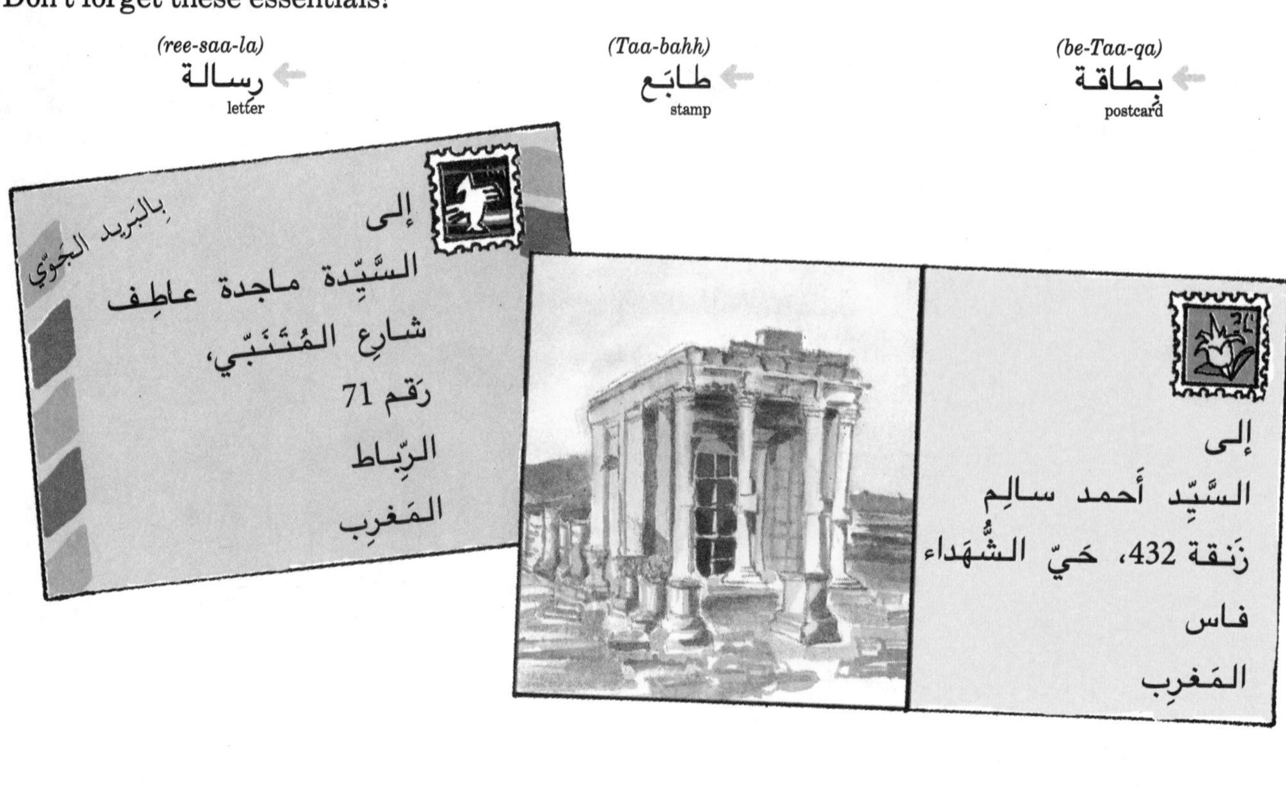

_____ رسالة _____ (letter)   _____ طابع _____ (stamp)   _____ بطاقة _____ (postcard)

The word "جَوّ (zhao) air" ← is also found in "بِالبَريد الجَوّي (bil-ba-reed) (al-zhao-we) by airmail." ← Note above that "إلى السَّيِّد (ee-la) (sy-yed) to Mr." ← and "إلى السَّيِّدة (ee-la) (sy-yeh-da) to Mrs." ← are used when addressing letters بِالعَرَبِيّة (bil-r-ra-be-ya) in Arabic. ←

الآن (al-ann) label these things in المَكتَب (al-mahk-tahb) the study ← with your stickers. Do not forget to say هَذِهِ (heh-da-he) these الكَلِمات (al-ka-lee-maat) words ← out loud whenever أَنتَ (n-ta) write them, أَنتَ (n-ta) see them وَ أَنتَ ← apply the stickers.

The word لا (la) no / not is extremely useful بِالعَرَبِيّة (bil-r-ra-be-ya). ← Add لا (la) no / not before most verbs وَ you negate the sentence.

← لا (la) not	أُرسِلُ (oor-see-loo) I send	رِسالة. (ree-saa-la) (a) letter

← أُرسِلُ (oor-see-loo) I send	رِسالة. (ree-saa-la) (a) letter

Simple, isn't it? الآن (al-ann), ← after you fill in the blanks on the next page, go back a second time

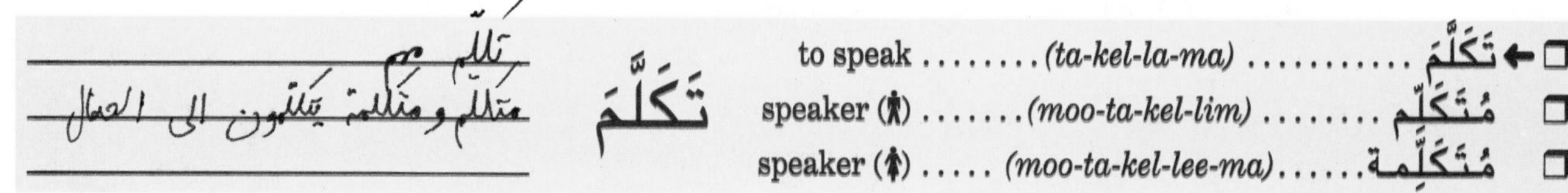

and negate all these sentences by adding لا (la) no/not before each verb. Practice saying these sentences out loud many times. Don't get discouraged! Just look at كَم (kem) how much ← you have already learned وَ think ahead to البَحر (al-ba-Har) the sea ← at عَقَبة (ah-qa-ba) Aqaba ← or sightseeing in مُرّاكُش (moor-raa-koosh) Marrakesh وَ (wa) القاهِرة (al-qaa-he-ra) Cairo.←

أتَّصِلُ (aht-ta-ssee-loo) I phone ← بِـ (be) _____

أنامُ (ah-naa-moo) I sleep ← _____

لي (lee) I have ← _____

أبيعُ (ah-be-roo) I sell ← _____

← أتَّصِلُ (aht-ta-ssee-loo) I phone _____ بِالفُندُق. (bil-foon-dooq) the hotel

تَتَّصِلُ (taht-ta-ssee-loo) you (♂) phone _____ بِالمَطعَم. (bil-ma-Tahm) the restaurant

تَتَّصِلين (taht-ta-ssee-lee-na) you (♀) phone _____ بِالبَيت. (bil-bait) the house

يَتَّصِلُ (yaht-ta-ssee-loo) he phones _____ بِطَنجة. (be-Tahn-zha) (to) Tangier

تَتَّصِلُ (taht-ta-ssee-loo) she phones _____ بِعَمّان. (be-ahm-maan) (to) Amman

نَتَّصِلُ (naht-ta-ssee-loo) we phone _____ بِكَندا. (be-ka-na-daa)

يَتَّصِلونَ (yaht-ta-ssee-loo-na) they phone _____ بِأمريكا. (be-ahm-ree-kaa) the U.S.A.

← لي (lee) I have _____ أخت. (ohkt) (a) sister

لَكَ (la-ka) you (♂) have _____ أخ. (ahk) (a) brother

لَكِ (la-kee) you (♀) have _____ اِبن. (ibn) (a) son

لَهُ (la-hoo) he has _____ بِنت. (bint) (a) daughter

لَها (la-haa) she has _____ صَديق. (ssa-deeq) (a) friend

لَنا (la-naa) we have _____ عائِلة كَبيرة. (aa-ee-la) family (ka-beer-ah) large

لَهُم (la-hoom) they have _____ عائِلة صَغيرة. (aa-ee-la) family (ssa-greer-ah) small

← أنامُ (ah-naa-moo) I sleep _____ في غُرفة النَّوم. (fee) (roor-fa) (ah-noum) the bedroom

تَنامُ (ta-naa-moo) you (♂) sleep / she sleeps _____ في غُرفة النَّوم. (roor-fa) (ah-noum)

تَنامينَ (ta-naa-me-na) you (♀) sleep _____ فَوقَ السَّرير. (fao-qa) on (ah-sa-reer) the bed

يَنامُ (ya-naa-moo) he sleeps _____ فَوقَ السَّرير. (fao-qa) (ah-sa-reer)

نَنامُ (na-naa-moo) we sleep _____ في الفُندُق. (al-foon-dooq)

يَنامونَ (ya-naa-moo-na) they sleep _____ في صالة الضُّيوف. (ssaa-laht) (ah-Doo-yoof) guesthouse

← أبيعُ (ah-be-roo) I sell _____ الطَّوابِع. (ah-Tao-waa-bihh) stamps

تَبيعُ (ta-be-roo) you (♂) sell / she sells _____ الطَّوابِع. stamps

تَبيعينَ (ta-be-ree-na) you (♀) sell _____ الجَرائِد. (al-zha-rair-id) newspapers

يَبيعُ (ya-be-roo) he sells _____ البِطاقات. (al-be-Taa-qaat) postcards

نَبيعُ (na-be-roo) we sell _____ الكُتُب. (al-koo-toob) books

يَبيعونَ (ya-be-roo-na) they sell _____ الزُّهور. (ah-zoo-hoor) flowers

تَكَلَّم

☐ كَلام ← speaking .... (keh-lahm) ....

☐ كَلِمة word .... (ka-lee-ma) ....

☐ كَلِمات words .... (ka-lee-maat) ....

Before (n-tee) أَنتِ (♀) proceed (mar) مَعَ the next step (fahD-lik) (min) مِن فَضلِك (♀) please ← identify all the items (ahs-fahl) أَسفَل below ←.

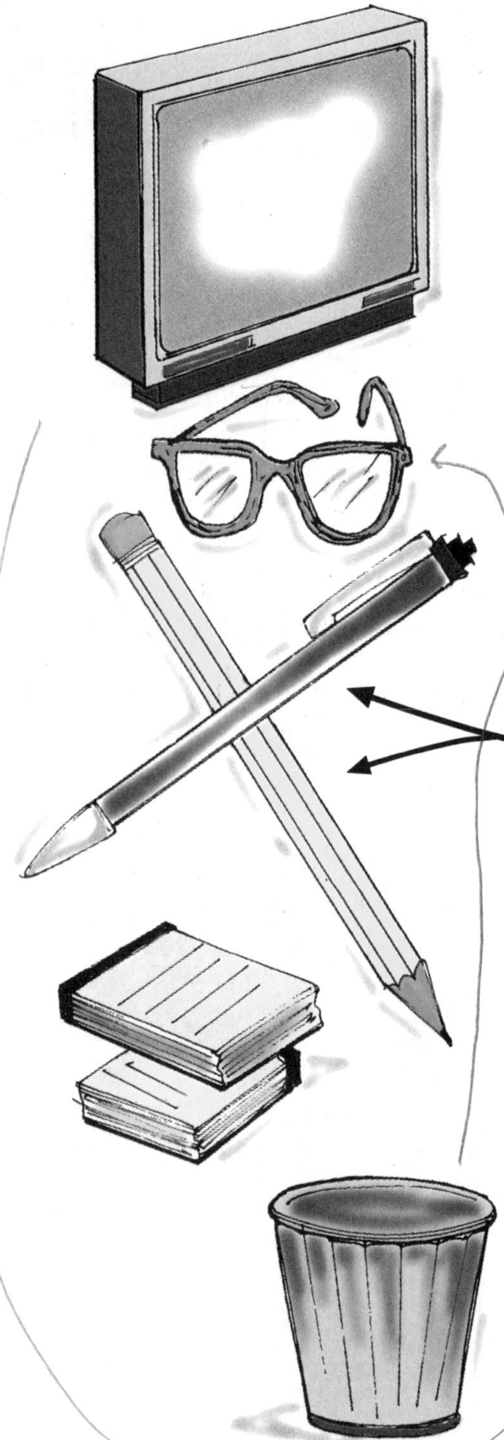

(zha-ree-da) جَريدة ←

(Taa-bahh) طابَع ←

(sahl-la) سَلّة ←

(be-Taa-qa) بِطاقة ←

(kee-taab) كِتاب ←

(wa-ra-qa) وَرَقة ←

(qa-lahm) قَلَم

(Teh-baa-ra) (aa-lit) آلة طِباعة

(ree-saa-la) رِسالة

(naTh-Thaa-ra) نَظّارة

(meh-zhel-la) مَجَلّة

(teh-lee-fiz-own) تِليفِزيون

(kohm-boo-tair) كَمبيوتر

The following are closely related even if not all in the same family.

أَرسَلَ

- ❑ ← to mail / send ....(air-sa-la)............... أَرسَلَ
- ❑ the mail ......(al-ba-reed)............... البَريد
- ❑ mailman .. (al-ba-reed)(seh-ree).. ساعي البَريد

البَريد (al-ba-reed) — the mail

أنتَ (n-ta) (you) know الآنَ (al-ann) how to count, كَيفَ (kay-fa, how) to ask أسئِلة (es-ee-la, questions), how to use verbs with the "plug-in" formula, كَيفَ (kay-fa, how) to make statements وَ how to describe something, be it the location of فُندُق (foon-dooq, (a) hotel) or the color of بَيت (bait, (a) house). Let's now take the basics that أنتَ (n-ta) have learned وَ expand them in special areas that will be most helpful in your travels. ماذا (may-daa, what) does everyone do on a holiday? Send بِطاقات (be-Taa-qaat, postcards), of course! Let's learn exactly كَيفَ (kay-fa, how) مَكتَب البَريد (mahk-tahb)(al-ba-reed), the post office, works.

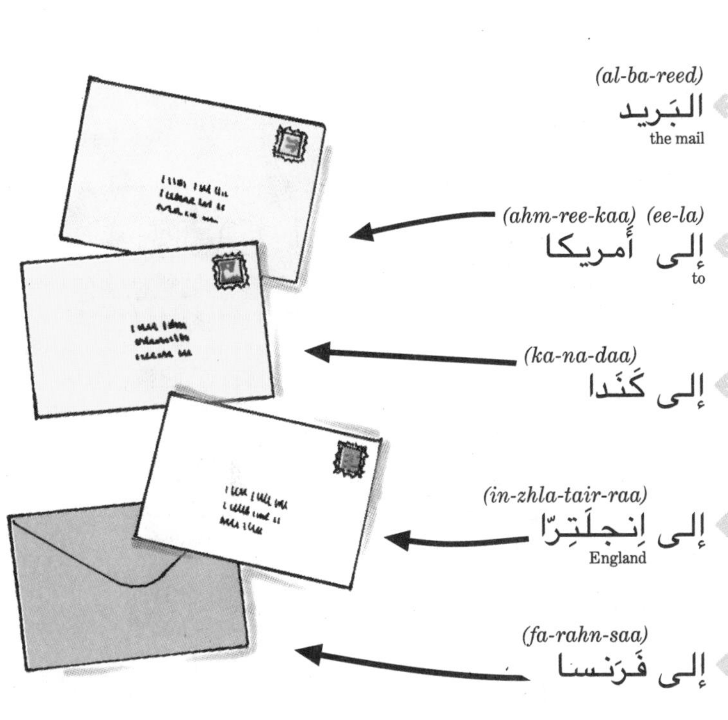

البَريد (al-ba-reed) — the mail

إلى أمريكا (ee-la) (ahm-ree-kaa) — to

إلى كَنَدا (ka-na-daa)

إلى إنجلَترّا (in-zhla-tair-raa) — England

إلى فَرَنسا (fa-rahn-saa)

مَكتَب البَريد (mahk-tahb)(al-ba-reed), the post office, has everything. مَكتَب البَريد (mahk-tahb)(al-ba-reed), the post office, is where أنتَ need to go to buy a طابَع (Taa-bahh, stamp), mail a package, and send بِطاقات (be-Taa-qaat, postcards) وَ رَسائِل (reh-saa-il, letters). مَكتَب البَريد (mahk-tahb)(al-ba-reed) is generally open, but not always, from الثّامِنة (ah-thaa-me-na, eight) وَ النِّصف (ah-nessf, half) صَباحاً (ssa-baa-Hahn) until السّادِسة (ah-saa-dee-sa, six) وَ النِّصف (ah-nessf) مَساءً (ma-saa-ahn) Sunday through Thursday in some countries and from Monday to Friday in other countries.

أرسَلَ

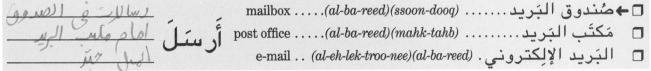

- ☐ صُندوق البَريد .... (al-ba-reed)(ssoon-dooq) ..... mailbox
- ☐ مَكتَب البَريد .... (al-ba-reed)(mahk-tahb) ..... post office
- ☐ البَريد الإلِكتروني . (al-eh-lek-troo-nee)(al-ba-reed) .. e-mail

(hoo-naa) هُنا ← the necessary (ka-lee-maat) كَلِمات for (al-ba-reed) (mahk-tahb) مَكتَب البَريد (the post office). ← Practice them aloud وَ write (al-ka-lee-maat) الكَلِمات in the blanks (ahs-fahl) أسفَل (below).

(ree-saa-la) رِسالة ← letter

(be-Taa-qa) بِطاقة ← postcard

(Tard) طَرد ← package

(ee-mail) إيميل ← email

(al-zhao-we) (bil-ba-reed) بِالبَريد الجَوّي ← by airmail

(faaks) فاكس ← fax

(Taa-bahh) طابَع ← stamp

(roo-moo-me) (haa-tif) هاتِف عُمومي ← public phone / booth

(al-ba-reed) (ssoon-dooq) صُندوق البَريد ← mailbox

(haa-tif) هاتِف ← telephone

(teh-lee-foon) تِليفون ← telephone

أرسَلَ

- ☐ ← رِسالة .... (ree-saa-la) .... letter / message
- ☐ الرَّسول .... (ah-ra-sool) .... the messenger
- ☐ بِالبَريد الجَوّي .. (al-zhao-we)(bil-ba-reed) .. by airmail

Next step — أنتَ (n-ta) (you) ask أسئلة (es-ee-la) (questions) like those أسفل (ahs-fahl) (below), depending on what تُريدُ (too-ree-do) (you want). Repeat these sentences aloud many times.

مِن أينَ أشتري الطَّوابِع مِن فَضلِك؟ (min) (eye-na) (esh-ta-ree) (ah-Tao-waa-bihh) (fahD-lahk) — from / where / do I buy / stamps / please ____________

مِن أينَ أشتري البطاقات مِن فَضلِك؟ (eye-na) (esh-ta-ree) (al-be-Taa-qaat) (fahD-lahk) — do I buy / postcards ____________

أينَ التِّليفون مِن فَضلِك؟ (eye-na) (ah-teh-lee-foon) — the telephone ____________

أينَ صُندوق البَريد مِن فَضلِك؟ (ssoon-dooq) (al-ba-reed) (fahD-lik) — the mailbox ____________

أينَ الهاتِف العُمومي مِن فَضلِك؟ (al-haa-tif) (al-roo-moo-me) (fahD-lik) — the public phone ____________

أينَ أُرسِلُ البطاقات مِن فَضلِك؟ (oor-see-loo) (al-be-Taa-qaat) (fahD-lik) — do I send / the postcards ____________

أينَ أُرسِلُ الفاكس مِن فَضلِك؟ (oor-see-loo) (al-faaks) — the fax ____________

الآنَ (al-ann) quiz yourself. See if أنتَ can translate the following thoughts إلى (ee-la) (into) العَرَبيّة (al-r-ra-be-ya).

1. Where is the public phone? ____________
2. From where do I buy the stamps? ____________
3. Where do I send the fax? ____________
4. Where do I send the postcards? ____________
5. Where is the post office? ____________
6. From where do I buy the postcards? ____________
7. By airmail? ____________
8. Where do I send the package? ____________

الأجوِبة

١ أينَ الهاتِف العُمومي؟
٢ مِن أينَ أشتري الطَّوابِع؟
٣ أينَ أُرسِلُ الفاكس؟
٤ أينَ أُرسِلُ البِطاقات؟
٥ أينَ مَكتَب البَريد؟
٦ مِن أينَ أشتري البِطاقات؟
٧ بِالبَريد الجَوّي؟
٨ أينَ أُرسِلُ الطَّرد؟

هُنا more verbs.

→ أكتُبُ (ahk-too-boo) I write ______	→ أعطيني (ah-Tee-nee) give me ______
→ أقرأ (ahq-ra-oo) I read ______	→ أدفَعُ (ahd-fa-roo) I pay ثَمَن ... (theh-men) the price of / for ______

Practice these verbs by not only filling in the blanks, but by saying them aloud many, many times until you are comfortable مَعَ (mar) the sounds وَ the words.

→ أكتُبُ (ahk-too-boo) I write ______ الرِّسالة. (ah-ree-saa-la) the letter	→ أعطيني (ah-Tee-nee) give me ______ القَلَم (al-qa-lahm) the pen مِن (min) فَضلِك. (fahD-lik) please
تَكتُبُ (tahk-too-boo) you write / she writes ______ الرِّسالة. (ah-ree-saa-la)	أعطيني (ah-Tee-nee) give me ______ القَلَم (al-qa-lahm) the pencil مِن فَضلِك.
تَكتُبينَ (tahk-too-be-na) you write ______ الكِتاب. (al-kee-taab) the book	أعطيني (ah-Tee-nee) ______ تَذكِرة (teth-kee-ra) (a) ticket مِن فَضلِك.
يَكتُبُ (yahk-too-boo) he writes ______ العُنوان. (al-roon-wen) the address	أعطيني ______ الطّابَع (ah-Taa-bahh) the stamp مِن فَضلِك. (fahD-lahk)
نَكتُبُ (nahk-too-boo) we write ______ الإسم. (al-eesm) the name	أعطيني ______ المِفتاح (al-mif-tair) the key مِن فَضلِك.
يَكتُبونَ (yahk-too-boo-na) they write ______ الفاكس. (al-faaks) the fax	أعطيني ______ الإسم (al-eesm) the name مِن فَضلِك.

→ أقرأ (ahq-ra-oo) I read ______ الكِتاب. (al-kee-taab) the book	→ أدفَعُ (ahd-fa-roo) I pay ثَمَن (theh-men) for ______ الفُندُق. (al-foon-dooq) the hotel
تَقرأ (tahq-ra-oo) you read / she reads ______ المَجَلّة. (al-meh-zhel-la) the magazine	تَدفَعُ (tahd-fa-roo) you pay / she pays ثَمَن (theh-men) ______ الفُندُق. (al-foon-dooq)
تَقرَئينَ (tahq-ra-eye-na) you read ______ المَجَلّة. (al-meh-zhel-la)	تَدفَعينَ (tahd-fa-ree-na) you pay ثَمَن (theh-men) ______ التّاكسي. (ah-taak-see) the taxi
يَقرأ (yahq-ra-oo) he reads ______ الجَريدة. (al-zha-ree-da) the newspaper	يَدفَعُ (yahd-fa-roo) he pays ثَمَن (theh-men) ______ الحافِلة. (al-Haa-fee-la) the bus
نَقرأ (nahq-ra-oo) we read ______ كَثيراً. (ka-thee-rahn) a lot	نَدفَعُ (nahd-fa-roo) we pay ثَمَن ______ التَّذكِرة. (ah-teth-kee-ra) the ticket
يَقرَؤونَ (yahq-ra-oo-na) they read ______ قَليلاً. (qa-lee-lahn) a little	يَدفَعونَ (yahd-fa-roo-na) they pay ثَمَن ______ المَطعَم. (al-ma-Tahm) the restaurant

رَحَلَ

- ❒ → رَحَلَ .... (ra-Ha-la) .... to move ______
- ❒ رَحّالة .... (raH-Haa-la) .... explorer ______
- ❒ رِحلة .... (reH-la) .... exploration / journey / excursion ______

١٧/17 Basic Traffic Signs and Conversions

Some of these signs you probably recognize, but take a couple of minutes to review them anyway.

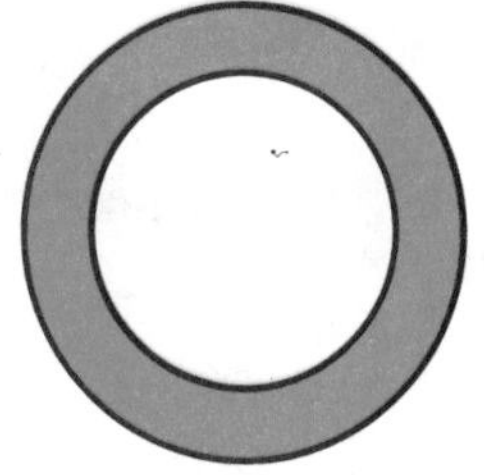

road closed to vehicles

(lee-sy-yaa-raat) (mooq-lahq) (ah-Ta-reeq)

الطَّريق مُغلَق لِلسَّيّارات

customs

(al-zha-mair-ik)

الجَمارِك

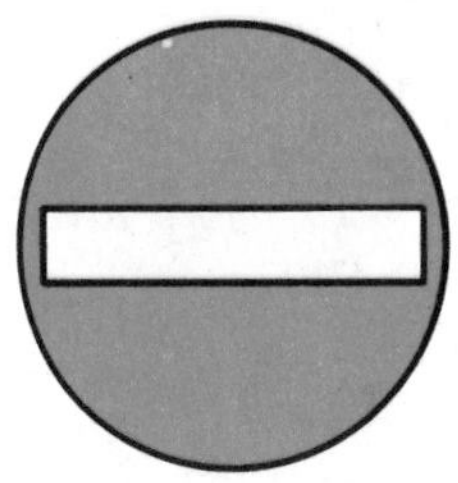

no entrance

(mem-noo') (ah-dook-hool)

الدُّخول مَمنوع

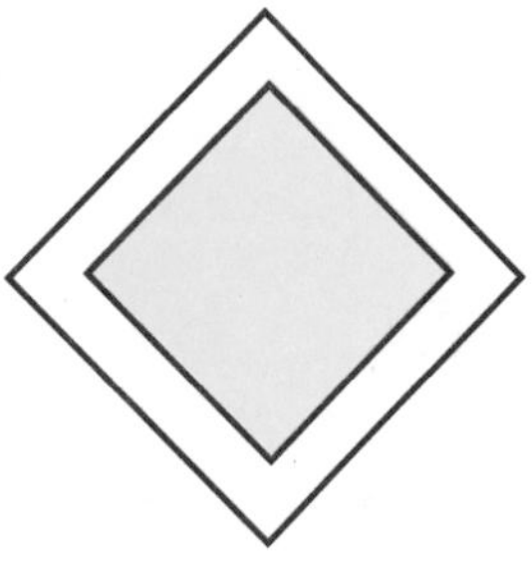

main road

(ra-ee-see-ya) (Ta-reeq)

طَريق رَئيسِيّة

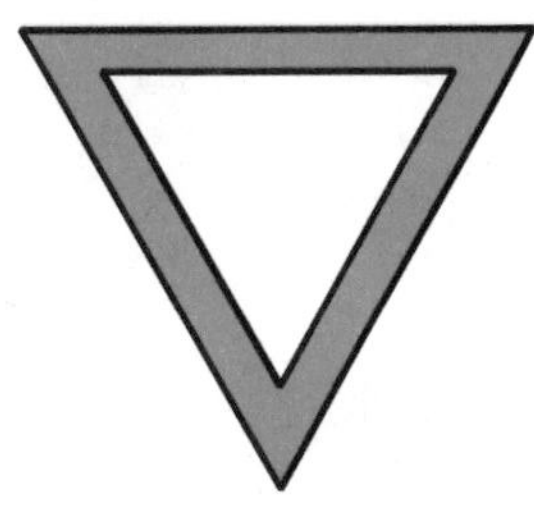

yield

(ah-soo-ra) (me-na)(hahf-fif)

خَفِّف مِنَ السُّرعة

speed limit

(meH-doo-da) (soo-ra)

سُرعة مَحدودة

no parking / no stopping

(mem-noo') (al-woo-goof)

الوُقوف مَمنوع

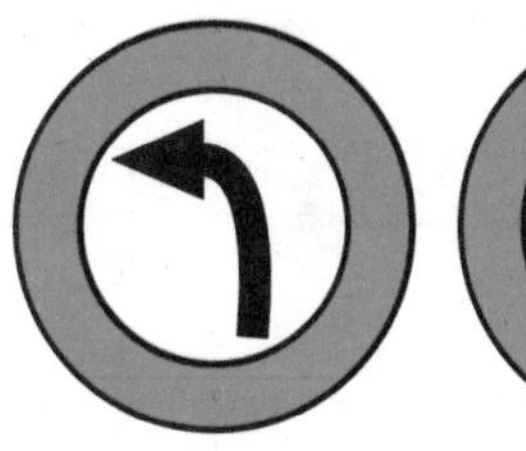

(al-ya-saar) (ee-la) (al-ya-meen) (ee-la)

إلى اليَمين / إلى اليَسار

to the right to the left

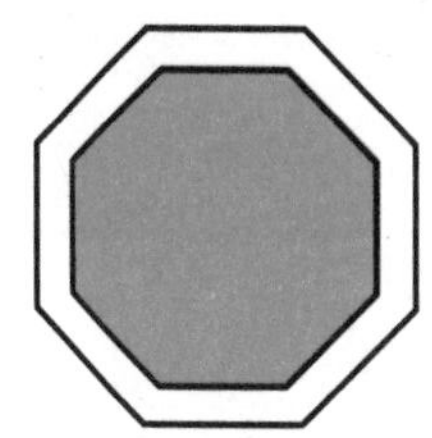

stop

(qef)

قِف

(mes-dood) (Ta-reeq)

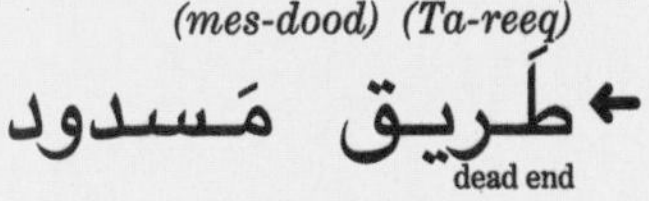

← طَريق مَسدود

dead end

What follows are approximate conversions, so when you order something by liters, kilograms or grams you will have an idea of what to expect and not find yourself being handed one piece of candy when you thought you ordered an entire bag.

To Convert		Do the Math		
liters (l) to gallons,	multiply by 0.26	4 liters x 0.26	=	1.04 gallons
gallons to liters,	multiply by 3.79	10 gal. x 3.79	=	37.9 liters
kilograms (kg) to pounds,	multiply by 2.2	2 kilograms x 2.2	=	4.4 pounds
pounds to kilos,	multiply by 0.46	10 pounds x 0.46	=	4.6 kg
grams (g) to ounces,	multiply by 0.035	100 grams x 0.035	=	3.5 oz.
ounces to grams,	multiply by 28.35	10 oz. x 28.35	=	283.5 g.
meters (m) to feet,	multiply by 3.28	2 meters x 3.28	=	6.56 feet
feet to meters,	multiply by 0.3	6 feet x 0.3	=	1.8 meters

For fun, take your weight in pounds and convert it into kilograms. It sounds better that way, doesn't it? How many kilometers is it from your home to school, to work, to the post office?

The Simple Versions		
one liter	=	approximately one US quart
four liters	=	approximately one US gallon
one kilo	=	approximately 2.2 pounds
100 grams	=	approximately 3.5 ounces
500 grams	=	slightly more than one pound
one meter	=	slightly more than three feet

The distance between عَمّان (ahm-maan) Amman ← وَ دِمَشق (deh-mahshk) Damascus is approximately 110 miles. How many kilometers would that be? The distance between القاهِرة (al-qaa-he-ra) Cairo ← وَ الرّباط (ah-ree-baaT) Rabat is 3,595 kilometers. How many miles is that?

kilometers (km.) to miles,	multiply by 0.62	1000 km. x 0.62	=	620 miles
miles to kilometers,	multiply by 1.6	1000 miles x 1.6	=	1,600 km.

Inches 1	2	3	4	5	6	7

To convert centimeters into inches, multiply by 0.39 Example: 9 cm. x 0.39 = 3.51 in.

To convert inches into centimeters, multiply by 2.54 Example: 4 in. x 2.54 = 10.16 cm.

cm 1	2	3	4	5	6	7	8	9	10	11	12	13	14	15	16	17	18

١٨/18 كَيفَ أَدفَعُ الحِساب

(kay-fa) (ahd-fa-roo) (al-Heh-saab)
how to pay the bill

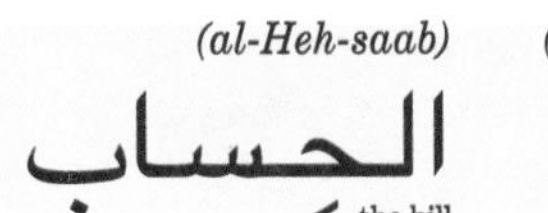
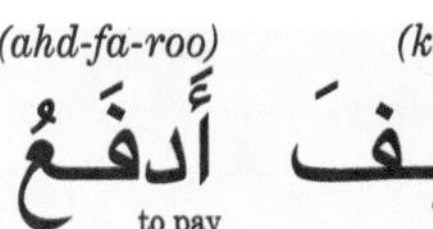

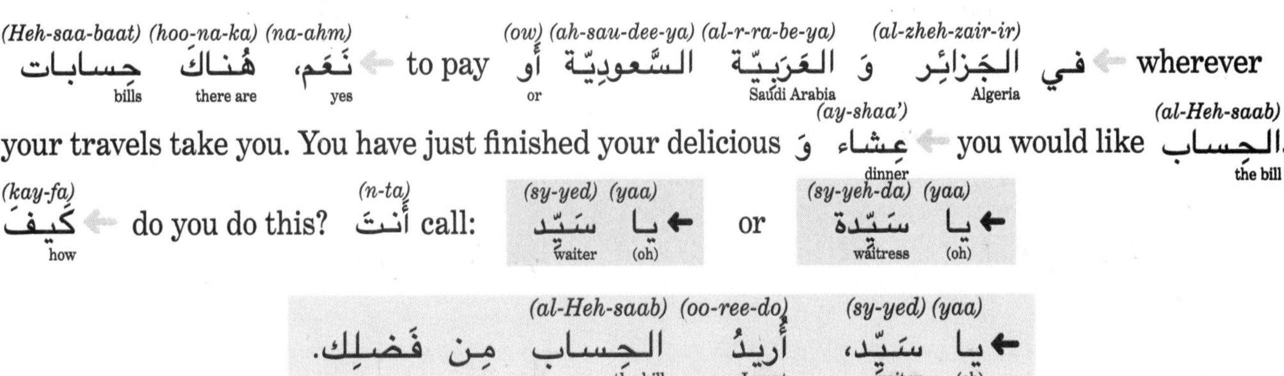

في (in) الجَزائِر (al-zheh-zair-ir, Algeria) وَ العَرَبِيّة السَّعودِيّة (al-r-ra-be-ya ah-sau-dee-ya, Saudi Arabia) أَو (ow, or) to pay حِسابات (Heh-saa-baat, bills) هُناكَ (hoo-na-ka, there are) نَعَم، (na-ahm, yes) wherever your travels take you. You have just finished your delicious عِشاء (ay-shaa', dinner) وَ you would like الحِساب (al-Heh-saab, the bill). كَيفَ (kay-fa, how) do you do this? أَنتَ (n-ta) call: يا سَيِّد (yaa sy-yed, oh waiter) or يا سَيِّدة (yaa sy-yeh-da, oh waitress)

يا سَيِّد، أُريدُ الحِساب مِن فَضلِك.
(yaa) (sy-yed) (oo-ree-do) (al-Heh-saab)
(oh) waiter I want the bill

The waiter will normally reel off what أَنتَ (n-ta) have eaten, while writing rapidly. هُوَ (hoo-wa, he) will then place a piece of paper on الطّاوِلة (ah-Taa-we-la, the table). "ثَلاثون ديناراً مِن فَضلِك." (tha-laa-thoon, 30) (dee-naa-rahn, dinars)
أَنتَ (n-ta) will pay the waiter or perhaps أَنتَ will pay الصُّندوق (ah-ssoon-dooq, the cashier)

Remember, the service may be included in الحِساب (al-Heh-saab, the bill). When أَنتَ dine out في سوريا (soo-ree-yaa, Syria) or في الجَزائِر (al-zheh-zair-ir), always make a reservation. It can be very difficult to get into a popular مَطعَم (ma-Tahm, restaurant). Remember, أَنتَ know enough عَرَبِيّة (r-ra-be-ya, Arabic) to make a reservation! Just speak slowly and clearly.

Tip: "يا" (yaa) is a friendly way to catch another's attention or to signal that you are speaking to that person as in "يا سَيِّد" (yaa sy-yed) above.

Remember these key كَلِمات (ka-lee-maat) when dining out بِالعَرَبِيّة (bil-r-ra-be-ya) *in Arabic*.

يا سَيِّدة (yaa) (sy-yeh-da) — (oh) waitress		يا سَيِّد (yaa) (sy-yed) — (oh) waiter
عَفواً (ahf-wahn) — you're welcome	عَفواً عَفواً عَفواً	حِساب (Heh-saab) — bill
رُسوم الخِدمة (roo-soom) (al-hid-ma) — service charge		لائحة الأكل (la-ee-Ha) (L-ah-kel) — the menu
شُكراً جَزيلاً (shook-rahn) (zha-zee-lahn) — thank you very much		مَعذِرة (mar-dee-ra) — excuse me
الوَصل (ah-wa-ssil) — receipt		مِن فَضلِك (min) (fahD-lahk) — please (♂) / مِن فَضلِك (min) (fahD-lik) (♀)

هَذا (heh-daa) *this* هُوَ (hoo-wa) *it (is)* a sample exchange about paying الحِساب (al-Heh-saab) *the bill*. Practice by writing it in the blanks.

جَليل (zha-leel) *Zhalil* : أُريدُ (oo-ree-do) *I want* أن (ahn) أدفَعَ (ahd-fa-ra) *pay* الحِساب (al-Heh-saab) مِن فَضلِك (♂).

____

البَوّاب (al-bao-web) *clerk* : أيُّ (eye-yoo) *which* غُرفة (roor-fa) *room* مِن فَضلِك؟

____

جَليل (zha-leel) : غُرفة (roor-fa) ثَلاثمِئة (tha-laa-thoo-me-ya) *300* وَ عَشرة *ten*.

____

البَوّاب (al-bao-web) : لَحظة (laH-Dha) *just a minute* مِن فَضلِك. ها (haa) *here* هُوَ (hoo-wa) *it (is)* الوَصل (ah-wa-ssil) *the receipt*. شُكراً جَزيلاً (zha-zee-lahn).

____

If أنتَ have any problems with الحِساب (al-Heh-saab), just ask someone to write out الأرقام (al-aar-qaam) *the numbers*, so that أنتَ can be sure you understand everything correctly,

مِن فَضلِك (fahD-lahk)، اِكتُب (eek-toob) *write out* الأرقام (al-aar-qaam) *the numbers*. شُكراً (shook-rahn).

Practice: ____
(Please write out the numbers. Thank you.)

عَلِمَ

- [ ] to know / learn / find out . . . . (ah-lee-ma) . . . . عَلِمَ
- [ ] scholar (♂) . . . . (aa-lim) . . . . عالِم
- [ ] scholar (♀) . . . . (aa-lee-ma) . . . . عالِمة

Let's take a break from الفُلوس *(al-foo-loos)* money وَ learn some fun جَديدة *(zha-dee-da)* new كَلِمات *(ka-lee-maat)*. You can always practice الكَلِمات *(al-ka-lee-maat)* هَذِهِ *(heh-da-he)* these by using your flash cards at the back of الكِتاب *(al-kee-taab)* هَذا *(heh-daa)* this. Carry these flash cards in your purse, pocket, briefcase أَو *(ow)* knapsack وَ use them!

(mef-tooH) مَفتوح ← open

مفتوح

(moog-lahq) مُغلَق ← closed

مغلق

(ka-beer) كَبير ← big

كبير

(ssa-greer) صَغير ← small

صغير

(sseH-He) صِحّي ← healthy

صحّي

(ma-reeD) مَريض ← sick

مريض

(zhy-yed) جَيِّد ← good

جيّد

(Dy-eef) ضَعيف ← bad (grades) / *(sy-yeh')* سَيِّء ← bad

weak

سيّء

(saak-hin) ساخِن hot (food) \ *(Har)* حارّ ← hot (weather)

حارّ ساخن

(bear-id) بارِد ← cold

بارد

knowledge .... *(ah-eh-lem)* .... العِلم ← ☐		
world .... *(ah-aa-lahm)*............... عالَم ☐	عَلِمَ	العالم كبير
flag .... *(ah-lahm)* .... عَلَم ☐		

طَويل (Ta-weel) long

قَصير (qa-sseer) short

120

25

سَريع (sa-reer) fast

بَطيء (ba-Tee') slow

قَصير (qa-sseer) short

طَويل (Ta-weel) tall

صَغير (ssa-greer) young

كَبير (ka-beer) old

رَخيص (ra-keess) cheap

ثَمين (tha-meen) / غالي (reh-lee) expensive

فَقير (fa-qeer) poor

غَنِيّ (ruh-nee) rich

قَليلاً (qa-lee-lahn) / شوَيّ (shway-yeh) a little

كَثيرًا (ka-thee-rahn) a lot

عَلِمَ

instructor (m) ..... (moo-ahl-lim) .... مُعَلِّم

instructor (f) ... (moo-ahl-lee-ma) .... مُعَلِّمة

landmark ...... (ma-aa-lim) .... مَعالِم

(hoo-naa) هُنا some new verbs. You can translate (ahn) (yeh-zhee-boo) يَجِبُ ← أن here simply as "I must." The second verb in the sentence needs to follow your pattern as you'll see in the examples below.

(yeh-zhee-boo) (ahn) ← يَجِبُ أن ______ it must be / I must

(ahs-ta-Tee-roo) (ahn) ← أستطيعُ أن ______ I can / am able to

(ah-qoo-loo) ← أقولُ ______ I say

(ahb-qa) ← أبقى ______ I stay

The word " أنْ " functions as a connector. You can translate it as "to" or "that" or sometimes a translation isn't even necessary.

(yeh-zhee-boo) (ahn) ← يَجِبُ أن ______ أدفَعَ الحِساب. it must be / I must ______ (I) pay (ahd-fa-ra) the bill (al-Heh-saab)

(yeh-zhee-boo) (ahn) يَجِبُ أن ______ أسافِرَ إلى القاهِرة. I must ______ (I) travel (oo-seh-fee-ra) (ee-la) Cairo (al-qaa-he-ra)

(yeh-zhee-boo) يَجِبُ أن ______ آكُلَ الآنَ. I must ______ eat (aa-koo-la) (al-ann)

(yeh-zhee-boo) يَجِبُ أن ______ أرى المَتحَف. ______ see (ah-ra) the museum (al-maht-Hahf)

(yeh-zhee-boo) يَجِبُ أن ______ أشرَبَ القَهوة. ______ drink (ahsh-ra-ba) (al-qa-wa)

يَجِبُ أن ______ أرى الأهرام. ______ see (ah-ra) the Pyramids (al-ah-raam)

(ah-qoo-loo) ← أقولُ ______ كَثيراً. I say ______ a lot (ka-thee-rahn)

(ta-qoo-loo) تَقولُ ______ كَثيراً. you (♂) say / she says ______ (ka-thee-rahn)

(ta-qoo-lee-na) تَقولينَ ______ قَليلاً. you (♀) say ______ a little (qa-lee-lahn)

(ya-qoo-loo) (la) لا يَقولُ ______ أيَّ شَيء. he says ______ nothing (eye) (shay')

(na-qoo-loo) نَقولُ ______ "لا". we say ______ no (la)

(ya-qoo-loo-na) يَقولونَ ______ "نَعَم". they say ______ yes (na-ahm)

(ahs-ta-Tee-roo) (ahn) ← أستطيعُ أن ______ أتَكَلَّمَ العَرَبِيّة. I can / am able to ______ speak (ah-ta-kel-la-ma) Arabic (al-r-ra-be-ya)

(tahs-ta-Tee-roo) (ahn) تَستطيعُ أن ______ تَتَكَلَّمَ العَرَبِيّة. you (♂) can / she can ______ speak (ta-ta-kel-la-ma)

(tahs-ta-Tee-ree-na) (ahn) تَستطيعينَ أن ______ تَفهَمي العَرَبِيّة. you (♀) can ______ understand (tahf-ha-mee)

(yahs-ta-Tee-roo) يَستطيعُ أن ______ يَقرَأَ العَرَبِيّة. he can ______ read (yahk-ra-ah)

(nahs-ta-Tee-roo) نَستطيعُ أن ______ نَتَكَلَّمَ الإنجليزِيّة. we can ______ speak (na-ta-kel-la-ma) English (al-in-zhlee-zee-ya)

(yahs-ta-Tee-roo-na) يَستطيعونَ أن ______ يَتَكَلَّموا الإنجليزِيّة. they can ______ speak (ya-ta-kel-la-moo)

(ahb-qa) ← أبقى ______ في الفُندُق. I stay ______ in (fee) the hotel (al-foon-dooq)

(tahb-qa) تَبقى ______ في صالة الضُّيوف. you (♂) stay / she stays ______ the guesthouse (ssaa-laht) (ah-Doo-yoof)

(tahb-qee-na) تَبقينَ ______ في البَيت. you (♀) stay ______ the house (al-bait)

(yahb-qa) يَبقى ______ في الشُّقّة. he stays ______ the apartment (ah-shooq-qa)

(nahb-qa) نَبقى ______ في قَطَر. we stay ______ Qatar (qa-Tar)

(yahb-qoo-na) يَبقونَ ______ في أبو ظَبي. they stay ______ Abu Dhabi (ah-boo) (da-bee)

عَلِمَ

☐ ← مُتَعَلِّم .... (moo-ta-ahl-lim) ..... educated person (♂) ______

☐ مُتَعَلِّمة .... (moo-ta-ahl-lee-ma) .... educated person (♀) ______

☐ تَعليم .... (ta-leem) .... education ______

Use the flash cards at the back of (al-kee-taab) الكِتاب (heh-daa) هَذا to drill these وَ other verbs. You saw that the verbs (ahs-ta-Tee-roo) أستَطيعُ (I can) and (yeh-zhee-boo) يَجِبُ (it must be) are joined with another verb by adding (ahn) أن.

← يَجِبُ (yeh-zhee-boo) it must be / I must — أن (ahn) — أتَكَلَّمَ (ah-ta-kel-la-ma) speak — العَرَبِيّة. (al-r-ra-be-ya)	← أستَطيعُ (ahs-ta-Tee-roo) I can — أن (ahn) — أتَكَلَّمَ (ah-ta-kel-la-ma) speak — العَرَبِيّة. (al-r-ra-be-ya)
← يَجِبُ أن أشتَرِيَ (esh-ta-ree-ya) buy — الكِتاب. (al-kee-taab) the book	← أستَطيعُ أن أفهَمَ (ahf-ha-ma) understand — العَرَبِيّة. (I can)
← يَجِبُ أن أسافِرَ (oo-seh-fee-ra) travel — إلى (ee-la) — العِراق. (al-ee-raaq) Iraq	← أستَطيعُ أن أكتُبَ (ahk-too-ba) write — بِالعَرَبِيّة. in Arabic

Did you notice that the verb following " أن " changed its last vowel from ُ (oo) (أتَكَلَّمُ) to َ (ah) (أتَكَلَّمَ)?

Can أنتَ translate the sentences below (ee-la) إلى العَرَبِيّة (into)? (al-ezh-we-ba) الأجوِبة (the answers) are below.

1. I can speak Arabic. انا اتكلم العربية
2. It must be that I pay the bill now. يجب ان ادفع الحساب الان
3. We do not know the address. لا نعرف العنوان
4. We can pay the bill. نستطيع ان ندفع الحساب
5. She stays in the hotel. هي تبقى في الفندق
6. You (♀) can speak Arabic. تَستَطيعينَ أن تَتَكَلَّمي العَرَبِيّة.
7. I say "yes." اقول "نعم"
8. We say "yes" in Arabic. نقول "نعم" بالعربية
9. I want to travel to Lebanon. اريد اسافر الى لبنان
10. She reads the newspaper. تقراء الجريدة

الأجوِبة

١ ← أستَطيعُ أن أتَكَلَّمَ العَرَبِيّة.
٢ يَجِبُ أن أدفَعَ الحِساب الآنَ.
٣ لا نَعرِفُ العُنوان.
٤ نَستَطيعُ أن نَدفَعَ الحِساب.
٥ تَبقى في الفُندُق.
٦ ← تَستَطيعينَ أن تَتَكَلَّمي العَرَبِيّة.
٧ أقولُ "نَعَم".
٨ نَقولُ "نَعَم" بِالعَرَبِيّة.
٩ أُريدُ أن أُسافِرَ إلى لُبنان.
١٠ تَقرَأُ الجَريدة.

(heh-da-he) هَذِهِ ← Use loud. out them say to forget Don't .(ahs-fahl) أسفَل ← opposites the (by-na) بَينَ ← lines draw الآنَ

Use هَذِهِ (heh-da-he) ← Don't forget to say them out loud. Actually:

Maybe أَنتَ will ride جَمَل (zha-mel) a camel around داخِل (daak-he-la) into حِصان (He-ssaan) a horse أو في مِصر (meess-ur) الأهرام (al-ah-raam) the Pyramids ← the Atlas Mountains ← في المَغرِب (al-ma-greb). You will have many wonderful new adventures وَ you will have them in Arabic!

سافَرَ

to travel........ (saa-fa-ra)............	سافَرَ
traveler (♂)........ (moo-seh-fer).........	مُسافِر
traveler (♀)...... (moo-seh-fee-ra)	مُسافِرة

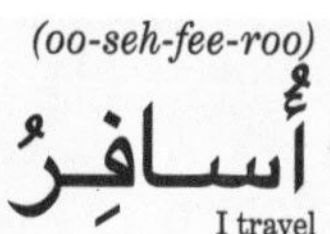

(oo-seh-fee-roo)
أُسافِرُ
I travel

(ahms) (al-yeh-men)
أمس في اليَمَن
yesterday Yemen

(al-yohm) (al-koo-wait)
اليَومَ في الكُوَيت
today Kuwait

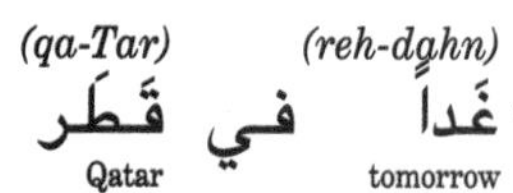

(reh-dghn) (qa-Tar)
غداً في قَطَر
tomorrow Qatar

(al-ha-mees) (al-oor-doon)
الخَميس في الأُردُن
Thursday Jordan

(ah-ith-nayn) (roo-maan)
الإثنَين في عُمان
Monday Oman

(al-ar-ba-aa') (leeb-yaa)
الأَربِعاء في ليبيا
Wednesday Libya

If you know a few key كَلِمات (ka-lee-maat), traveling in an Arabic-speaking بَلَد (ba-lahd) country will be so much easier, more enjoyable وَ rewarding.

(kay-fa) (too-seh-fee-roo)
كَيفَ تُسافِرُ؟
how do you (♀) travel

(ka-reem) (yoo-seh-fee-roo) (bil-qee-Taar)
كَريم يُسافِرُ بِالقِطار.
Karim travels by train

(moo-Hahm-med) (yoo-seh-fee-roo) (bih-sy-yaa-ra)
مُحَمَّد يُسافِرُ بِالسَّيّارة.
Muhammed travels

(mehzh-da) (too-seh-fee-roo) (bil-Haa-fee-la)
ماجدة تُسافِرُ بِالحافِلة.
Mezhda travels by bus

(na-beel) (yoo-seh-fee-roo) (bih-Taa-ee-ra)
نَبيل يُسافِرُ بِالطّائِرة.
Nabil travels by airplane

(ah-mee-na) (too-seh-fee-roo) (bil-bear-he-ra)
أمينة تُسافِرُ بِالباخِرة.
Amina by boat

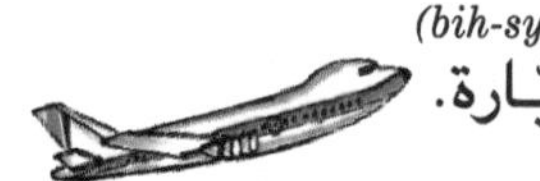

(aH-mahd) (yoo-seh-fee-roo) (bih-sy-yaa-ra)
أحمَد يُسافِرُ بِالسَّيّارة.
Ahmed

DATELINE
RUSSIA
NORTH AMERICA
SATURDAY
SUNDAY
AFRICA
SOUTH AMERICA

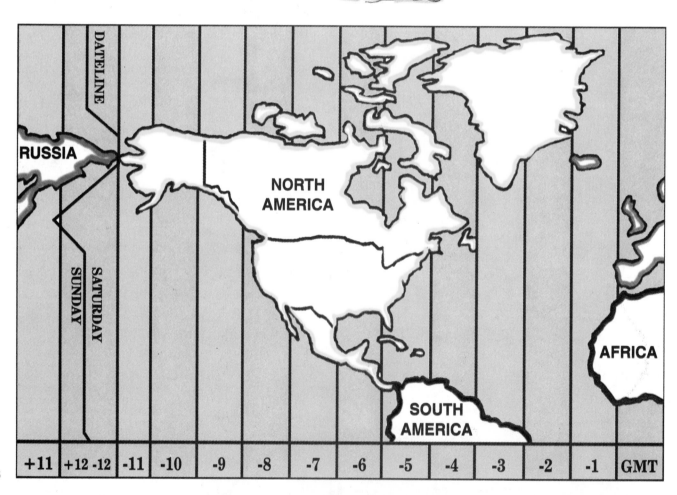

+11	+12 -12	-11	-10	-9	-8	-7	-6	-5	-4	-3	-2	-1	GMT

When أنتَ (n-ta) (♂) are traveling, أنتَ will want to tell others your nationality and أنتَ will meet people from all corners of the world. Can you guess where someone is from if they say one of the following? الأجوبة (al-ezh-we-ba) (the answers) ← are in your glossary beginning on page 108.

← أنا (ah-naa) I (am) مِن (min) from أمريكا (ahm-ree-kaa). ______________	← أنا (ah-naa) I (am) مِن (min) from العَربيّة (al-r-ra-be-ya) السَّعوديّة (ah-sau-dee-ya). ______________
أنا مِن كَنَدا (ka-na-daa). ______________	أنا مِن فَلَسطين (fa-les-Teen). ______________
أنا مِن إنجلَتِرّا (in-zhla-tair-raa). ______________	أنا مِن ليبيا (leeb-yaa). ______________
أنا مِن أُستُراليا (oos-too-raa-lee-ya). ______________	أنا مِن العِراق (al-ee-raaq). ______________
أنا مِن السّودان (ah-soo-daan). ______________	أنا مِن الكُوَيت (al-koo-wait). ______________
أنا مِن الأُردُن (al-oor-doon). ______________	أنا مِن تونُس (too-noos). ______________
أنا مِن مِصر (meess-ur). ______________	أنا مِن المَغرِب (al-ma-greb). ______________
أنا مِن سوريا (soo-ree-yaa). ______________	أنا مِن الجَزائِر (al-zheh-zair-ir). ______________

EUROPE
ASIA
AFRICA
DATELINE
SATURDAY
SUNDAY

-1	GMT	+1	+2	+3	+4	+5	+6	+7	+8	+9	+10	+11	+12 -12

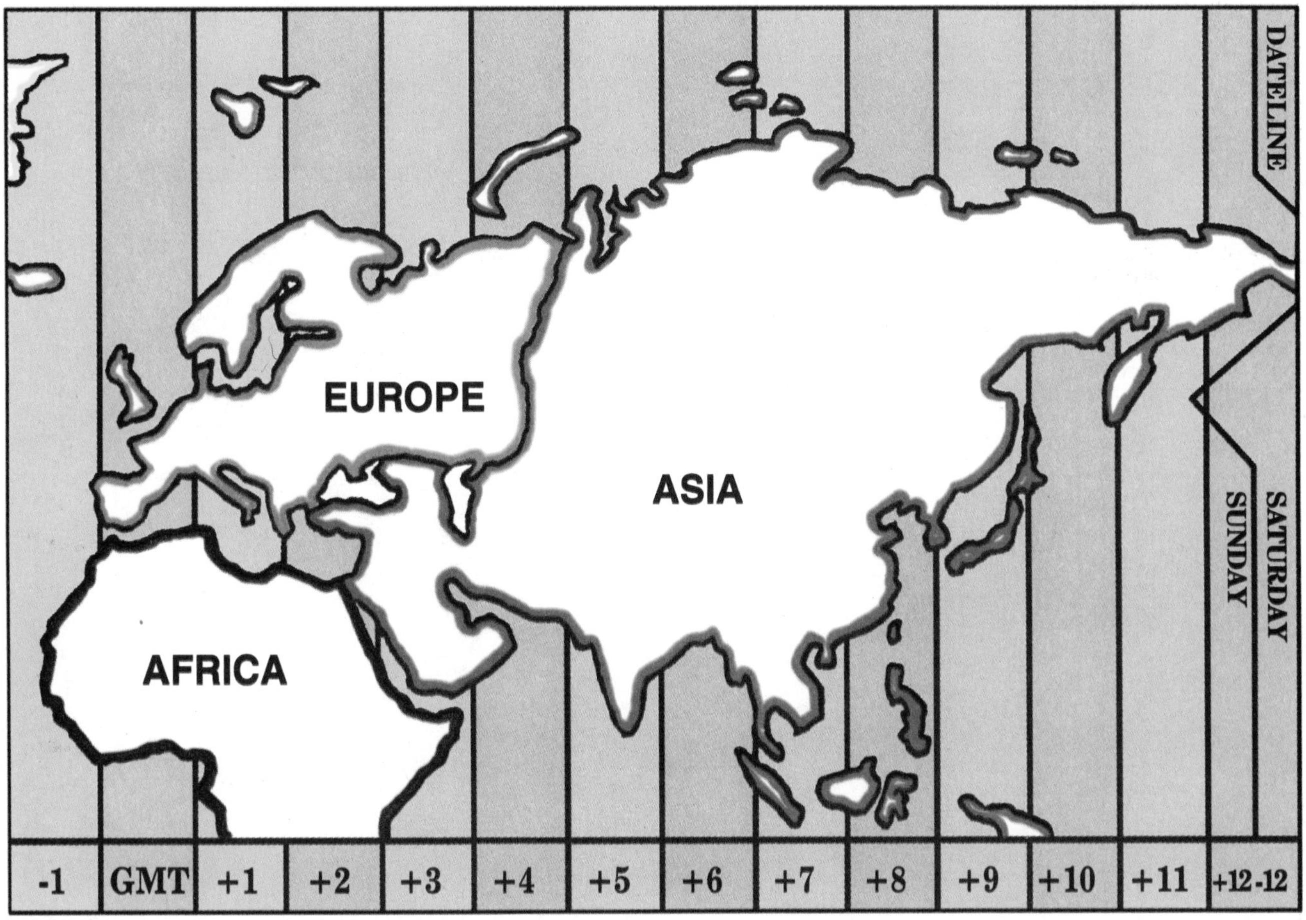

Most people love to travel so it is no wonder to find كَلِمات كَثيرة (ka-thee-ra) many revolving around the concept of سَفَر (sa-far) travel which is exactly what تُريدُ (too-ree-do) you want to do. Practice saying the following كَلِمات many times. أَنتَ will see them often.

مَكتَب سَفَر (mahk-tahb) (sa-far) travel agency ______________________

أُسافِرُ (oo-seh-fee-roo) I travel ______________________

سَفَر (sa-far) trip ______________________

مُسافِر (moo-seh-fer) traveler ______________________

If أَنتَ choose to travel بِالسَّيّارة (bih-sy-yaa-ra) by car, here are a few key كَلِمات.

مَحَطّة البِنزين (ma-HahT-Taht) (al-ben-zeen) gas station ______________________

طَريق (Ta-reeq) road / freeway ______________________

زَنَقة / زُقاق (za-na-qa) (zoo-qaak) small street ______________________

شارِع (sheh-re') big street ______________________

Here are some basic signs which أَنتَ should learn to recognize quickly بِدون (be-doon) without the vowels.

خَرَجَ (ha-ra-zha) to exit ______________________

دَخَلَ (dahk-ha-la) to enter ______________________

خروج

دخول

خُروج (hoo-roozh) exit ______________________

دُخول (dook-hool) entrance ______________________

الخُروج مَمنوع (al-hoo-roozh) (mem-noo') no exit ______________________

الدُّخول مَمنوع (ah-dook-hool) (mem-noo') no entrance ______________________

اغلق

افتح

إِغلَق (ear-lahq) pull ______________________

إِفتَح (if-taH) push ______________________

سافَرَ

- ❑ سَفَر ← trip / journey........ (sa-far) .... ______________________
- ❑ مَكتَب سَفَر travel agency.... (sa-far)(mahk-tahb).. ______________________
- ❑ شيكات سَفَر traveler's checks.... (sa-far)(shee-ket)... ______________________

Take out a piece of paper وَ make up your own sentences with these الكَلِمات الجَديدة (al-zha-dee-da) *new*. Follow the same pattern you have in previous Steps, but note that "هُناكَ" (hoo-naa-ka) *there is, there are* does not change its form!

أَسوقُ (ah-soo-qoo) — I drive ______________________

أَزورُ (ah-zoo-roo) — I visit ______________________

أَحجِزُ (aH-zhee-zoo) — I reserve ______________________

أَدخُلُ (ahd-hoo-loo) — I enter ______________________

أَحزِمُ (aH-zee-moo) — I pack ______________________

أَصِلُ (ah-ssee-loo) — I arrive ______________________

هُناكَ (hoo-naa-ka) — there is, there are ______________________

أُغادِرُ (oo-raa-dee-roo) — I leave, depart ______________________

هُنا (hoo-na) some كَلِمات جَديدة (zha-dee-da) *new* for your سَفَر (sa-far) *trip*.

المَطار (al-ma-Taar) — airport

____

مَحَطّة الحافِلات (ma-HahT-Taht) (al-Haa-fee-laat) — bus station

____

التَّوقيت (ah-tao-qeet) — timetable

مِن القاهِرة (al-qaa-he-ra) إلى الرياض (ah-ree-yaaD)		
الوُصول (al-woo-ssool) arrival	طَيَران (Ta-ya-raan) flight	الذَّهاب (ah-da-haab) departure
10:30	50	8:00
12:30	19	10:00
15:30	10	13:00
18:30	4	16:00
22:30	22	20:00

____

مَحَطّة القِطار (ma-HahT-Taht) (al-qee-Taar) — train station

____

طَلَب

- [ ] to order / ask . . . . (Ta-la-ba) . . . . طَلَبَ
- [ ] application . . . . (Ta-lahb) . . . . طَلَب
- [ ] order form . . . . (Ta-lahb) . . . . طَلَب

____
____
____

(n-ta) (heh-da-he) (sa-far)

الكَلِمات أَنتَ مَعَ هَذِهِ ← are ready for any سَفَر (trip) anywhere. أَنتَ should have no problem مَعَ these verbs, just remember the basic "plug-in" formula أَنتَ learned already. Use that knowledge to translate the following thoughts إلى (ee-la) (into) العَرَبِيّة.

1. I reserve a car. ______________________________
2. I drive to Rabat (الرِّباط). ______________________________
3. The bus leaves at 9:30. ______________________________
4. We arrive tomorrow in Jordan. ______________________________
5. You (🚹) travel to Cairo. ______________________________
6. They travel to Qatar. ______________________________
7. Where is the bus to Amman? ______________________________
8. How do we travel to Morocco? ______________________________

هُنا some جِدّاً (zhid-dahn) (very) important words for the traveler.

(da-haab)
← ذَهاب ______________________________
departure

(mahsh-rool)
← مَشغول ______________________________
occupied

(woo-ssool)
← وُصول ______________________________
arrival

(sheh-rir)
← شاغِر ______________________________
free

(raa-la-me)
← عالَمي ______________________________
international

(koor-see)
← كُرسي ______________________________
seat

(ma-Hahl-lee)
← مَحَلّي ______________________________
domestic

(neh-fee-da)
← نافِذة ______________________________
window

الأجوبة

١ ← أحجِزُ سَيّارة.
٢ أسوقُ إلى الرِّباط.
٣ الحافِلة تُغادِرُ في التّاسِعة وَ النِّصف.
٤ نَصِلُ غَداً إلى الأُردُن.
٥ تُسافِرُ إلى القاهِرة.
٦ يُسافِرونَ إلى قَطَر.
٧ أينَ الحافِلة إلى عَمّان؟
٨ كَيفَ نُسافِرُ إلى المَغرِب؟

Increase your travel كَلِمات by writing out (ahs-fahl) أسفَل (below) الكَلِمات and practicing the sample sentences out loud. Practice asking (eye-na) "أيـنَ" questions. It will help you later.

(ee-la) إلى (to) ______________________

أينَ الحافِلة إلى الإسكَندَريّة؟ (Alexandria)

(teth-kee-ra) تَذكِرة (ticket) ______________________

بِكَم التَّذكِرة إلى الإسكَندَريّة؟

(min) مِن (from) ______________________

أينَ الحافِلة القادِمة مِن البَتراء؟ (coming) (Petra)

(al-ir-sheh-daat) (mahk-tahb) مَكتَب الإرشادات (office) (information) ______________________

أينَ مَكتَب الإرشادات؟

(al-moo-seh-fee-reen) (How-weh-izh)(mahk-tahb) مَكتَب حَوائِج المُسافِرين (left-luggage office) ______________________

أينَ مَكتَب حَوائِج المُسافِرين؟

(ah-ra-ba) عَرَبة (luggage cart / trolley) ______________________

أينَ العَرَبة؟

(koor-see) كُرسي (seat) ______________________

مِن فَضلِك، هَل هَذا الكُرسي مَشغول؟ (occupied)

(sheh-rir) شاغِر (free) ______________________

مِن فَضلِك، هَل هَذا الكُرسي شاغِر؟

(shoob-bek) شُبّاك (counter) ______________________

مِن فَضلِك، أينَ الشُّبّاك رَقم ثَمانِية؟ (number)

(fa-les-Teen) (too-seh-fee-roo) ؟ إلى فَلَسطين تُسافِرُ (do you travel) ______ ______ (when)

(oo-ree-do) ؟ تُريدُ (do you (♂) want) ______ ______ (what)

طَلَب

- ❐ ← طالِب .... (Taa-leeb) .... student (♂) ______________________
- ❐ طالِبة .... (Taa-lee-ba) .... student (♀) ______________________
- ❐ مُتَطَلَّبات ... (moo-ta-Tahl-leh-bet) ..... requirements ______________________

Can أَنتِ (n-tee) (♀) read the following?

أُسافِرُ (oo-seh-fee-roo) إلى المَغرِب (al-ma-greb). أو (ow)

أُسافِرُ (oo-seh-fee-roo) إلى الأُردُن (al-oor-doon). أو

أُسافِرُ (oo-seh-fee-roo) إلى الكُوَيت (al-koo-wait).

عِندي (rin-dee) فُلوس (foo-loos).

عِندي (rin-dee) تَذكِرة (teth-kee-ra)، جَواز (zhao-wez) سَفَر (sa-far) (passport)، وَ حَقيبة (Ha-qee-ba) (suitcase) جَديدة (zha-dee-da) (new).

أَنا سائِح (saa-eH) (tourist ♂) أَو أَنا سائِحة (saa-ee-Ha) (♀).

أَصِلُ (ah-ssee-lo) غَداً (reh-dahn) في العاشِرة (al-ah-she-ra) (ten o'clock) صَباحاً (ssa-baa-Hahn).

سَفَر سَعيد (sy-yeed)!
Have a good trip!

في سوريا (soo-ree-yaa) (Syria) أَو الأُردُن (al-oor-doon) (Jordan) وَ most Arabic-speaking countries the bus is the most common form of transport. Make sure أَنتَ find out in advance if أَنتَ need قِطعة (qeh-Tart) (a token) نُقود (noo-qood) أَو possibly a special bus card. In any case, be sure أَنتَ have enough قِطَع (qeh-Tar) (coins) نَقدِيّة (nahq-dee-ya) with you.

This should help you identify various ways of food preparation.

______________	baked . . . . (mahk-booz) . . . . مَخبوز	☐
______________	broiled . . . .(magh-lee) . . . . مَغلي	☐
______________	steamed . . . . (moo-bahk-khur) . . . . مُبَخَّر	☐

Knowing these travel كَلِمات (ka-lee-maat) will make your holiday twice as enjoyable وَ at least three times as easy. Review هَذِهِ (heh-da-he) الكَلِمات الجَديدة (al-zha-dee-da) new by doing the crossword puzzle أسفَل (ahs-fahl) below. Drill yourself on this Step by selecting other destinations وَ ask your own أسئِلة (es-ee-la) questions about طائِرات (Taa-ee-raat) airplanes وَ حافِلات (Haa-fee-laat) buses قِطارات، (qee-Taa-raat) trains that go there. Select كَلِمات (ka-lee-maat) جَديدة (zha-dee-da) from your قاموس (qaa-moos) dictionary وَ ask your own أسئِلة (es-ee-la) questions that begin with مَتى (meh-ta) when أينَ (eye-na) where بِكَم (be-kem) how much. الأجوِبة (al-ezh-we-ba) to the crossword puzzle are at the bottom of the next page.

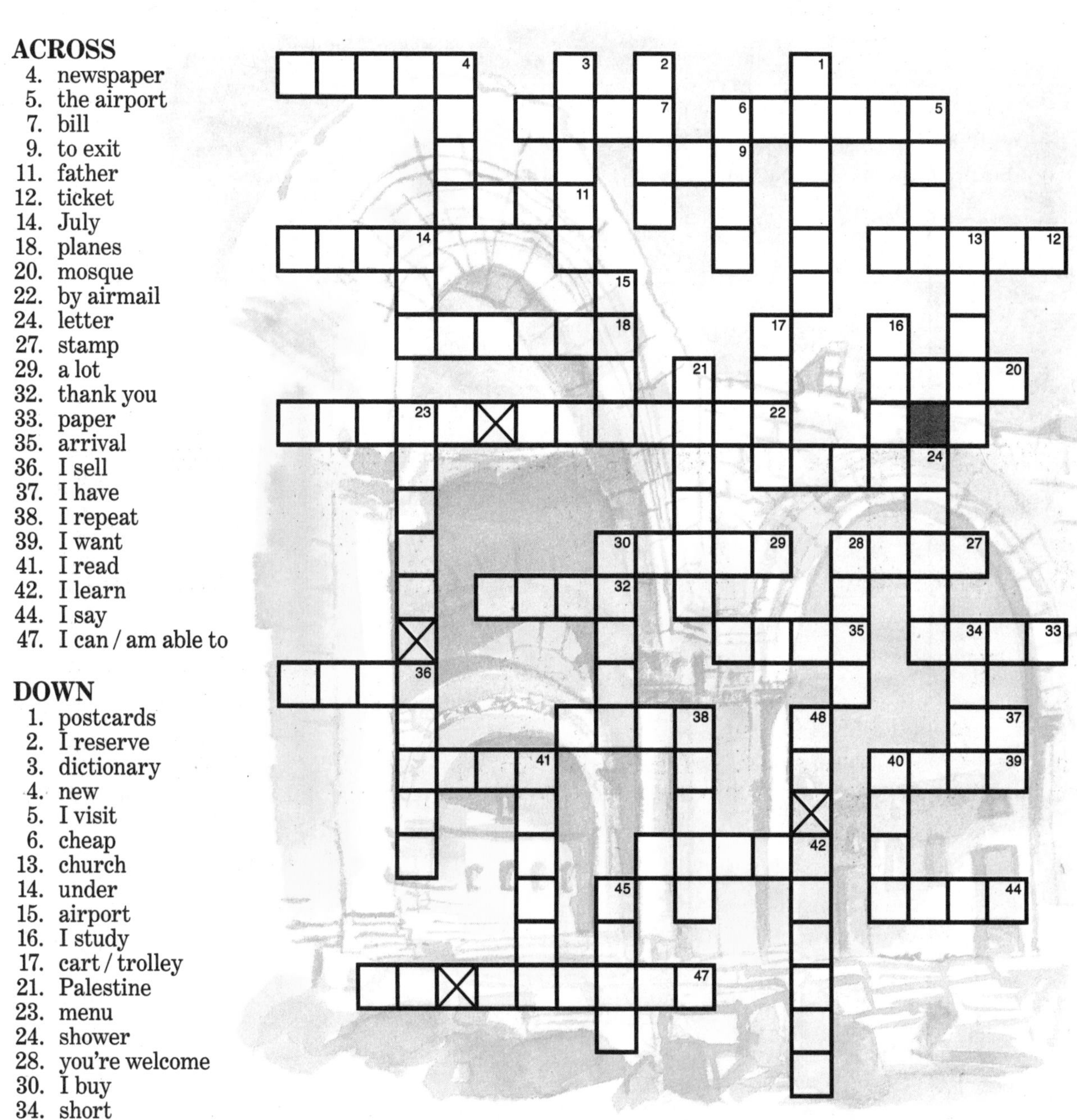

ACROSS

4. newspaper
5. the airport
7. bill
9. to exit
11. father
12. ticket
14. July
18. planes
20. mosque
22. by airmail
24. letter
27. stamp
29. a lot
32. thank you
33. paper
35. arrival
36. I sell
37. I have
38. I repeat
39. I want
41. I read
42. I learn
44. I say
47. I can / am able to

DOWN

1. postcards
2. I reserve
3. dictionary
4. new
5. I visit
6. cheap
13. church
14. under
15. airport
16. I study
17. cart / trolley
21. Palestine
23. menu
24. shower
28. you're welcome
30. I buy
34. short
37. no
38. I speak
40. entrance
41. give me
45. I write
48. What time is it?

Remember: When you do your crossword puzzles, you do not need to use any of the vowels.

What about inquiring about the price of تَذكِرة (teth-kee-ra) (a) ticket? Remember, العَرَبِيّة (al-r-ra-be-ya) تَتَكَلَّمُ (ta-ta-kel-la-moo) you (♂) speak and

أن (ahn) تَستَطيعُ (tahs-ta-Tee-roo) you (♂) can ask الأسئِلة (al-es-ee-la) questions هَذِهِ. (heh-da-he) these

بِكَم (be-kem) how much التَّذكِرة (ah-teth-kee-ra) the ticket إلى القاهِرة؟ (al-qaa-he-ra) ____________________

بِكَم التَّذكِرة (ah-teth-kee-ra) إلى مُرّاكُش؟ (moor-raa-koosh) Marrakesh ____________________

بِكَم التَّذكِرة (ah-teth-kee-ra) إلى تونُس؟ (too-noos) ____________________

رِحلة (reH-la) trip "ذَهاب" (da-haab) one-way أو "إيّاب" (ee-yeb) ____________________

هَذِهِ. (heh-da-he) الأسئِلة (al-es-ee-la) questions also ask تَستَطيعُ (tahs-ta-Tee-roo) you (♂) can أن (ahn)? وُصول (woo-ssool) arrival and ذَهاب (da-haab) departure about times of ماذا (may-daa) what

مَتى (meh-ta) when تُغادِرُ (too-raa-dee-roo) leaves الحافِلة (al-Haa-fee-la) the bus إلى الجَزائِر؟ (al-zheh-zair-ir) Algeria ____________________

مَتى (meh-ta) تُغادِرُ (too-raa-dee-roo) leaves الحافِلة إلى طَرابلُس؟ (Ta-raa-bloos) Tripoli ____________________

مَتى تَصِلُ (ta-ssee-loo) arrives الحافِلة مِن (from) دِمَشق؟ (deh-mahshk) Damascus ____________________

مَتى تَصِلُ (ta-ssee-loo) الطّائِرة (ah-Taa-ee-ra) the plane مِن (min) بَيروت؟ (bay-root) Beirut ____________________

مَتى تُغادِرُ (too-raa-dee-roo) leaves الطّائِرة (ah-Taa-ee-ra) إلى شَرم (sharm) Sharm الشّيخ؟ (ah-sheek) Al-Sheik ____________________

Well, tell that to the person at تُريدُ (oo-ree-do) you (♂) want أن تُسافِرَ (too-seh-fee-ra) you (♂) travel إلى عَمّان. (ahm-maan) أنتَ في المَطار. (al-ma-Taar) the airport

التَّذاكِر. (ah-theh-daa-kair) tickets selling الشّبّاك (ah-shoob-bek) the counter

سَفَر سَعيد (sy-yeed) Have a good trip

الأجوِبة TO THE CROSSWORD PUZZLE

ACROSS

4. جريدة
5. المطار
7. حساب
9. خرج
11. والد
12. تذكرة
14. تموز
18. طائرات
20. مسجد
22. بالبريد الجوي
24. رسالة
27. طابع
29. كثيرا
32. شكرا
33. ورقة
35. وصول
36. ابيع
37. لي
38. اعيد
39. اريد
41. اقرا
42. اتعلم
44. اقول
47. استطيع ان

DOWN

1. بطاقات
2. احجز
3. قاموس
4. جديد
5. ازور
6. رخيص
13. كنيسة
14. تحت
15. المطار
16. ادرس
17. عربة
21. فلسطين
23. لائحة الاكل
24. رشاشة
28. عفوا
30. اشتري
34. قصير
37. لا
38. اتكلم
40. دخول
41. اعطيني
45. اكتب
48. كم الساعة؟

(al-ann) الآنَ that *(ta-ree-foo)* تَعرِفُ (you (♂) know) the words essential for traveling – to Bahrain, Tunisia, Iraq, Yemen *(ow)* أو Morocco – what are some speciality items أنتَ might go in search of?

(moo-zhao-ha-ret) مُجَوهَرات
jewelry

(meh-leh-bes) مَلابِس
clothing

(koo-oos) (wa) (qa-wa) (ee-breeq) إبريق قَهوة وَ كُؤوس
coffee set

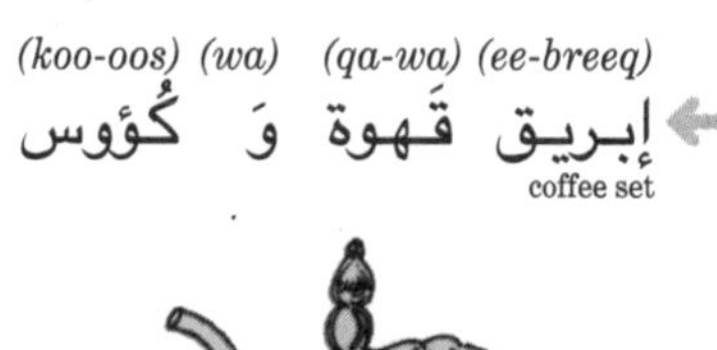

______________________ ______________________ ______________________

(lao-Het) لَوحات
paintings

(za-haa-rif) زَخارِف
decorative arts / ornamentation

(sahzh-zheh-det) سَجّادات
rugs / carpets

______________________ ______________________ ______________________

Consider using ARABIC *a language map®* as well. ARABIC *a language map®* is the perfect companion for your travels when أَنتَ may not wish to take along *(al-kee-taab)* الكِتاب (book) *(heh-daa)* هَذا. Each section focuses on essentials for your *(sa-far)* سَفَر. Your *Language Map®* is not meant to replace learning العَرَبيّة, but will help you in the event أَنتَ forget something and need a little bit of help. For more information about the *Language Map®* Series, please turn to page 132.

______________________	fried . . . . *(mahq-lee)* . . . . مَقلي ☐
______________________	roasted . . . . *(mesh-we)* . . . . مَشوي ☐
______________________	boiled . . . . *(mahss-looq)* . . . . مَصلوق ☐

٢٠ / 20 لائِحة الأكل

(L-ah-kel) (la-ee-Ha) — the menu

أنتَ في بَيروت. أنتَ في الفُندُق. أنتَ جوعان. هَل هُناك مَطعَم جَيِّد؟

(n-ta) (bay-root) (al-foon-dooq) (zhao-aan) hungry *(hel) (hoo-naa-ka)* is there *(ma-Tahm) (zhy-yed)*

First of all, there are different types of places to eat. Let's learn them.

مَطعَم *(ma-Tahm)* restaurant

____

Many different national cuisines are represented, so أنتَ have plenty of interesting choices.

مَقهى *(mahq-ha)* café

____

serves food وَ is your afternoon stop for coffee

كافيتيريا *(kaa-fee-tair-ree-aa)* cafeteria

____

serves a variety of dishes

مَحلَبة *(maH-la-ba)* creamery / deli

____

serves small pastries, breads, snacks, cheese, coffee, milk, juice

خَيمة *(hy-ma)* tent

____

tent offering traditional and regional dishes

You may want to begin your meal with a plate of حَلوى *(hel-wa)* pastries or خُبز وَ حُمُّص *(hoobz)* bread *(hoom-mooss)* hummus. Before beginning your وَجبة *(wehzh-ba)* meal, be sure to wish those sharing your table: وَجبة طَيِّبة. *(Ty-yee-ba) (wehzh-ba)* enjoy your meal

____
(enjoy your meal)

And at least one more time for practice!

____
(enjoy your meal)

أَكَلَ

- ☐ أَكَلَ ← to eat .... *(aa-ka-la)* .... _______________
- ☐ لائِحة الأكل the menu ... *(L-ah-kel)(la-ee-Ha)* ... _______________
- ☐ بَيت الأكل the dining room ..... *(L-ah-kel)(bait)* ...... _______________

Do not pass up the opportunity to enjoy فَلافِل (fa-laa-fel) [falafel] or fresh خُبز (hoobz) [bread] at a falafel stand.

Once you have found a ← مَطعَم جَيِّد (ma-Tahm) (zhy-yed) [restaurant] [good] enter المَطعَم (al-ma-Tahm) and find طاوِلة (Taa-we-la) [(a) table]. أنتَ call ← "يا سَيِّد" (yaa) (sy-yed) أو (ow) "يا سَيِّدة" (yaa) (sy-yeh-da) and say: ← يا سَيِّد، (yaa) (sy-yed) لائِحة (la-ee-Ha) الأكل (L-ah-kel) مِن فَضلِك.

____

(Waiter, the menu please.)

If your waiter asks: ← كَيفَ (kay-fa) الوَجبة؟ (al-wehzh-ba) [the meal] You may simply say, شُكراً (shook-rahn) [thank you] or if you are feeling confident, say,

← "هَذِهِ مائِدة (may-ee-da) رائِعة!" (raa-ee-ya)

This conveys that the food, service وَ the setting were all excellent. Be sure to enjoy the custom في many المَطاعِم (al-ma-Taa-im) [restaurants] of cleansing your hands before وَ after the meal مَعَ ← ماء الوَرد. (maa') (al-weard) [rosewater]

الآن (al-ann), it may be breakfast time at home, but أنتَ are ← في عَمّان (ahm-maan) [Amman] and it is 20:00. Some المَطاعِم (al-ma-Taa-im) [restaurants] post ← لائِحة (la-ee-Ha) الأكل (L-ah-kel) [the menu] outside. Always read it before entering so تَعرِفُ (ta-ree-foo) [you (♂) know] what type of meals وَ prices أنتَ will encounter inside.

إحتَفَلَ

____________________	to celebrate	(iH-ta-fa-la)	← إحتَفَلَ ☐
____________________	party	(Haf-la)	حَفلة ☐
____________________	celebration	(iH-tee-fel)	إحتِفال ☐

(tha-laa-tha) (hoo-naa-ka) ثَلاثة three هُناكَ there are ← main meals to enjoy every (yohm) يَوم day, plus (shay) شاي tea وَ (qa-wa) قَهوة coffee ← and perhaps (Hel-wa) حَلوى little sweets for the tourist (ah-Doo-hur) (ba-da) بَعدَ الظُّهر (in) the afternoon. ←

(al-foo-Toor) ← الفُطور breakfast
breakfast may include bread, butter, cheese, eggs, olives, olive oil as well as قَهوة or شاي

(al-ree-deh') ← الغِذاء lunch
the main meal of the day – usually served between 12:00 and 14:00

(al-ay-shaa') ← العِشاء dinner
usually served from 18:00 until the very late evening

هُنا a preview of delights to come . . . . At the back of (al-kee-taab) (heh-daa) هَذا الكِتاب you will find a sample (L-ah-kel) (la-ee-Ha) لائِحة الأكل menu. ← Read (L-ah-kel) (la-ee-Ha) لائِحة الأكل ← today وَ learn (al-zha-dee-da) (al-ka-lee-maat) الكَلِمات الجَديدة new ! ← (rin-da-maa) عِندَما when you are ready to leave for (al-ow-sahT) (ah-shark) الشَّرق الأوسَط the Middle East أو (al-ha-leezh) الخَليج the Gulf (ef-ree-qee-yaa) (sheh-mel) شَمال إفريقيا North Africa, ← cut out (L-ah-kel) (la-ee-Ha) لائِحة الأكل, ← fold it وَ carry it in your pocket, wallet أو purse. (na-qoo-loo) (kay-fa) كَيفَ how نَقولُ do we say ← these (tha-laa-tha) ثَلاثة three phrases which are so very important for the hungry traveler?

I am hungry. ______________________________ ←

Waiter, the menu, please. ______________________________ ←

Enjoy your meal! ______________________________ ←

← ________ (who) (yahsh-ra-boo) يَشرَبُ drinks (ah-shay) الشّاي؟

← ________ (who) (yaa-koo-loo) يَأكُلُ eats (ah-shoor-ba) الشّوربة؟ soup

________ (who)

← ________ (who) (yoo-seh-fee-roo) يُسافِرُ (ah-ree-yahD) إلى الرِّياض؟ Riyadh

إحتَفَلَ

- ☐ concert . . (moo-see-qee-ya)(Hahf-la) . . حَفلة موسيقِيّة ← ______________
- ☐ festival . . . . (Hahfl) . . . . حَفل ______________
- ☐ the people celebrating . . . (al-mooH-ta-fee-loon) . . . . المُحتَفِلون ______________

(ahs-fahl) (L-ah-kel) (la-ee-Ha) (al-ma-Taa-im)
أسفَل الأكل لائِحة ← has the main categories أَنت will find in most المَطاعِم. Learn them
below / restaurants

(al-yohm) (tahs-ta-Tee-roo) (loob-naan)
اليَوم ← so that تَستَطيعُ easily recognize them when you dine out أَو في لُبنان ←
today / you (♀) can

(meess-ur)
في مِصر. ← Be sure to write الكَلِمات in the blanks below.

أَطعَم

- ❑ ← أَطعَم .... (ah-Ta-ma) .... to feed
- ❑ مَطعَم .... (ma-Tahm) .... restaurant
- ❑ طَعام .... (Taam) .... food

أَنتَ will also get خُضار (hoo-Daar) [vegetables] with your عِشاء (ay-shaa') [dinner] and perhaps a سَلَطة (sa-la-Ta) [salad]. One day at السّوق (ah-sook) [the market] will teach you ← الأسماء (ah-ees-maa') [the names] for all the different kinds of الخُضار (al-hoo-Daar) [the vegetables] and الفَواكِه (al-fa-waa-kih) [the fruit], plus it will be a delightful experience for you. أَنتَ can always consult your menu guide at the back of الكِتاب هَذا (heh-daa) if أَنتَ forget the correct الإسم (al-eesm) [name]. ← الآن (al-ann) you are seated and the waiter يَجيء (ya-zhee-oo) [comes].

← الفُطور (al-foo-Toor) [breakfast] is delicious. ← الفُطور (al-foo-Toor) includes cheese, eggs, olives, وَ bread أو rolls. أَسفَل (ahs-fahl) [below] is a sample of ← ما (maa) [what] تَستَطيع (tahs-ta-Tee-roo) [you (♂) can] أن expect to greet you في الصَّباح (ah-ssa-baaH).

(aa-koo-loo) ← آكُل I eat
(hoobz) خُبز
(zhoob-na) جُبنة cheese
(by-eD) بَيض eggs
(zy-toon) زَيتون olives
(he-yaar) خِيار cucumbers
(Ta-maa-Tem) طَماطِم tomatoes
(moo-rahb-ba) مُرَبّى jam
(ahsh-ra-boo) ← أشرَبُ I drink
(qa-wa) قَهوة
(qa-wa) (Ha-leeb) قَهوة مَعَ حَليب milk
(shay) شاي
(ra-sseer) ← عَصير juice
(toof-feH) تُفّاح apple
(boor-too-qaal) بُرتُقال orange
(ry-nahb) عِنَب grape

أَطعَمَ

- ☐ feeding . . . . . . (ih-Taam) . . . . إطعام ←
- ☐ someone who feeds (♂) . . . . . (moo-Time) . . . . . . مُطعِم
- ☐ someone who feeds (♀) . . . (moo-Ty-ee-ma) . . مُطعِمة

(hoo-naa) هُنـا an example of أَنـتَ (maa) مـا (what) might select for your evening meal. Using your menu guide on pages 117 and 118, as well as أَنـتَ مـا have learned in this Step, fill in the blanks (bil-een-zhlee-zee-ya) بِـالإِنـجـلـيـزِيّة (in English) with أَنـتَ مـا believe the waiter will bring you. (al-ezh-we-ba) الأَجوِبـة أَسـفَل.

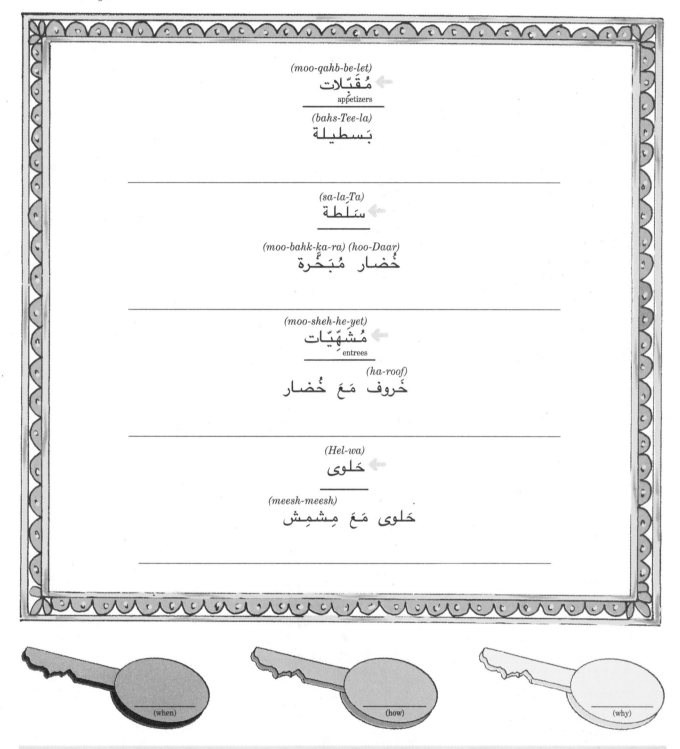

(moo-qahb-be-let)
مُقَبّلات
appetizers

(bahs-Tee-la)
بَسطيلة

____

(sa-la-Ta)
سَلَطة

(moo-bahk-ka-ra) (hoo-Daar)
خُضار مُبَخَّرة

____

(moo-sheh-he-yet)
مُشَهّيات
entrees

(ha-roof)
خَروف مَعَ خُضار

____

(Hel-wa)
حَلوى

(meesh-meesh)
حَلوى مَعَ مِشمِش

____

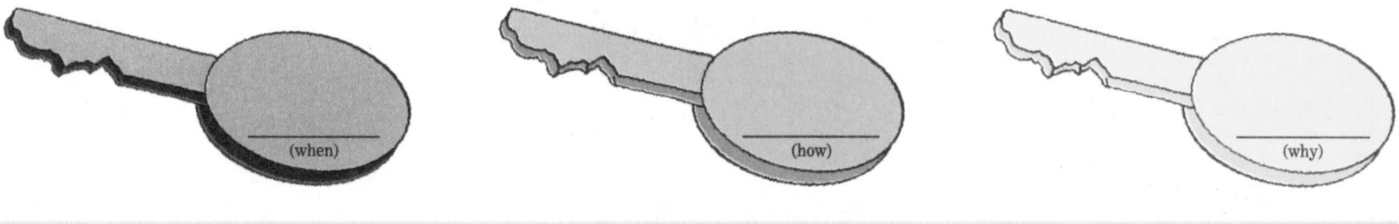

(when) (how) (why)

الأَجوِبـة

Appetizers: bastilla: chicken with spices, almonds, onion, garlic and parsley
Salad: steamed vegetables
Entrees: lamb with vegetables
Desserts: cake with apricots

(al-ann) الآن it is a good time for a quick review. Draw lines (by-na) بَينَ (between) الكَلِمات العَرَبِيّة وَ their English equivalents.

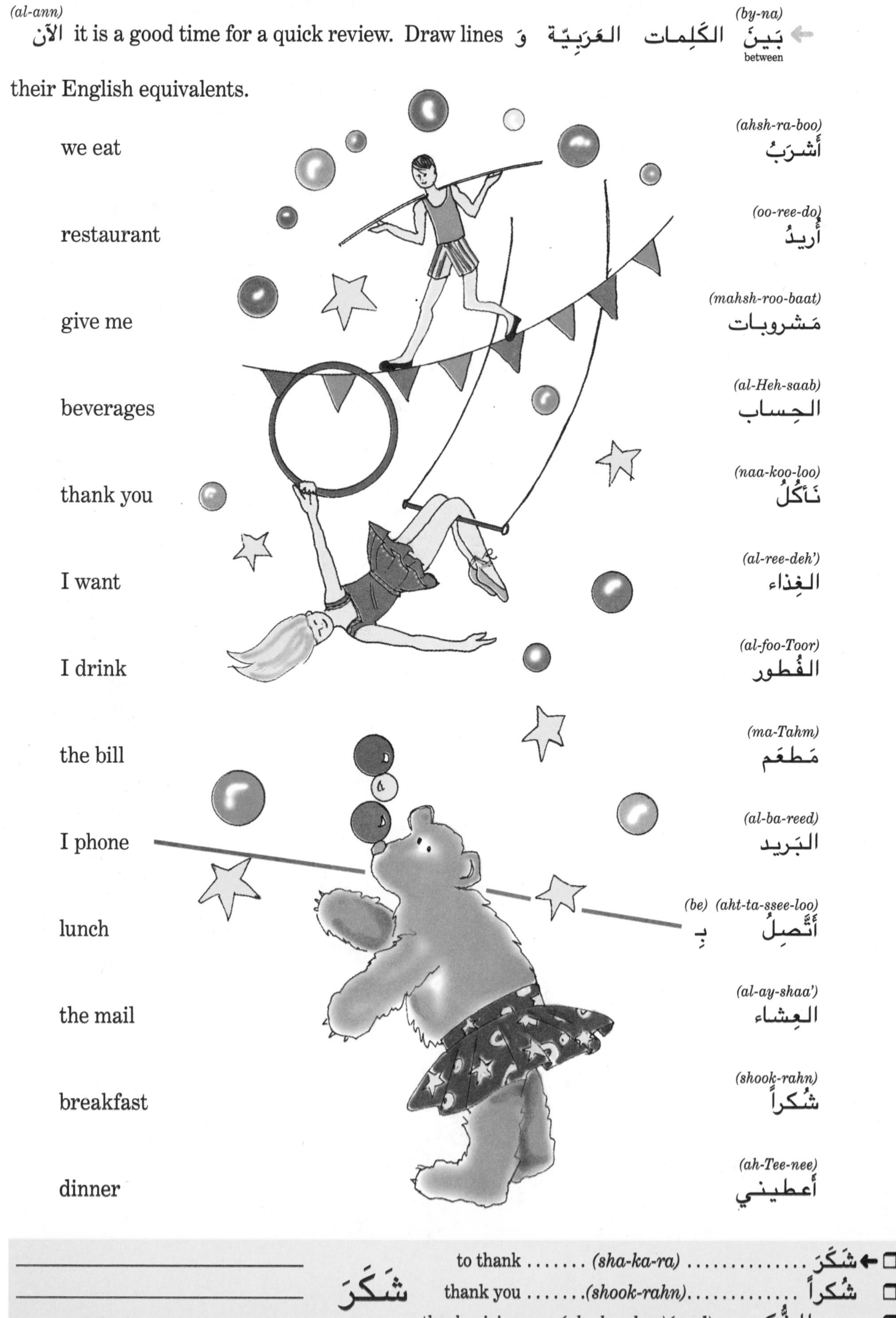

we eat	(ahsh-ra-boo) أَشرَبُ
restaurant	(oo-ree-do) أُريدُ
give me	(mahsh-roo-baat) مَشروبات
beverages	(al-Heh-saab) الحِساب
thank you	(naa-koo-loo) نَأكُلُ
I want	(al-ree-deh') الغِذاء
I drink	(al-foo-Toor) الفُطور
the bill	(ma-Tahm) مَطعَم
I phone	(al-ba-reed) البَريد
lunch	(aht-ta-ssee-loo) (be) أَتَّصِلُ بِـ
the mail	(al-ay-shaa') العِشاء
breakfast	(shook-rahn) شُكراً
dinner	(ah-Tee-nee) أعطيني

شَكَرَ

- ❒ to thank .... (sha-ka-ra) .... شَكَرَ ←
- ❒ thank you ....(shook-rahn)............. شُكراً
- ❒ thanksgiving ....(ah-shoo-kur)(reed).... عيد الشُّكر

٢١/21 (ah-teh-lee-foon) (al-haa-tif) الهاتِف / التِّليفون ← the telephone

(maa) ما what is different about (al-haa-tif) الهاتِف the telephone ← في (al-koo-wait) الكُوَيت وَ (al-ma-greb) المَغرِب؟ Well, أنتِ never notice such things until (taH-teh-zhee-na) تَحتاجينَ you (♀) need إلى ← use them. (al-haa-tif) الهاتِف ← allows you to reserve your (foon-dooq) فُندُق hotel in another city, call (al-ahss-dee-qaa') الأصدِقاء friends, order tickets, make emergency calls, check on ← (saa-raat) ساعات the hours (al-maht-Haft) المَتحَف (of) the museum and all those other (al-eh-shee') الأشياء things which أنتِ do on a daily basis.

For many telephones أنتِ must buy

← (qeh-Tart) قِطعة (noo-qood) نُقود a token أو (be-Taa-qa) بِطاقة (teh-lee-foo-nee-ya) تِليفونيّة a phone card

before أن (tahs-ta-Tee-ree-na) تَستَطيعين you (♀) can use them. You can buy

← (qeh-Tart) قِطعة (noo-qood) نُقود a token أو (be-Taa-qa) بِطاقة (teh-lee-foo-nee-ya) تِليفونيّة a phone card

at the post office or at a newstand.

Let's learn how to operate (al-haa-tif) الهاتِف.

Instructions can look complicated, but remember, some of الكَلِمات (heh-da-he) هَذِهِ you should be able to recognize already. Ready? Well, before you turn the page it would be a good idea to go back وَ review all your (aar-qaam) أرقام numbers one more time.

To dial from the United States to any other country أنتِ need that country's international area code. Your (kee-taab) كِتاب (ah-teh-lee-foon) التِّليفون telephone book at home should have a listing of international area codes. When

Here are some useful words built around the word "تِليفون."

________________	operator ...... (moo-ta-kel-lim)................. مُتَكَلِّم ← ☐
________________	public telephone .. (roo-moo-me)(teh-lee-foon) .. تِليفون عُمومي ☐

(ow) *(al-oos-ra)* *(al-ahss-dee-qaa')*

أَنتِ leave your contact numbers أَو الأُسْرَة، مَعَ الأَصْدِقاء ← business colleagues, أَنتِ should
family *friends*

include your destination country's area code وَ city code whenever possible . For example,

Country Codes		City Codes	
Egypt	20	Cairo	2
Iraq	964	Baghdad	1
Jordan	962	Amman	6
Morocco	212	Rabat	7

When calling from within the country, say from Cairo to Alexandria, or from Casablanca to Rabat,

you need to use "0" with the city code. So now أَن تَسْتَطيعينَ ← use التِّليفون to make a call
(tahs-ta-Tee-ree-na) *(ah-teh-lee-foon)*
you (♀) can *the telephone*

while traveling abroad. هُناكَ also more city codes called وَ رَقْم المَدينة ← these are
(hoo-naa-ka) *(al-meh-dee-na)* *(rahq-m)*
there are *city codes*

listed في كِتاب التِّليفون. ←
(ah-teh-lee-foon) (kee-taab)

Do not be surprised if your first public telephone does not work. You may need to locate a second

one in order to make your call. This can be a common occurrence.

When answering أَنتِ التِّليفون ← pick up the receiver وَ say: "نَعَم" ←
(ah-teh-lee-foon) *(na-ahm)*
yes

When saying goodbye, أَنتِ say: "مَعَ السَّلامة" ← Your turn —
(ah-sa-laa-ma) (mar)
goodbye

_____ _____
(goodbye)   (yes)

Do not forget that أَن تَسْتَطيعينَ ask . . .
(tahs-ta-Tee-ree-na)
you (♀) can
_____ بِكَم المُكالَمة إلى دِمَشق؟ ←
(deh-mahshk) (ee-la) (al-moo-kaa-la-ma) (be-kem)
Damascus *the call* *how much*

_____ بِكَم المُكالَمة إلى بَيروت؟ ←
(bay-root) *(al-moo-kaa-la-ma)*
Beirut

_____ telephone book . . .(ah-teh-lee-foon)(kee-taab).. كِتاب التِّليفون ← ☐

_____ phone conversation . . (teh-lee-foo-nee)(Heh-waar)... حِوار تِليفوني ☐

_____ call . . . .(moo-kaa-la-ma) . . . . مُكالَمة ☐

94

(hoo-naa) *(ahs-fahl)*
هُنـا some sample sentences for the telephone. Write them in the blanks أسفَل.

(be-she-kaa-goo) (aht-ta-ssee-la) (ahn) (oo-ree-do)
أُريدُ أن أَتَّصِلَ بِشيكاغو. ____________________
Chicago / I phone / I want

(al-ma-gree-be-ya) (al-zha-we-ya) (bil-hoo-TooT) (aht-ta-ssee-la) (oo-ree-do)
أُريدُ أن أَتَّصِلَ بِالخُطوط الجَوّيّة المَغرِبِيّة. ____________________
Maroc / airline

(al-ir-sheh-daat) (be-mahk-tahb) (aht-ta-ssee-la)
أُريدُ أن أَتَّصِلَ بِمَكتَب الإرشادات. ____________________
information

(ah-teh-lee-foon) (rahq-m) (hoo-wa) (maa)
ما هُوَ رَقم التِّليفون؟ ____________________
number / (is) / what

(hoo-wa) (ah-teh-lee-foon) (rahq-m)
رَقم التِّليفون هُو: ٢٦-٨٧-٢٦. ____________________
number

(al-foon-dooq) (teh-lee-foon) (rahq-m) (hoo-wa)
ما هُوَ رَقم تِليفون الفُندُق؟ ____________________
(of) the hotel / number

(fahD-lik) (la-teef) (ah-sy-yed) (ah-ta-kel-la-ma) (na-ahm) (aH-mahd)
أحمَد: نَعَم أُريدُ أن أَتَكَلَّمَ مَعَ السَّيِّد لَطيف مِن فَضلِك.
Ahmed / I speak / Mr. / Latif

____

(mahsh-rool) (al-hahT) (laH-Da) (sek-ree-tair-ah)
سِكرتيرة: لَحظة مِن فَضلِك، الخَطّ مَشغول.
secretary / just a moment / the line / busy

____

(fahD-lik) (be-booT') (ah-ree-dee) (ook-ra) (mar-ra) (aH-mahd)
أحمَد: مَرّة أُخرى مِن فَضلِك، أعيدي بِبُطء مِن فَضلِك.
once / more / repeat (♀) / slowly

____

(mahsh-rool) (al-hahT) (sek-ree-tair-ah)
سِكرتيرة: الخَطّ مَشغول.

____

(ah-sa-laa-ma) (mar) (zha-zee-lahn) (shook-rahn) (aH-mahd)
أحمَد: شُكراً جَزيلاً مَعَ السَّلامة.
very much

____

الآن, you are ready to use any تِليفون from Cairo to Dubai. Just speak slowly وَ clearly.

- ❒ ← الشُّرطة .... *(ah-shoor-Ta)* .... police ____________________
- ❒ الإسعاف .... *(al-ees-aaf)* .... first aid ____________________
- ❒ الحَريق .... *(al-Ha-reeq)* .... fire brigade ____________________

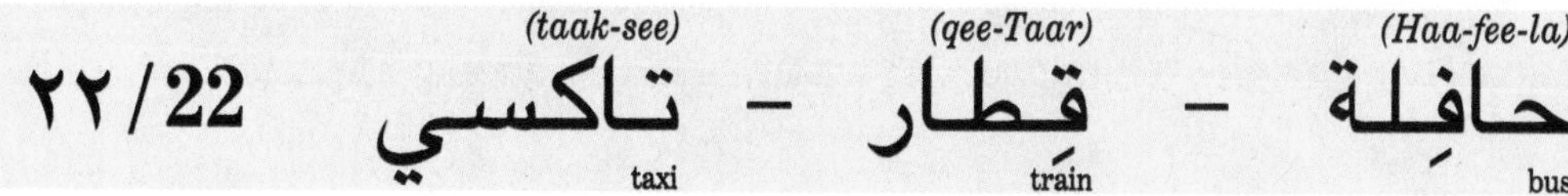

٢٢ / 22 تاكسي - قِطار - حافِلة

(taak-see) taxi – (qee-Taar) train – (Haa-fee-la) bus

In most Arabic-speaking countries, people يُسافِرونَ (oo-seh-fee-roo-na) travel بِالحافِلة (bil-Haa-fee-la) by bus، بِالسَّيّارة (bih-sy-yaa-ra) by car أو بِالتّاكسي (bih-taak-see) by taxi.

Keep in mind, the buses can be very crowded.

(qee-Taar)
قِطار
train

(Haa-fee-la)
حافِلة
bus

_______________________________ _______________________________

(taak-see)
تاكسي
taxi

(ma-HahT-Taht) (al-Haa-fee-laat)
مَحَطّة الحافِلات
bus stop

_______________________________ _______________________________

Don't forget, you can always, hail a تاكسي (taak-see) taxi on الشّارِع (ah-sheh-re') the street as well.

Other than having foreign words, the bus systems in Beirut أو Tunis function just like those in San Francisco, New York أو Boston. Locate your destination, select the correct line on your practice حافِلة (Haa-fee-la) bus و hop on board.

	مَنَحَ	
_______________	to give .... (ma-na-Ha) .... مَنَحَ	☐
_______________	scholarship .... (meen-Ha)........... مِنحة	☐
_______________	grant .... (meen-Ha)........... مِنحة	☐

(ahs-fahl) أسفَل is an imaginary (ha-ree-Ta) خَريطة (map) which gives you a chance to practice key كَلِمات which can be found in most cities. Ready? Start at the post office وَ practice traveling to all the destinations. Ask when, where وَ how much!

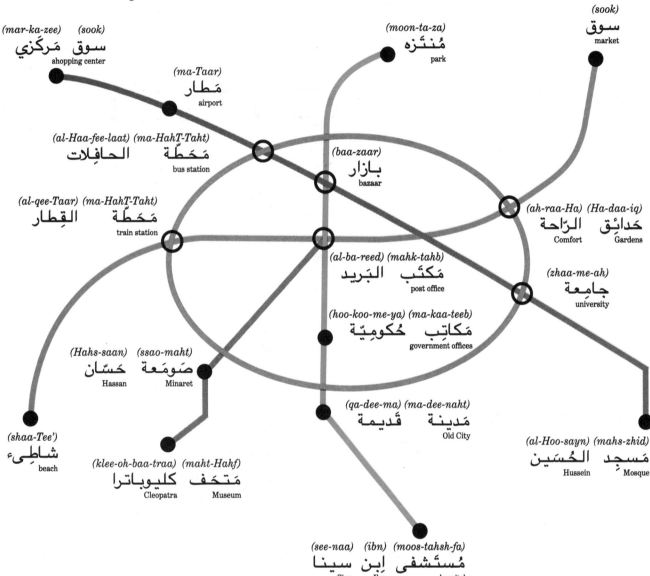

(mar-ka-zee) (sook)
سوق مَركَزي
shopping center

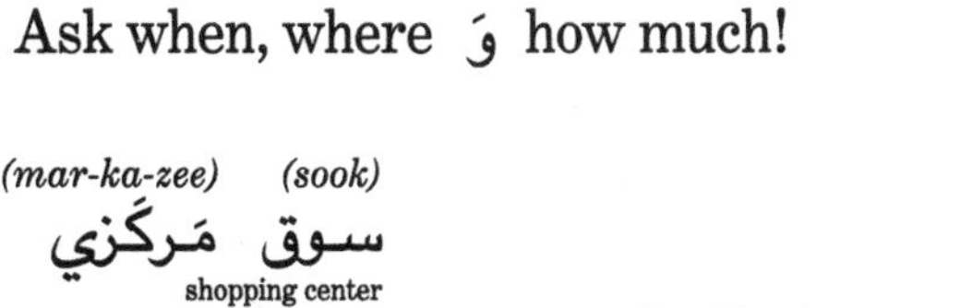

(ma-Taar)
مَطار
airport

(moon-ta-za)
مُنتَزه
park

(sook)
سوق
market

(al-Haa-fee-laat) (ma-HahT-Taht)
مَحَطّة الحافِلات
bus station

(baa-zaar)
بازار
bazaar

(al-qee-Taar) (ma-HahT-Taht)
مَحَطّة القِطار
train station

(ah-raa-Ha) (Ha-daa-iq)
حَدائِق الرّاحة
Comfort Gardens

(al-ba-reed) (mahk-tahb)
مَكتَب البَريد
post office

(zhaa-me-ah)
جامِعة
university

(hoo-koo-me-ya) (ma-kaa-teeb)
مَكاتِب حُكومِيّة
government offices

(Hahs-saan) (ssao-maht)
صَومَعة حَسّان
Hassan Minaret

(qa-dee-ma) (ma-dee-naht)
مَدينة قَديمة
Old City

(shaa-Tee')
شاطِئ
beach

(klee-oh-baa-traa) (maht-Hahf)
مَتحَف كليوباترا
Cleopatra Museum

(al-Hoo-sayn) (mahs-zhid)
مَسجِد الحُسَين
Hussein Mosque

(see-naa) (ibn) (moos-tahsh-fa)
مُستَشفى اِبن سينا
Sina Ibn hospital

Practice these questions aloud many times.

(al-Haa-fee-laat) (ma-HahT-Taht) (eye-na)
← أينَ مَحَطّة الحافِلات؟
station where (is)

(ah-taak-see)
← أينَ مَحَطّة التّاكسي؟

(al-qee-Taar)
← أينَ مَحَطّة القِطار؟

مَنَح

☐ ← مَنح .... (menH) .... donation
☐ مانِح .... (men-eH) .... donator (m)
☐ مانِحة .... (men-ee-Ha) .... donator (f)

____
____
____

Practice the following basic أَسئِلة (es-ee-la) questions out loud وَ then write them in the blanks عَلى (ah-la) to اليَسار (al-ya-saar) the left.

1. مَتى (meh-ta) when تَجيءُ (ta-zhee-oo) comes الحافِلة (al-Haa-fee-la) إلى (ee-la) تونُس؟ (too-noos) Tunis ______

مَتى تَجيءُ (ta-zhee-oo) comes الحافِلة إلى فاس؟ (fes) Fez ______

مَتى تَجيءُ (ta-zhee-oo) الحافِلة إلى المَطار؟ (al-ma-Taar) airport ______

2. مَتى يُغادِرُ (yoo-raa-dee-roo) leaves القِطار؟ (al-qee-Taar) the train ______

مَتى تُغادِرُ (too-raa-dee-roo) leaves الحافِلة؟ (al-Haa-fee-la) ______

مَتى تُغادِرُ (too-raa-dee-roo) الحافِلة إلى الجَزائِر؟ (al-zheh-zair-ir) ______

3. بِكَم (be-kem) how much تَذكِرة (teth-kee-ra) ticket الحافِلة؟ (al-Haa-fee-la) (of) the bus ______

بِكَم تَذكِرة (teth-kee-ra) القِطار؟ (al-qee-Taar) (of) the train ______

بِكَم التَّذكِرة (ah-teth-kee-ra) the ticket إلى أَسوان؟ (ahs-won) Aswan ______

4. مِن (min) from أَينَ (eye-na) where أَشتَري (esh-ta-ree) do I buy تَذكِرة (teth-kee-ra) الحافِلة؟ ______

مِن أَينَ أَشتَري (esh-ta-ree) تَذكِرة القِطار؟ (al-qee-Taar) train ______

Let's change directions وَ learn ثَلاثة (tha-laa-tha) three new verbs. تَعرِفُ (ta-ree-foo) you (♂) know the basic "plug-in" formula, so write out your own sentences using these new verbs.

أَغسِلُ (ar-see-loo) I wash ______

يَأخُذُ (yek-hoo-doo) it takes ______

أَفعَلُ (ahf-ah-loo) I do ______

حَصَلَ عَلى

- ❒ حَصَلَ عَلى . . (Ha-ssa-la)(ah-la) . . to obtain ______
- ❒ مُحَصِّل . . . . (moo-Ha-ssil) . . . tax collector ______
- ❒ مَحصول . . . . . . (maH-ssool) . . . . harvest / result ______

٢٣/23 (esh-ta-ree) أَشتَري I buy وَ (ah-be-roo) أَبيعُ I sell

Shopping abroad is exciting. The simple everyday task of buying (lee-tair) لِتر (maa') ماء water أو (toof-faa-Ha) تُفّاحة (an) apple becomes a challenge that أَنتَ should (al-ann) الآن be able to meet quickly وَ easily. Of course, أَنتَ will purchase (Ta-waa-bihh) طَوابِع، stamps (be-Taa-qaat) بِطاقات postcards وَ (teth-kaar) تِذكار (a) souvenir but don't forget those many other (al-eh-shee') الأشياء things ranging from shoelaces to (ahq-raass) أَقراص aspirin that أَنتَ might need unexpectedly. Locate your store, draw a line to it وَ as always, write your كَلِمات (zha-dee-da) جَديدة in the blanks provided.

(see-neh-maa) سينِما cinema ______________________

(ma-Ha-laat) (tee-zhaa-ree-ya) مَحَلّات تِجارِيّة department stores ______________________

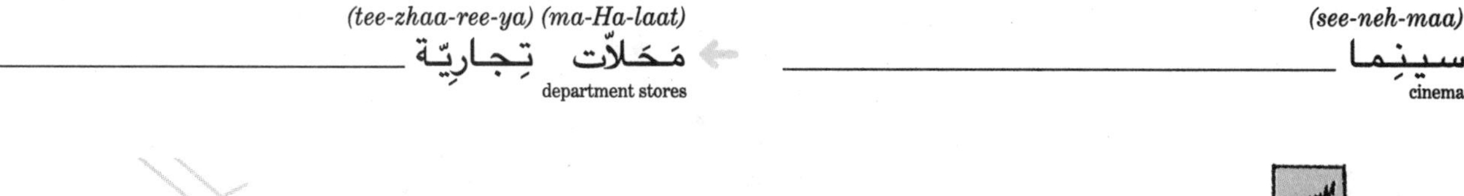

(bahnk) بَنك bank ______________________

(mahk-tahb) (al-ba-reed) مَكتَب البَريد post office ______________________

(ma-HahT-Taht) (al-ben-zeen) مَحَطّة البَنزين gas station ______________________

(foon-dooq) فُندُق hotel ______________________

(min) (mef-too-Ha) (al-ma-Ha-laat)
← المَحَلاّت مَفتوحة مِن
the stores / open / from

(al-ha-mees) (al-ah-Hahd)
الأَحَد إلى الخَميس.
Sunday / Thursday

(al-zhahz-zair)
الجَزّار
butcher shop

(al-mahk-ta-ba)
← المَكتَبة
bookstore

(mahss-ba-na)
← مَصبَنة ____________________
dry cleaners

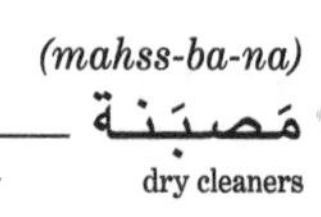

(ah-sy-da-lee-ya)
← الصَّيدَلِيّة ____________________
pharmacy

(al-ma-HahT-Ta)
← المَحَطّة ____________________
parking lot (station)

(al-zha-raa-id) (ma-Hahl)
← مَحَلّ الجَرائِد ____________________
newspaper kiosk

(maH-la-ba)
← مَحلَبة ____________________
delicatessen

(al-ha-dair-yaa) (ma-Hahl)
← مَحَلّ الهَدايا ____________________
gift store

(sook) (be-haa) (qar-ya) (meh-dee-na) (kool-loo)
← كُلّ مَدينة وَ قَرية بِها سوق.
every / town / village / has / (a) market

Start your shopping list now!

(sa-far) (mahk-tahb)
مَكتَب سَفَر
travel agency

(ah-shoor-Ta)
← الشُّرطة
police station

(al-Ha-lao-we-yet) (ma-Hahl)
مَحَلّ الحَلَوِيّات
candy store

(ah-zoo-hoor) (ma-Hahl)
مَحَلّ الزُّهور
flower shop

(ah-sa-mahk) (sook)
سوق السَّمَك ______________
fish market

(ah-tahss-wair) (ma-Hahl)
مَحَلّ التَّصوير ______________
camera shop

(sook)
سوق ______________
market

(dook-ken)
دُكّان ______________
grocery store / greengrocer

(al-moo-zhao-ha-ret) (maht-zhar)
مَتجَر المُجَوهَرات ______________
jewelry store

(mahk-beh-za)
مَخبَزة ______________
bakery

(mahq-ha)
مَقهى ______________
coffee house / café

(mahss-ba-na)
مَصبَنة ______________
laundry

(hy-yaa-Ta) (hy-yaaT)
خَيّاط / خَيّاطة
tailor (♂) / (♀)

(Ha-laa-qa) (Ha-laaq)
حَلاّق / حَلاّقة
barber / hairdresser

ground floor	=	← الطّابَق الأَرضي	(ah-Taa-bahq) (al-ar-Dee)
first floor	=	← الطّابَق الأَوَّل	(ah-Taa-bahq) (ah-ow-wel)
second floor	=	← الطّابَق الثّاني	(ah-Taa-bahq) (ah-thaa-nee)

٢٤ / 24 ← مَحَلّات تِجارِيّة

(ma-Ha-laat) (tee-zhaa-ree-ya)
department stores

At this point, أَنتِ should just about be ready for your ← سَفَر (sa-far). ← أَنتِ have gone shopping for those last-minute odds 'n ends. Most likely, the store directories at your local ← مَحَلّات تِجارِيّة (ma-Ha-laat) (tee-zhaa-ree-ya) department stores do not look like the one ← أَسفَل (ahs-fahl). ← تَعرفين (ta-ree-fee-na) you know that الأَطفال (al-ahT-faal) is Arabic for "children," so if ← تَحتاجين (taH-teh-zhee-na) you need إِلى something for a child you would probably look on ← الطّابَق (ah-Taa-bahq) the floor الثّاني (ah-thaa-nee) second wouldn't you?

4.	الخَزَف البِلَّور أَواني	أَدوات مُلَمِّع	كريستال أَسِرّة أَغطِية
3.	مَطعَم جَرائِد مَجَلّات	مَذاييع آلات موسيقِيّة مَحَطّة	كمبيوترات تَلفَزات
2.	مَوادّ التَّجميل أَثاث سَجّادات	مَلابِس الرِّجال مَلابِس الرُّضَّع آلة التَّصوير	مَلابِس الأَطفال مَلابِس النِّساء
1.	مُعِدّات سَجائِر مَخبَزة	مَلابِس سِباحة أَحذِية كُتُب	مُعِدّات السَّيّارة مَلابِس داخِلِيّة مَفاتِح
0.	ساعات عِطر مَقهى	جِلد جَوارِب أَحزِمة	خَرائِط قُبَّعات مُجَوهَرات

Let's start a checklist for your سَفَر (sa-far) trip. Besides clothing, ← ماذا (may-daa) what تَحتاجين؟ (taH-teh-zhee-na) do you need As you learn these words, assemble these items in زاوِية (zair-we-ah) a corner of your بَيت (bait). Check وَ make sure that they are clean وَ ready for your سَفَر. Be sure to do the same مَعَ the rest of the clothing that أَنتِ pack. On the next pages, match each item to its picture, draw a line to it and write out the word many times. As you organize these things, check them off on this list. Do not forget to take the next group of sticky labels and label these things اليَومَ (al-yohm).

(sa-far) (zhao-wez)
جَواز سَفَر
passport

(teth-kee-ra)
تَذكِرة
ticket

(Ha-qee-ba)
حَقيبة
suitcase

(yed) (Ha-qee-bet)
حَقيبة يَد
handbag

(mehH-fa-Tha)
مِحفَظة
wallet

(foo-loos)
فُلوس
money

فُلوس فُلوس فُلوس

(bahn-kee-ya) (be-Taa-qaht)
بِطاقة بَنكِيّة
credit card

(sa-far) (shee-ket)
شيكات سَفَر
traveler's checks

(tahss-wair) (aa-lit)
آلة تَصوير
camera

(feelm)
فيلم
film

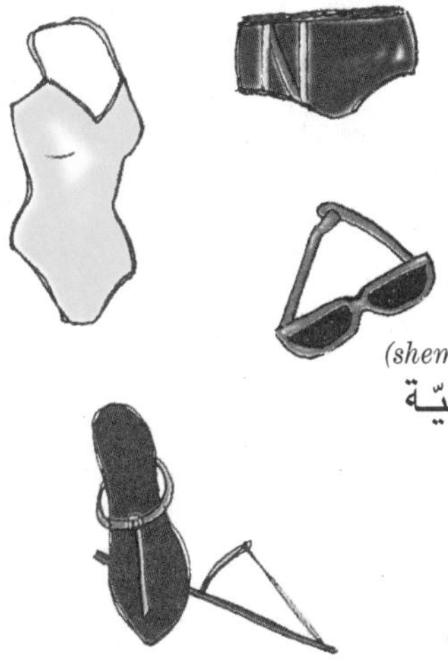

(see-baa-Ha) (leh-bes)
لِباس سِباحة
swimsuit

(nahl)
نَعل
sandals / slippers

(shem-see-ya) (naTh-Thaa-ra)
نَظّارة شَمسِيّة
sunglasses

(foor-shet)
فُرشاة
toothbrush

(al-es-naan) (ma-zhoon)
مَعجون الأَسنان
toothpaste

(ssaa-boon)
صابون
soap

(shahf-ra)
شَفرة
razor

(Teeb)
طيب
deodorant

(reh-Tur)
عِطر
perfume

(meshT)
مِشط
comb
(meer-Tahf)
مِعطَف
overcoat / raincoat
(me-Thahl-la)
مَظَلّة
umbrella
(foos-ten)
فُستان
dress
(qa-meess)
قَميص
sweater
(soot-ra)
سُترة
blouse
(tahn-noo-ra) (thohb)
ثَوب / تَنّورة
skirt
(He-dair')
حِذاء
shoes
(ree-yaa-Da) (He-dair')
حِذاء رِياضة
tennis shoes
(hoof-fez)
خُفّاز
gloves
(qoob-ba)
قُبَّعة
hat
(beed-la)
بِدلة
suit
(rahb-Ta)
رَبطة
tie
(qa-meess)
قَميص
shirt / T-shirt
(min-deel)
مِنديل
handkerchief
(soot-ra)
سُترة
jacket / blazer
(seer-wel)
سِروال
trousers / jeans / shorts
(zheenz)
"دجينز"
jeans
(short)
"شورت"
shorts
خُفّاز خُفّاز خُفّاز خُفّاز

(bil-r-ra-be-ya) (daak-he-lee-ya) (meh-leh-bes)
بِالعَرَبِيّة the phrase مَلابِس داخِلِيّة tends to refer to a variety of undergarments for both men وَ women.

(daak-he-lee-ya) (meh-leh-bes)
مَلابِس داخِلِيّة
underclothing

(zha-wear-rib)
جَوارِب
socks

(noum) (meh-leh-bes)
مَلابِس نَوم
pajamas

(Hahm-maam) (thohb)
ثَوب حَمّام
bathrobe

(meh-leh-bes)
So أَنتِ have assembled your مَلابِس (clothing). Here are some clothing items which أَنتِ might encounter on your سَفَر (sa-far). أَنتِ will hear a variety of words for these items.

(koo-fee-ya)
كوفِية
men's head covering

(thohb)
ثَوب
men's wrap to hold the head covering

(He-zhaab)
حِجاب
veil

(ah-by-ya)
عَباية
women's long-sleeved outer garment

(zhil-beb)
جلباب
women's long-sleeved outer garment

(kahf-Taan)
قَفطان
women's long-sleeved outer garment

(zhil-beb)
جلباب
men's long, shirt-like garment

(boor-noos)
بورنوس
burnus

From now on, أَنتِ have "صابون" (ssaa-boon, soap) and not "soap." Having assembled these الأَشياء (al-eh-shee', things) you are ready for your سَفَر (sa-far). Let's add these important shopping phrases to your basic repertoire.

(qee-yes) (eye-yoo)
أيُّ قِياس؟
which size

(qee-yeh-sook) (heh-daa)
هَذا قِياسُك.
this fits

(qee-yeh-sook) (lay-sa)
لَيسَ قِياسُك.
it does not fit

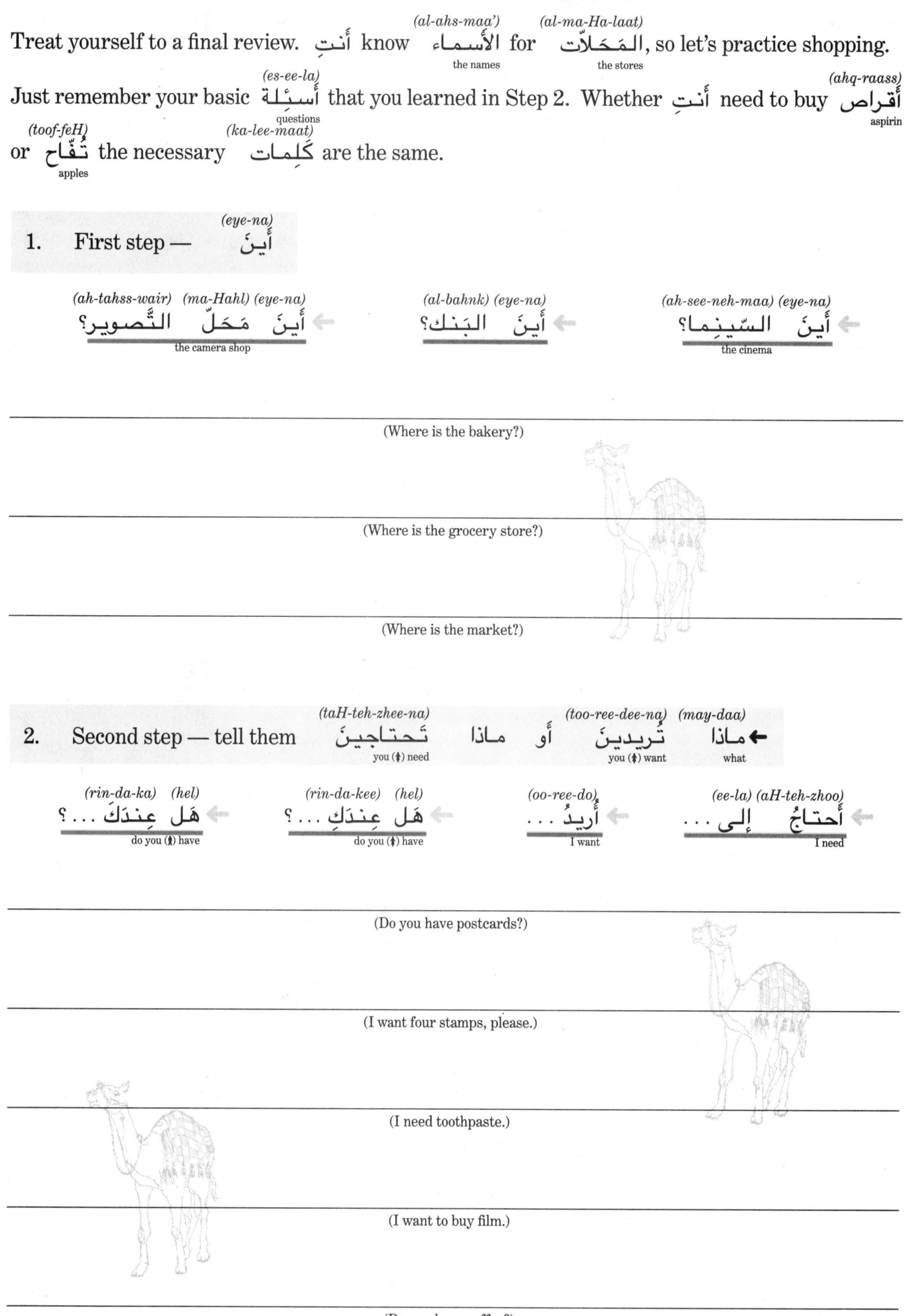

Treat yourself to a final review. أَنتِ know الأسماء (al-ahs-maa') the names for المَحَلّات (al-ma-Ha-laat) the stores, so let's practice shopping. Just remember your basic أَسئِلة (es-ee-la) questions that you learned in Step 2. Whether أَنتِ need to buy أَقراص (ahq-raass) aspirin or تُفّاح (toof-feH) apples the necessary كَلِمات (ka-lee-maat) are the same.

1. First step — أَينَ (eye-na)

← أَينَ السّينِما؟ (ah-see-neh-maa) (eye-na) — the cinema

← أَينَ البَنك؟ (al-bahnk) (eye-na)

← أَينَ مَحَلّ التَّصوير؟ (ah-tahss-wair) (ma-Hahl) (eye-na) — the camera shop

____

(Where is the bakery?)

____

(Where is the grocery store?)

____

(Where is the market?)

2. Second step — tell them ماذا (may-daa) what ← تُريدينَ (too-ree-dee-na) you (♀) want أو ماذا تَحتاجينَ (taH-teh-zhee-na) you (♀) need

← أَحتاجُ إلى ... (aH-teh-zhoo) (ee-la) — I need

← أُريدُ ... (oo-ree-do) — I want

← هَل عِندَكِ ...؟ (hel) (rin-da-kee) — do you (♀) have

← هَل عِندَكَ ...؟ (hel) (rin-da-ka) — do you (♂) have

____

(Do you have postcards?)

____

(I want four stamps, please.)

____

(I need toothpaste.)

____

(I want to buy film.)

____

(Do you have coffee?)

Go through the glossary at the end of (al-kee-taab) الكِتاب (heh-daa) هَذا and select (ka-lee-maat) كَلِمات (’ah-shar) عَشَر (ten). Drill the above patterns (al-ka-lee-maat) الكَلِمات (heh-da-he) هَذِهِ (these) مَعَ (with). Drill them (al-yohm) اليَومَ. Now, take (’ah-shar) عَشَر more كَلِمات from your glossary وَ do the same.

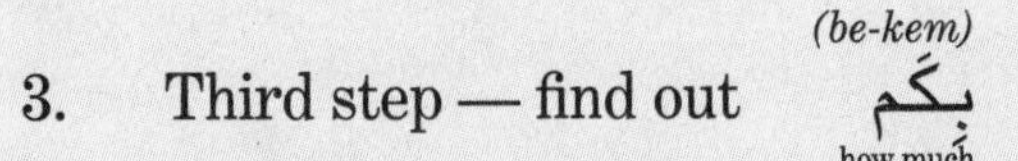

3. Third step — find out (be-kem) بِكَم (how much)

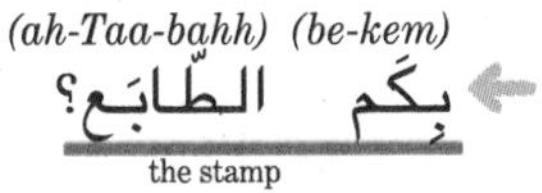

(ah-Taa-bahh) (be-kem) بِكَم الطّابَع؟ (the stamp)

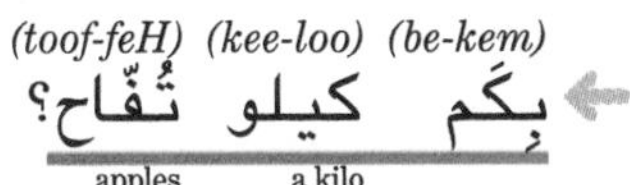

(toof-feH) (kee-loo) (be-kem) بِكَم كيلو تُفّاح؟ (a kilo / apples)

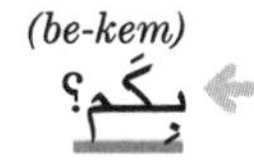

(be-kem) بِكَم؟

____
(How much is the toothpaste?)

____
(How much is the soap?)

____
(How much is a cup of tea?)

4. Fourth step — success! I found it!

Once أَنتِ find what (too-ree-dee-na) تُريدينَ (you want) – say,

_______________________________ (fahD-lik) (min) (heh-daa) (oo-ree-do) أُريدُ هَذا مِن فَضلِك. (this)

_______________________________ (fahD-lik) (min) (heh-da-he) (oo-ree-do) أُريدُ هَذِهِ مِن فَضلِك. (this)

Or, if أَنتِ would not like it,

_______________________________ (shook-rahn) (heh-daa) (oo-ree-do) (la) لا أُريدُ هَذا شُكراً. (I do not want)

or

_______________________________ (shook-rahn) (la) لا شُكراً. (thank you / no)

(ma-brook) مَبروك! (congratulations) You have finished. By now you should have stuck your labels, flashed your cards, cut out your menu guide and packed your suitcases. You should be very pleased with your accomplishment. You have learned what it sometimes takes others years to achieve and you hopefully had fun doing it. (sy-yeed) (sa-far) سَفَر سَعيد! (Have a good trip!)

Glossary

This glossary contains words used in this book only. It is not meant to be a dictionary. Consider purchasing a dictionary which best suits your needs - small for traveling, large for reference, or specialized for specific vocabulary needs.

A

a little..... *(shway-yeh)* شـوَيَ / *(qa-lee-lahn)* قَليلاً
a lot.......... *(ka-thee-rahn)* كَثيراً
about.......... *(rahn)* عَن
address (the).......... *(al-roon-wen)* العُنوان
after.......... *(ba-da)* بَعدَ
afternoon........ *(ah-Doo-hur) (ba-da)* بَعدَ الظُّهر
air.......... *(zhao)* جَوّ
airline.. *(al-zha-we-ya)(al-hoo-TooT)* الخُطوط الجَوِّيّة
airplane.......... *(Taa-ee-ra)* طائِرة
airport.......... *(ma-Taar)* مَطار
alarm clock.......... *(saa-ra)* ساعة
Algeria.......... *(al-zheh-zair-ir)* الجَزائِر
also.......... *(eye-Dahn)* أيضاً
am not.......... *(les-too)* لَستُ
America.......... *(ahm-ree-kaa)* أمريكا
American (♀).......... *(ahm-ree-kee-ya)* أمريكِيّة
American (♂).......... *(ahm-ree-kee)* أمريكي
and.......... *(wa)* وَ
answer (the).......... *(al-zha-web)* الجَواب
apartment.......... *(shooq-qa)* شُقّة
appetizers.......... *(moo-qa-be-let)* مُقَبِّلات
apple.......... *(toof-faa-Ha)* تُفّاحة
apples.......... *(toof-feH)* تُفّاح
appliances.......... أدَوات
apricots.......... *(meesh-meesh)* مِشمِش
April.......... *(ah-breel)* أبريل
Arabic.......... *(r-ra-be-ya)* عَرَبِيّة
Arabic (the).......... *(al-r-ra-be-ya)* العَرَبِيّة
arrival.......... *(woo-ssool)* وُصول
aspirin.......... *(ahq-raass)* أقراص
at.......... *(fee)* في
August.......... *(rohsht)* غُشت
aunt (maternal).......... *(khaa-la)* خالة
Australia.......... *(oos-too-raa-lee-yaa)* أستُراليا
Australian (♀).......... *(oos-too-raa-lee-ya)* أستُرالِيّة
Australian (♂).......... *(oos-too-raa-lee)* أستُرالي
auto accessories.......... مُعِدّات السَّيّارة

B

baby department.......... مَلابِس الرُّضَّع
bad.......... *(sy-yeh')* سَيِّء
bad (grades).......... *(Dy-eef)* ضَعيف
bad (weather).......... *(ra-dee')* رَديء
bakery.......... *(mahk-beh-za)* مَخبَزة
bank.......... *(bahnk)* بَنك
barber.......... *(Ha-laaq)* حَلّاق
basement.......... *(ka-boo)* قَبو
bathrobe.......... *(Hahm-maam)(thohb)* ثَوب حَمّام
bathroom / toilet.......... *(Hahm-maam)* حَمّام
bazaar.......... *(baa-zaar)* بازار
beach.......... *(shaa-Tee')* شاطِيء
bed.......... *(sa-reer)* سَرير
bed linens.......... *(ree-Ta')* غِطاء
bedroom.......... *(ah-noum)(roor-fa)* غُرفة النَّوم
beds.......... أسِرّة
before.......... *(qahb-la)* قَبلَ
behind.......... *(wa-raa-ah)* وَراءَ
behind.......... *(hahl-fa)* خَلفَ
below.......... *(ahs-fahl)* أسفَل
belts.......... أحزِمة
between.......... *(by-na)* بَينَ
beverages.......... *(mahsh-roo-baat)* مَشروبات
bicycle.......... *(dar-raa-zha)* دَرّاجة
big, old.......... *(ka-beer)* كَبير
bill.......... *(Heh-saab)* حِساب
bills (currency), money.......... *(foo-loos)* فُلوس
black.......... *(ahs-wed)* أسوَد
blouse.......... *(soot-ra)* سُترة
blue.......... *(ahz-rahq)* أزرَق
book.......... *(kee-taab)* كِتاب
books.......... *(koo-toob)* كُتُب
bookstore.......... *(al-mahk-ta-ba)* المَكتَبة
bread.......... *(hoobz)* خُبز
breakfast.......... *(al-foo-Toor)* الفُطور
brother.......... *(ahk)* أخ
brown.......... *(boon-nee)* بُنّي
bus.......... *(Haa-fee-la)* حافِلة
bus (the).......... *(al-oo-too-bees)* الأوتوبيس
bus station / stop..........
(al-Haa-fee-laat)(ma-HahT-Taht) مَحَطّة الحافِلات
but.......... *(la-kin)* لَكِن
butcher shop.......... *(al-zhahz-zair)* الجَزّار
butter.......... *(zoob-da)* زُبدة

by airmail. . . *(al-zhao-we)(bil-ba-reed)* بِالبَريد الجَوّي
by boat . . . . *(bil-bear-he-ra)* بِالباخِرة

C

café . . . . *(mahq-ha)* مَقهى
cafeteria. . . . . *(kaa-fee-tair-ree-aa)* كافيتيريا
calendar (the) . . . . *(ah-ta-queem)* التَّقويم
call (the). . . . . *(al-moo-kaa-la-ma)* المُكالَمة
camel . . . . *(zha-mel)* جَمَل
camera . . . . *(tahss-wair) (aa-lit)* آلة تَصوير
camera shop . . . .
. . . . *(ah-tahss-wair)(ma-Hahl)* مَحَلّ التَّصوير
Canada. . . . . *(ka-na-daa)* كَنَدا
candy store . . . .
. . . . . . *(al-Ha-lao-we-yet)(ma-Hahl)* مَحَلّ الحَلَوِيّات
car. . . . . *(sy-yaa-ra)* سَيّارة
carpet. . . . . *(sahzh-zheh-da)* سَجّادة
cashier (the). . . . . *(ah-ssoon-dooq)* الصُّندوق
cat. . . . . *(keT-Ta)* قِطّة
ceramics. . . . . الخَزَف
chair . . . . *(koor-see)* كُرسي
cheap . . . . *(ra-keess)* رَخيص
cheese. . . . . *(zhoob-na)* جُبنة
children (the). . . . . *(al-ahT-faal)* الأطفال
children's clothing . . . . مَلابِس الأطفال
Christian (♀). . . . . *(meh-see-He-ya)* مَسيحِيّة
Christian (♂). . . . . *(meh-see-He)* مَسيحي
church . . . . *(ka-nee-sa)* كَنيسة
cinema . . . . *(see-neh-maa)* سينِما
city, town . . . . *(meh-dee-na)* مَدينة
city codes. . . *(al-meh-dee-na) (rahq-m)* رَقم المَدينة
class (the). . . . . *(ah-ssahf)* الصَّفّ
clock, alarm clock . . . . *(saa-ra)* ساعة
closed . . . . *(moog-lahq)* مُغلَق
closet, wardrobe, cupboard. . . . . . *(hee-zaa-na)* خِزانة
clothing . . . . *(meh-leh-bes)* مَلابِس
cloudy. . . . . *(raa-im)* غائِم
coffee . . . . *(qah-wa)* قَهوة
coffee house / café. . . . . *(mahq-ha)* مَقهى
coffee set . . . .
(koo-oos)(wa)(qa-wa)(ee-breeq) إبريق قَهوة وَ كُؤوس
coins . . . . *(nahq-dee-ya) (qeh-Tar)* قِطَع نَقدِيّة
cold . . . . *(bear-id)* بارِد
colorful. . . . . *(moo-la-wen)* مُلَوَّن
colors (the). . . . . *(ahl-wen)* الألوان
comb. . . . . *(meshT)* مِشط

computer . . . . *(kohm-boo-tair)* كَمبيوتر
concert (the) . . . .
. . . . *(moo-see-qee-ya)(Hahf-la)* حَفلة موسيقِيّة
congratulations. . . . . *(ma-brook)* مَبروك
conversations (the). . . . . . *(al-He-waa-raat)* الحِوارات
corner (the). . . . . *(al-zair-we-ya)* الزّاوِية
cosmetics . . . . مَوادّ التَّجميل
counter. . . . . *(shoob-bek)* شُبّاك
country. . . . . *(ba-lahd)* بَلَد
credit card. . . . .
. . . . *(bahn-kee-ya) (be-Taa-qaht)* بِطاقة بَنكِيّة
crystal . . . . كريستال
cucumbers . . . . *(he-yaar)* خِيار
cup . . . . *(feen-zhaan)* فِنجان
curtain . . . . *(see-taa-ra)* سِتارة

D

dad . . . . *(ahb)* أب
daughter . . . . *(bint)* بِنت / *(ib-na)* اِبنة
day . . . . *(yohm)* يَوم
December . . . . *(dee-sem-br)* ديسَمبر
decorative arts / ornamentation. . *(za-haa-rif)* زَخارِف
delicatessen, creamery . . . . *(maH-la-ba)* مَحلَبة
deodorant. . . . . *(Teeb)* طيب
department stores . . . .
. . . *(tee-zhaa-ree-ya) (ma-Ha-laat)* مَحَلّات تِجارِيّة
departure. . . . . *(da-haab)* ذَهاب
desk . . . . *(mahk-tahb)* مَكتَب
dessert, little sweets. . . . . *(Hel-wa)* حَلوى
dictionary. . . . . *(qaa-moos)* قاموس
dinars . . . . *(dee-naar)* دينار
dining room . . . . *(L-ah-kel) (bait)* بَيت الأكل
dinner. . . . . *(ay-shaa')* عِشاء
dirhams . . . . *(deh-raa-him)* دَراهِم
dishes . . . . أواني
Do you have (♀)? . . . . *(rin-da-kee)(hel)* هَل عِندَكِ
Do you have (♂)? . . . . *(rin-da-ka)(hel)* هَل عِندَكَ
doctor (the) . . . . *(ah-dook-toor)* الدُّكتور
dog . . . . *(kelb)* كَلب
Dome of the Rock (the) . . . .
. . . . *(ah-ssahk-ra)(qoob-baht)* قُبّة الصَّخرة
domestic. . . . . *(ma-Hahl-lee)* مَحَلّي
door . . . . *(baab)* باب
downstairs (the). . . . .
. . . . *(ah-soo-flee)(ah-Taa-bahq)* الطّابَق السُّفلي
dress. . . . . *(foos-ten)* فُستان
dry cleaners, laundry. . . . . *(mahss-ba-na)* مَصبَنة

E

east . . . . *(ah-shark)* الشَّرق

eggs . . . . *(by-eD)* بَيض

Egypt . . . . *(meess-ur)* مِصر

eight . . . . *(tha-maa-nee-ya)* ثَمانِية

eight (o'clock) . . . . *(ah-thaa-me-na)* الثّامِنة

eighteen . . *('ah-shar)(tha-maa-nee-ya)* ثَمانِية عَشَر

eighty . . . . *(tha-maa-noon)* ثَمانون

eleven . . . . *('ah-shar)(ah-Hahd)* أَحَد عَشَر

email . . . . *(ee-mail)* إيميل

England . . . . *(in-zhla-tair-raa)* إنجلَترا

English (language) . . . *(al-in-zhlee-zee-ya)* الإنجليزيّة

English (🚺) . . . . *(in-zhlee-zee-ya)* إنجليزيّة

English (🚹) . . . . *(in-zhlee-zee)* إنجليزي

enjoy your meal / excellent meal . . . .
. . . . *(Ty-yee-ba) (wehzh-ba)* وَجبة طَيِّبة

entrance . . . . *(dook-hool)* دُخول

evening (the) . . . . *(al-ma-saa')* المَساء

evenings / in the evening . . . . *(ma-saa-ahn)* مَساءً

every . . . . *(kool-loo)* كُلُّ

everything . . . . *(shay')(kool)* كُلّ شَيء

excuse me . . . . *(mar-dee-ra)* مَعذِرة

excuse me / I'm sorry / pardon (🚺) . . . *(eh-sih-fa)* آسِفة

excuse me / I'm sorry / pardon (🚹) . . . . . *(eh-sif)* آسِف

exit . . . . *(hoo-roozh)* خُروج

expensive . . . . *(tha-meen)* ثَمين / *(reh-lee)* غالي

extended family . . . . *(aa-ee-la)* عائِلة

eyeglasses . . . . *(naTh-Thaa-ra)* نَظّارة

F

falafel . . . . *(fa-laa-fel)* فَلافِل

fall (the) . . . . *(al-ha-reef)* الخَريف

family . . . . *(oos-ra)* أُسرة

fast . . . . *(sa-reer)* سَريع

father . . . . *(weh-lid)* والِد

fax . . . . *(faaks)* فاكس

February . . . . *(feh-bry-yar)* فِبراير

fifteen . . . . *('ah-shar) (hahm-sa)* خَمسة عَشَر

fifty . . *(hahm-seen)* خَمسين / *(hahm-soon)* خَمسون

film, movie . . . . *(feelm)* فيلم

first floor . . . *(ah-ow-wel)(ah-Taa-bahq)* الطّابَق الأوَّل

fish . . . . *(sa-mahk)* سَمَك

fish market . . . . . *(ah-sa-mahk) (sook)* سوق السَّمَك

five . . . . *(hahm-sa)* خَمسة

five hundred . . . . *(hahm-soo-me-ya)* خَمسُمِئة

flight . . . . *(Ta-ya-raan)* طَيَران

flower . . . . *(zah-ra)* زَهرة

flower shop . . *(ah-zoo-hoor)(ma-Hahl)* مَحَلّ الزُّهور

flowers . . . . *(zoo-hoor)* زُهور

fork . . . . *(shoo-ka)* شوكة

forty . . . . *(ar-ba-oon)* أربَعون

four . . . . *(ar-ba-ah)* أربَعة

fourteen . . . . *('ah-shar) (ar-ba-ah)* أربَعة عَشَر

France . . . . *(fa-rahn-saa)* فَرَنسا

free, available . . . . *(sheh-rir)* شاغِر

French . . . . *(al-fa-rahn-see-ya)* الفَرَنسيّة

Friday . . . . *(al-zhoo-moo-ah)* الجُمُعة

friend (🚹) . . . . *(ssa-deeq)* صَديق

friends (the) . . . . *(al-ahss-dee-qaa')* الأصدِقاء

from . . . . *(min)* مِن

fruit . . . . *(faa-kee-ha)* فاكِهة

furniture . . . . أثاث

G

garage . . . . *(ma-raab)* مَرأب

garden . . . . *(Ha-dee-qa)* حَديقة

gas station . . . .
. . . . *(al-ben-zeen) (ma-HahT-Taht)* مَحَطّة البِنزين

gentlemen . . . . *(ah-ree-zhel)* الرِّجال

German . . . . *(al-ahl-maa-nee-ya)* الألمانيّة

gift store . . *(al-ha-dair-yaa) (ma-Hahl)* مَحَلّ الهَدايا

give me . . . . *(ah-Tee-nee)* أعطيني

glass . . . . *(kess)* كَأس

gloves . . . . *(hoof-fez)* خُفّاز

go! (🚺) . . . . *(eed-ha-bee)* اِذهَبي

go! (🚹) . . . . *(eed-hahb)* اِذهَب

good . . . . *(zhy-yed)* جَيِّد

good evening . . . . *(al-hair)(ma-saa')* مَساء الخَير

good luck . . . . *(sy-yeed) (Hahth)* حَظّ سَعيد

good morning . . . . *(al-hair)(ssa-baaH)* صَباح الخَير

good night . . . .
(hair)(ah-la)(tooss-beh-Hoo-na) تُصبِحونَ عَلى خَير

goodbye . . . . *(ah-sa-laa-ma) (mar)* مَعَ السَّلامة

grandfather . . . . *(zhed)* جَدّ

grandmother . . . . *(zhed-da)* جَدّة

grape . . . . *(ry-nahb)* عِنَب

gray . . . . *(reh-maa-dee)* رَمادي

green . . . . *(ahk-Dar)* أخضَر

grocery store / greengrocer . . . . *(dook-ken)* دُكّان

ground floor . . . .
. . . . *(al-ar-Dee)(ah-Taa-bahq)* الطّابَق الأرضي

guesthouse . . . .
. . . . *(ah-Doo-yoof)(ssaa-laht)* صالة الضُّيوف

Gulf (the) . . . . *(al-ha-leezh)* الخَليج

H

hairdresser . . . . *(Ha-laa-qa)* حَلاَّقة
half (time) . . . . *(ah-nessf)* النِّصف
handbag . . . . *(yed) (Ha-qee-bet)* حَقيبة يَد
handkerchief . . . . *(min-deel)* مِنديل
hat . . . . *(qoob-ba)* قُبّعة
Have a good trip! . . . *(sy-yeed) (sa-far)* سَفَر سَعيداً!
he, it (♂) . . . . *(hoo-wa)* هُوَ
he has . . . . *(la-hoo)* لَهُ
healthy . . . . *(sseH-He)* صِحّي
Hebrew . . . . *(al-ay-bree-ya)* العِبريّة
hello . . . . *(mar-Ha-baa)* مَرحَبا
here . . . . *(haa)* ها
here (are) / here (is) . . . . *(hoo-naa)* هُنا
home, house . . . . *(bait)* بَيت
horse . . . . *(He-ssaan)* حِصان
hot (food) . . . . *(saak-hin)* ساخِن
hot (weather) . . . . *(Har)* حارّ
hotel . . . . *(foon-dooq)* فُندُق
hour . . . . *(saa-ra)* ساعة
house . . . . *(bait)* بَيت
how . . . . *(kay-fa)* كَيفَ
How are you (♂)? . . . . *(Haa-lik)(kay-fa)* كَيفَ حالُكِ؟
How are you (♂)? . . . *(Haa-lahk)(kay-fa)* كَيفَ حالُكَ؟
how many, how much . . . . *(kem)* كَم
how much (price) . . . . *(be-kem)* بِكَم
hummus . . . . *(hoom-mooss)* حُمُّص
hundred (one) . . . . *(me-ya)* مِئة
hungry . . . . *(zhao-aan)* جوعان

I

I . . . . *(ah-naa)* أنا
I am able to . . . . . *(ahn) (ahs-ta-Tee-roo)* أستَطيعُ أن
I arrive . . . . *(ah-ssee-loo)* أَصِلُ
I buy . . . . *(esh-ta-ree)* أَشتَري
I can . . . . *(ahn) (ahs-ta-Tee-roo)* أستَطيعُ أن
I come . . . . *(ah-zhee-oo)* أَجيءُ
I do . . . . *(ahf-ah-loo)* أَفعَلُ
I drink . . . . *(ahsh-ra-boo)* أَشرَبُ
I drive . . . . *(ah-soo-qoo)* أَسوقُ
I eat . . . . *(aa-koo-loo)* آكُلُ
I enter . . . . *(ahd-hoo-loo)* أَدخُلُ
I go to . . . . *(ee-la)(ahd-ha-boo)* أَذهَبُ إلى
I have . . . . *(lee)* لي
I have . . . . *(rin-dee)* عِندي
I know . . . . *(ah-ree-foo)* أَعرِفُ
I learn . . . . *(ah-ta-rahl-la-moo)* أَتَعَلَّمُ
I leave, depart . . . . *(oo-raa-dee-roo)* أُغادِرُ
I live . . . . *(es-koo-noo)* أَسكُنُ
I need . . . . *(ee-la)(aH-teh-zhoo)* أَحتاجُ إلى
I pack . . . . *(aH-zee-moo)* أَحزِمُ
I pay for . . . . *(theh-men)(ahd-fa-roo)* أَدفَعُ ثَمَن
I phone . . . . *(be)(aht-ta-ssee-loo)* أَتَّصِلُ بِـ
I read . . . . *(ahq-ra-oo)* أَقرَأُ
I repeat . . . . *(oor-ee-do)* أُعيدُ
I reserve . . . . *(aH-zhee-zoo)* أَحجِزُ
I say . . . . *(ah-qoo-loo)* أَقولُ
I see . . . . *(ah-ra)* أرى
I sell . . . . *(ah-be-roo)* أَبيعُ
I send . . . . *(oor-see-loo)* أُرسِلُ
I sleep . . . . *(ah-naa-moo)* أَنامُ
I speak . . . . *(ah-ta-kel-la-moo)* أَتَكَلَّمُ
I stay . . . . *(ahb-qa)* أبقى
I study . . . . *(ah-droo-soo)* أَدرُسُ
I travel . . . . *(oo-seh-fee-roo)* أُسافِرُ
I understand . . . . *(ahf-ha-moo)* أَفهَمُ
I visit . . . . *(ah-zoo-roo)* أَزورُ
I want . . . . *(oo-ree-do)* أُريدُ
I wash . . . . *(ar-see-loo)* أَغسِلُ
I work . . . . *(ah-ma-loo)* أَعمَلُ
I write . . . . *(ahk-too-boo)* أَكتُبُ
ice cream . . *(boo-Da)* بوضة / *(kreem)(ice)* آيس كريم
important . . . . *(moo-him)* مُهِمّ
in . . . . *(fee)* في
in Arabic . . . . *(bil-r-ra-be-ya)* بِالعَرَبيّة
in English . . . . *(bil-een-zhlee-zee-ya)* بِالإنجليزيّة
in front of . . . . *(ah-maa-ma)* أَمامَ
signals a question / no meaning . . . . *(hel)* هل
information office . . . .
. . . . *(al-ir-sheh-daat) (mahk-tahb)* مَكتَب الإرشادات
international . . . . *(raa-la-me)* عالَمي
into . . . . *(ee-la)* إلى / *(daak-he-la)* داخِلَ
Iraq . . . . *(al-ee-raaq)* العِراق
it (♀), she . . . . *(he-ah)* هِيَ
it (♂), he . . . . *(hoo-wa)* هُوَ
it is . . . . *(in-na-haa)* إنَّها
it must be / I must . . . *(ahn) (yeh-zhee-boo)* يَجِبُ أن
it takes . . . . *(yek-hoo-doo)* يَأخُذُ
Italian . . . . *(al-ee-Taa-lee-ya)* الإيطاليّة

J / K

jacket / blazer . . . . *(soot-ra)* سُترة
jam . . . . *(moo-rahb-ba)* مُرَبّى
January . . . . *(ya-ny-yar)* يَناير

jeans . . . . (zheenz) "دجينز"
jewelry . . . . (moo-zhao-ha-ret) مُجَوهَرات
jewelry store . . . .
(al-moo-zhao-ha-ret)(maht-zhar) مَتجَر المُجَوهَرات
Jordan . . . . (al-oor-doon) الأُردُن
juice . . . . (ra-sseer) عَصير
July . . . . (yoo-lee-yoo) يوليو
June . . . . (yoo-nee-yoo) يونيو
just a minute . . . . (laH-Dha) لَحظة
key . . . . (mif-tair) مِفتاح
keys . . . . مَفاتِح
kilo . . . . (kee-loo) كيلو
kitchen . . . . (mahT-bahk) مَطبَخ
knife . . . . (sik-keen) سِكّين
Kuwait . . . . (al-koo-wait) الكُوَيت

L

ladies . . . . (ah-nee-seh') النِّساء
lamb . . . . (ha-roof) خَروف
lamp . . . . (miss-baaH) مِصباح
large, old . . . . (ka-beer) كَبير
laundry . . . . (mahss-beh-na) مَصبَنة
lavatory (the) . . . . (al-meer-HaaD) المِرحاض
leather goods . . . . جِلد
Lebanon . . . . (loob-naan) لُبنان
left . . . . (ya-saar) يَسار
left-luggage office . . . . (al-moo-seh-fee-reen)
(How-weh-izh)(mahk-tahb) مَكتَب حَوائِج المُسافِرين
letter . . . . (ree-saa-la) رِسالة
Libya . . . . (leeb-yaa) ليبيا
light snacks . . . . (ha-feef) (ah-kel) أكل خَفيف
lighting . . . . مُلَمِّع
line (the) . . . . (al-hahT) الخَطّ
linens . . . . أغطِية
lingerie . . . . مَلابِس داخِلِيّة
liter . . . . (lee-tair) لِتر
living room . . . . (L-zhoo-loos) (bait) بَيت الجُلوس
long, tall . . . . (Ta-weel) طَويل
luggage cart / trolley . . . . (ah-ra-ba) عَرَبة
lunch . . . . (al-ree-deh') الغِذاء

M

magazine . . . . (meh-zhel-la) مَجَلّة
mail . . . . (al-ba-reed) البَريد
mailbox . . . (al-ba-reed) (ssoon-dooq) صُندوق البَريد
man . . . . (ra-zhool) رَجُل
many . . . . (ka-thee-ra) كَثيرة
map . . . . (ha-ree-Ta) خَريطة
March . . . . (maars) مارس
market . . . . (sook) سوق
May . . . . (may) ماي
meal . . . . (wehzh-ba) وَجبة
meat . . . . (laHm) لَحم
men's clothing . . . . مَلابِس الرِّجال
menu . . . . (L-ah-kel) (la-ee-Ha) لائِحة الأكل
Middle East (the) . . . .
. . . . (al-ow-sahT) (ah-shark) الشَرق الأوسَط
milk . . . . (Ha-leeb) حَليب
minaret . . . . (ssao-maht) صَومَعة
minus . . . . (ee-la) إلاّ
minute . . . . (da-qee-qa) دَقيقة
mirror . . . . (mir-et) مِرآة
mom . . . . (oom) أُمّ
Monday . . . . (ah-ith-nayn) الإثنَين
money . . . . (foo-loos) فُلوس
months (the) . . . . (ah-shoo-hoor) الشُّهور
more . . . . (ahk-thar) أكثَر
morning (the) . . . . (ah-ssa-baaH) الصَّباح
mornings, in the morning . . . . (ssa-baa-Hahn) صَباحاً
Morocco . . . . (al-ma-greb) المَغرِب
mosque . . . (zhaa-mehh) جامِع / (mahs-zhid) مَسجِد
mother . . . . (weh-lee-da) والِدة
motorcycle . . (neh-ree-ah) (dar-raa-zha) دَرّاجة نارِيّة
Mr . . . . (sy-yeed) سَيِّد
Mrs . . . . (sy-yee-da) سَيِّدة
museum . . . . (maht-Hahf) مَتحَف
musical instruments . . . . آلات موسيقِيّة
Muslim (♀) . . . . (moos-lee-ma) مُسلِمة
Muslim (♂) . . . . (moos-lim) مُسلِم
my name (is) . . . . (ees-me) إسمي

N

name . . . . (eesm) إسم
napkin, handkerchief . . . . (min-deel) مِنديل
new . . . . (zha-deed) جَديد
newspaper . . (ssa-He-fa) صَحيفة / (zha-ree-da) جَريدة
newspaper kiosk . . . .
. . . . (al-zha-raa-id) (ma-Hahl) مَحَلّ الجَرائِد
next to . . . . (be-zhaa-nee-be) بِجانِبِ
nice to meet you . . . . (ta-shar-rahf-naa) تَشَرَّفنا
night (the) . . . . (ah-lail) اللَّيل
nine . . . . (tis'ah) تِسعة
nineteen . . . . ('ah-shar) (tis'ah) تِسعة عَشَر
ninety . . . . (tis'oon) تِسعون

no, not. . . . . (la) لا
no entrance. . (mem-noo')(ah-dook-hool) الدُّخول مَمنوع
no exit. . . . (mem-noo')(al-hoo-roozh) الخُروج مَمنوع
north. . . . . (eh-sheh-mel) الشَّمال
nothing. . . . . (shay')(eye). . . (la) لا . . . أيّ شَيء
November . . . . (noo-wen-br) نُوَنبِر
now. . . . . (al-ann) الآن
number. . . . . (rahq-m) رَقم
numbers (the) . . . . (al-aar-qaam) الأرقام

O

occupied. . . . . (mahsh-rool) مَشغول
October . . . . (ook-too-br) أُكتوبر
of. . . . . (me-na) مِنَ
office. . . . . (mahk-tahb) مَكتَب
old, large . . . . (ka-beer) كَبير
old. . . . . (qa-deem) قَديم
olives. . . . . (zy-toon) زَيتون
Oman . . . . (roo-maan) عُمان
on . . . . (ah-la) عَلى
once more . . . . (ook-ra) (mar-ra) مَرّة أُخرى
one . . . . (waa-Hahd) واحِد
one-way . . . . (ee-yeb) (ow) (da-haab) ذَهاب أو إيّاب
open . . . . (mef-tooH) مَفتوح
or. . . . . (ow) أو
orange (color) . . . . (boor-too-qaa-lee) بُرتُقالي
orange (fruit). . . . . (boor-too-qaal) بُرتُقال
out of . . . . (haa-ree-zha) خارِجَ
over, above. . . . . (fao-qa) فَوقَ
overcoat, raincoat. . . . . (meer-Tahf) مِعطَف

P

package . . . . (Tard) طَرد
page . . . . (ssahf-Ha) صَفحة
paintings . . . . (lao-Het) لَوحات
pajamas . . . . (noum) (meh-leh-bes) مَلابِس نَوم
Palestine . . . . (fa-les-Teen) فَلَسطين
paper, piece of paper . . . . (wa-ra-qa) وَرَقة
parents (the) . . . . (al-weh-lee-dane) الوالِدَين
parking lot, station. . . . . (al-ma-HahT-Ta) المَحَطّة
passport. . . . . (sa-far) (zhao-wez) جَواز سَفَر
pastries, small cakes . . . . (Hel-wa) حَلوى
pen, pencil . . . . (qa-lahm) قَلَم
pepper . . . . (ahs-wed) (fool-fool) فُلفُل أَسوَد
perfume . . . . (reh-Tur) عِطر
pharmacy. . . . . (ah-sy-da-lee-ya) الصَّيدَلِيّة
phone card. . . . .
. . . (teh-lee-foo-nee-ya)(be-Taa-qa) بِطاقة تِليفونيّة

picture . . . . (ssoo-ra) صورة
pillow . . . . (we-seh-da) وِسادة
pink. . . . . (zeh-ree) زَهري
plate . . . . (Ta-bahq) طَبَق
pleasant . . . . (la-Teef) لَطيف
please (♀) . . . . (fahD-lik) (min) مِن فَضلِك
please (♂) . . . . (fahD-lahk) (min) مِن فَضلِك
police station . . . . (ah-shoor-Ta) الشُّرطة
poor. . . . . (fa-qeer) فَقير
porcelain . . . . البِلَّور
post office. . . (al-ba-reed) (mahk-tahb) مَكتَب البَريد
postcard. . . . . (be-Taa-qa) بِطاقة
poultry . . . . (da-zhaazh) دَجاج
printer . . . . (Teh-baa-ra) (aa-lit) آلة طِباعة
public phone / booth. . . . .
. . . . (roo-moo-me) (haa-tif) هاتِف عُمومي
pull . . . . (ear-lahq) اِغلَق
push . . . . (if-taH) اِفتَح
Pyramids (the) . . . . (al-ah-raam) الأهرام

Q / R

Qatar . . . . (qa-Tar) قَطَر
quarter (time) . . . . (ah-roo-boy) الرُّبع
question . . . . (soo-wel) سُؤال
questions . . . . (es-ee-la) أَسئِلة
radios . . . . مَذاييع
rainy. . . . . (moom-Tair) مُمطِر
razor. . . . . (shahf-ra) شَفرة
receipt (the). . . . . (ah-wa-ssil) الوَصل
red. . . . . (aH-mar) أَحمَر
refrigerator. . . . . (tha-laa-zha) ثَلاّجة
relatives (the) . . . . (al-ah-qaa-rib) الأقارِب
religion. . . . . (deen) دين
repeat! (♀). . . . . (ah-ree-dee) أَعيدي
repeat! (♂). . . . . (ah-rid) أَعِد
restaurant . . . . (ma-Tahm) مَطعَم
rich . . . . (ruh-nee) غَنِيّ
right . . . . (ya-meen) يَمين
road / freeway . . . . (Ta-reeq) طَريق
room . . . . (roor-fa) غُرفة
round-trip . . . (ee-yeb) (wa) (da-haab) ذَهاب وَ إيّاب
rugs, carpets . . . . (sahzh-zheh-det) سَجّادات

S

salad. . . . . (sa-la-Ta) سَلَطة
salt . . . . (melH) مِلح
sandals / slippers . . . . (nahl) نَعل
Saturday . . . . (ah-sahbt) السَّبت

Saudi Arabia ... (ah-sau-dee-ya) (al-r-ra-be-ya) العَرَبِيّة السّعودِيّة
school ... (ma-dra-sa) مَدرَسة
sea (the) ... (al-ba-Har) البَحر
seat ... (koor-see) كُرسي
second (number) ... (ah-thaa-nee) الثّاني
second floor ... (ah-thaa-nee) (ah-Taa-bahq) الطّابَق الثّاني
second (time) ... (thaa-nee-ya) ثانِية
September ... (seb-tem-br) سِبتَمبر
service charge (al-hid-ma) (roo-soom) رُسوم الخِدمة
seven ... (sahb'ah) سَبعة
seventeen ... ('ah-shar)(sahb'ah) سَبعة عَشَر
seventy ... (sahb'oon) سَبعون
she, it (♀) ... (he-ah) هِيَ
shirt / T-shirt ... (qa-meess) قَميص
shoes ... (He-dair') حِذاء
shopping center ... (mar-ka-zee)(sook) سوق مَركَزي
short ... (qa-sseer) قَصير
shorts ... (short) شورت
shower ... (rahsh-shair-sha) رَشّاشة
sick ... (ma-reeD) مَريض
sink / washstand ... (meer-sahl) مِغسَل
sister ... (ohkt) أُخت
six ... (seet-teh) سِتّة
six (o'clock) ... (ah-saa-dee-sa) السّادِسة
sixteen ... ('ah-shar)(seet-teh) سِتّة عَشَر
sixty ... (seet-toon) سِتّون
size ... (qee-yes) قِياس
skirt ... (tahn-noo-ra) تَنّورة / (thohb) ثوب
slow ... (ba-Tee') بَطيء
slowly ... (be-booT') بِبُطء
small ... (ssa-greer) صَغير
small street ... (za-na-qa) زَنَقة / (zoo-qaak) زُقاق
snowy ... (mooth-leezh) مُثلِج
soap ... (ssaa-boon) صابون
socks ... (zha-wear-rib) جَوارِب
sofa ... (ka-na-ba) كَنَبة / (ah-ree-ka) أريكة
son ... (ibn) اِبن
soup ... (shoor-ba) شوربة
souvenir ... (teth-kaar) تِذكار
south ... (al-zha-noob) الجَنوب
Spanish ... (al-ees-baa-nee-ya) الإسبانِيّة
spoon ... (mil'a-qa) مِلعَقة
spring (the) ... (ar-ra-be-ya) الرَّبيع
stamp ... (Taa-bahh) طابَع
stationery ... مَحَطّة
steamed ... (moo-bahk-ka-ra) مُبَخّرة
stop ... (qef) قِف
stores (the) ... (al-ma-Ha-laat) المَحَلّات
stove ... (foorn) فُرن
straight ahead ... (tool) (ah-la) عَلى طول
street (big) ... (sheh-re') شارِع
study (the) ... (al-mahk-tahb) المَكتَب
Sudan ... (ah-soo-daan) السّودان
suit ... (beed-la) بِدلة
suitcase ... (Ha-qee-ba) حَقيبة
summer (the) ... (ah-ssife) الصَّيف
Sunday ... (al-ah-Hahd) الأحَد
sunglasses ... (shem-see-ya) (naTh-Thaa-ra) نَظّارة شَمسِيّة
sweater ... (qa-meess) قَميص
swimsuit ... (see-baa-Ha)(leh-bes) لِباس سِباحة
Syria ... (soo-ree-yaa) سوريا

T

table ... (Taa-we-la) طاوِلة
tailor (♀) ... (hy-yaa-Ta) خَيّاطة
tailor (♂) ... (hy-yaaT) خَيّاط
tall, long ... (Ta-weel) طَويل
taxi ... (taak-see) تاكسي
tea ... (shay) شاي
telephone .. (teh-lee-foon) تِليفون / (haa-tif) هاتِف
telephone book ... (ah-teh-lee-foon) (kee-taab) كِتاب التِّليفون
television ... (teh-lee-fiz-own) تِليفِزيون
ten (♀) ... ('ah-sha-ra) عَشَرة
ten (♂) ... ('ah-shar) عَشَر
tennis shoes ... (ree-yaa-Da) (He-dair') حِذاء رِياضة
tent ... (hy-ma) خَيمة
thank you ... (shook-rahn) شُكراً
thank you very much ... (zha-zee-lahn) (shook-rahn) شُكراً جَزيلاً
there is / there are ... (hoo-na-ka) هُناكَ
these, this (♀) ... (heh-da-he) هَذِهِ
they ... (hoom) هُم
things ... (eh-shee') أشياء
third (number) ... (ah-thaa-leeth) الثّالِث
third (time) ... (ah-thoo-looth) الثُّلُث
thirteen ... ('ah-shar) (tha-laa-tha) ثَلاثة عَشَر
thirty ... (tha-laa-thoon) ثَلاثون
this (♀) ... (heh-da-he) هَذِهِ
this (♂) ... (heh-daa) هَذا
this fits ... (qee-yeh-sook)(heh-daa) هَذا قِياسُك

thousand (one) *(alf)* أَلف
three *(tha-laa-tha)* ثَلاثة
three hundred *(tha-laa-thoo-me-ya)* ثَلاثُمِئة
Thursday *(al-ha-mees)* الخَميس
ticket *(teth-kee-ra)* تَذكِرة
tie *(rahb-Ta)* رَبطة
timetable (the) *(ah-tao-qeet)* التَّوقيت
to *(ee-la)* إلى
to enter *(dahk-ha-la)* دَخَلَ
to exit *(ha-ra-zha)* خَرَجَ
tobacco سَجائِر
today, the day *(al-yohm)* اليَوم
toilet *(Hahm-maam)* حَمّام
token *(noo-qood)(qeh-Tart)* قِطعة نُقود
tomatoes *(Ta-maa-Tem)* طَماطِم
tomorrow *(reh-dahn)* غَداً
tools مُعِدّات
toothbrush *(foor-shet)* فُرشاة
toothpaste *(al-es-naan) (ma-zhoon)* مَعجون الأَسنان
tourist (♀) *(saa-ee-Ha)* سائِحة
tourist (♂) *(saa-eH)* سائِح
towels *(foo-ahT)* فُوَط
train *(qee-Taar)* قِطار
train station *(al-qee-Taar) (ma-HahT-Taht)* مَحَطّة القِطار
travel, trip *(sa-far)* سَفَر
travel agency *(sa-far) (mahk-tahb)* مَكتَب سَفَر
traveler *(moo-seh-fer)* مُسافِر
traveler's checks *(sa-far) (shee-ket)* شيكات سَفَر
trousers / jeans / shorts *(seer-wel)* سِروال
Tuesday *(ah-thoo-la-thaa')* الثُّلاثاء
Tunisia *(too-noos)* تونُس
twelve *('ah-shar) (ith-naa)* اِثنا عَشَر
twenty *(aysh-roon)* عِشرون / *(aysh-reen)* عِشرين
two *(ith-nayn)* اِثنَين

U / V

U.S.A. (the) *(ahm-ree-kaa)* أَمريكا
umbrella *(me-Thahl-la)* مِظَلّة
uncle *(ahm)* عَمّ
under *(taH-ta)* تَحتَ
underclothing *(daak-he-lee-ya) (meh-leh-bes)* مَلابِس داخِلِيّة
university *(zhaa-me-ah)* جامِعة
upstairs (the) *(al-rool-we)(ah-Taa-bahq)* الطّابَق العُلوي
vegetables *(hoo-Daar)* خُضار
very *(zhid-dahn)* جِدّاً
village *(qar-ya)* قَرية

W

waiter (oh)! *(sy-yed) (yaa)* يا سَيِّد
waitress (oh)! *(sy-yeh-da) (yaa)* يا سَيِّدة
wallet *(mehH-fa-Tha)* مِحفَظة
wastepaper basket *(sahl-la)* سَلّة
water *(maa')* ماء
we *(naH-noo)* نَحنُ
we have *(rin-da-naa)* عِندَنا
we want *(noo-ree-do)* نُريدُ
weather (the) *(al-zhao)* الجَوّ
Wednesday *(al-ar-ba-aa')* الأَربِعاء
week (the) *(al-oos-boo')* الأُسبوع
west *(al-greb)* الغَرب
what *(may-daa)* ماذا
what *(maa)* ما
What is your name? *(ees-mook)(maa)* ما إسمُك؟
What time is it? *(ah-saa-ra) (kem)* كَم السّاعة؟
when *(rin-da-maa)* عِندَما
when (in questions) *(meh-ta)* مَتى
where *(eye-na)* أَينَ
which *(eye-yoo)* أَيُّ
white *(ah-be-yahD)* أَبيَض
who *(men)* مَن
why *(lee-may-daa)* لِماذا
wind *(ree-yaaH)* رياح
window *(neh-fee-da)* نافِذة
winter (the) *(ah-shee-taa')* الشِّتاء
with *(mar)* مَعَ
without *(be-doon)* بِدون
women's clothing مَلابِس النِّساء
word *(ka-lee-ma)* كَلِمة
write out! (♂) *(eek-toob)* اُكتُب

Y

year (the) *(ah-seh-na)* السَّنة
yellow *(ahss-far)* أَصفَر
Yemen *(al-yeh-men)* اليَمَن
yes *(na-ahm)* نَعَم
yesterday *(ahms)* أَمس
you (♀) *(n-ta)* أَنتَ
you (♂) *(n-tee)* أَنتِ
you all *(ahn-toom)* أَنتُم
you're welcome *(ahf-wahn)* عَفواً
young *(ssa-greer)* صَغير
zero *(sif-fur)* صِفر

٢٥ / 25 Beverage and Menu Guides

This Beverage Guide is intended to explain the variety of beverages available to you while traveling الخَليج (al-ha-leezh) the Gulf أو شَمال اِفريقيا (sheh-mel) (ef-ree-qee-yaa) North Africa أو في الشّرق الأوسَط (fee) (ah-shark) (al-ow-saht) the Middle East. It is by no means complete. Some of the experimenting has been left up to you, but this should get you started.

مَشروبات ساخِنة (mahsh-roo-baat) (saak-hih-na) hot beverages

coffee .... قَهوة
coffee with cream .... قَهوة مَعَ كريم
black coffee .... قَهوة سَوداء
Turkish coffee .... قَهوة تُركِيّة
espresso .... قَهوة مُعَصَّرة

tea .... شاي
tea with milk .... شاي مَعَ حَليب
tea with lemon .... شاي مَعَ لَيمون
mint tea .... شاي بِالنَّعناع
spiced tea .... شاي مُعَطَّر
hot chocolate .... شوكولاتة ساخِنة

tisane .... اللّويزة
pomegranate syrup .... شَراب الرُّمّان
rosewater syrup .... شَراب الوَرد
wine .... نبيذ
beer .... بيرّا
arak .... عَرق
ice cubes .... مُكَعَّبات
bottle .... آنِية

مَشروبات بارِدة (mahsh-roo-baat) (bear-ee-da) cold beverages

mineral water .... ماء طَبيعي
soda water .... ماء غازِي
lemonade .... عَصير لَيمون
milk .... حَليب

عَصير فَواكِه (ra-sseer) (fa-waa-kih) juice fruit

You can buy a glass of freshly-squeezed juice from street vendors. It's delicious!

orange juice .... عَصير بُرتُقال
apple juice .... عَصير تُفّاح
prune juice .... عَصير بَرقوق
apricot juice .... عَصير مِشمِش
peach juice .... عَصير خوخ
tomato juice .... عَصير طَماطِم

The coffee house is an institution! Sit outside at one of the sidewalk cafes and sample one of the many varieties of coffee.

CUT ALONG DOTTED LINE, FOLD AND TAKE WITH YOU

خُضار
vegetables

zucchini	كوسة
carrots	جَزَر
potatoes	بَطاطِس
green peas	بازِلاّء
peppers	فُلفُل
cucumber	خِيار
tomatoes	طَماطِم
eggplant	باذِنجان
green beans	فاصوليا خَضراء
onions	بَصَل
parsley	بَقدونِس
garlic	ثوم

Specialties

hummus	حُمُّص
tehina	طَحينة
stuffed vine leaves	وَرَق عِنَب مَحشُوّة
couscous	كوسكوس
falafel	فَلافِل
bastilla	بَسطيلة
tagine	طَجين
mixed pistachios with peanuts, butter and sugar	خَليط مِن المُكَسَّرات والزُّبدة والسُّكَّر
crepes	فَطائِر
baba ganoush	بابا غَنّوش
dates stuffed with nuts, served with cold milk	تَمَر مَحشو بِالمُكَسَّرات، يُقَدَّمُ مَعَ حَليب بارِد

FOLD HERE

لُحوم بَيضاء
poultry

chicken	دَجاج
quail	سُماني
turkey	الدّيك الرّومي
goose	وَزّة
pigeon	حَمام
chicken with lemon and olives	دَجاج بِاللَّيمون وَ الزَّيتون

حَلَويّات
desserts

braewat	بريوات
ice-cream	آيس كريم / بوظة
fekkas	فَقّاص
sweets	حَلَويّات
fruit salad	سَلَطة فَواكِه
fruit cake	فَطيرة فَواكِه
baklava	بَقلاوة

(Ty-yee-ba) (wehzh-ba)

وَجبة طَيّبة

enjoy your meal

FOLD HERE

لائحة الأكل
the menu

عامّ
general

jam	مُرَبّى
butter	زُبدة
honey	عَسَل
salt	مِلح
pepper	فُلفُل أَسوَد
vinegar	خَلّ
oil	زَيت
ketchup	كيتشاب
cheese	جُبن
olives	زَيتون
olive oil	زَيت الزَّيتون
almonds	اللّوز
cake	فَطيرة
fresh nuts	مُكَسَّرات طَرِيّة
dried nuts	مُكَسَّرات مُجَفَّفة
sandwich	شَطيرة / ساندويتش
pancakes	فَطائِر
raisins	عِنَب
french fries	بَطاطِس مَقلِيّة
popcorn	فُشار
rice	رُزّ
sugar	سُكَّر
mint	نَعناع
chamomile	قُرفة
steamed	مُبَخَّر

مُقَبِّلات
appetizers

vegetables and spices	خُضار وتَوابِل
olives with vegetables and spices	زَيتون مَعَ خُضار وتَوابِل
stuffed tomatoes	طَماطِم مَحشُوّة
minced meat wrapped in pastry	كُفتة مَحشُوّة
sardines	سَمَك السَّردين

شوربة
soup

clear broth	حِساء
harara	حَريرة
chicken soup	شوربة بِالدَّجاج
lentil soup	شوربة بِالعَدَس
mushroom soup	شوربة بِالفِطرِيّات
onion soup	شوربة بِالبَصَل
pea soup	شوربة بِالبازِلاّء
tomato soup	شوربة بِالطَّماطِم
vegetable soup	شوربة بِالخُضار

خُبز
bread

white bread	خُبز أبيَض
whole wheat bread	خُبز القَمح
black bread	خُبز أسوَد
baguette	خَبز فَرَنسي
rolls	خُبز مُدَوَّر
special bread	خُبز خاصّ
loaf	مُستَطيل
round	مُدَوَّر
flat	مُلَوَّح
pita (flat)	خُبز مُلَوَّح

FOLD HERE

سَمَك
fish

calamari	كَلَماري
salmon	سالمون
shrimp	شريم / جَمبَري
sole	صول
tuna	تونة
white fish	سَمَك أبيض

بَيض
eggs

hard-boiled egg	بَيض مَصلوق
fried egg	بَيض مَقلي
omelette with tomatoes and onions	بَيض مَقلي بِالطَّماطِم وَ البَصَل
scrambled eggs	بَيض مَخلوط

اللَّحم
meat

lamb	لَحم الخَروف
lamb shoulder	كَتِف الخَروف
lamb leg	رِجل الخَروف
lamb ribs	ضُلوع الخَروف
steak	لَحم بَقَر مُصَفَّف
veal	لَحم رَأس الخَروف
kebab	كَباب
shawarmah	شَوارمة
goulash	لَحم المَعِز
meatballs	كُفتة
mechoui (BBQ)	مِشوي

FOLD HERE

سَلَطة
salad

carrot salad	سَلَطة جَزَر
cucumber salad	سَلَطة خِيار
eggplant salad	سَلَطة باذِنجان
green salad	سَلَطة خَضراء
potato salad	سَلَطة بَطاطِس
tomato salad	سَلَطة طَماطِم
zucchini salad	سَلَطة كوسة

فَواكِه
fruit

apples	تُفّاح
apricots	مِشمِش
bananas	مَوز / بَنان
cantaloupe	بَطّيخ أصفَر
cherries	كَرَز
dates	تَمَر
figs	تين
grapefruit	بُرتُقال أحمَر
grapes	عِنَب
lemons	لَيمون
mandarin oranges	يوسُفي
nuts	مُكَسَّرات
oranges	بُرتُقال
peaches	خوخ
pears	إجّاص
plums	بَرقوق
pomegranates	رُمّان
prunes	بَرقوق جافّ
strawberries	فَراولة
watermelon	بَطّيخ أحمَر

(ah-naa) أَنــا	*(hoo-wa)* هُــوَ
(he-ah) هِــيَ	*(naH-noo)* نَــحنُ
(n-tee) أَنــتِ	*(hoom)* هُــم
(n-ta) أَنــتَ	*(esh-ta-ree)* أَشــتَري
(ah-ta-rahl-la-moo) أَتَــعَلَّمُ	*(oor-ee-do)* أُعيــدُ
(ahf-ha-moo) أَفــهَمُ	*(ah-ta-kel-la-moo)* أَتَــكَلَّمُ

he

I

we

she

they

you (female symbol)

I buy

you (male symbol)

I repeat

I learn

I speak

I understand

(es-koo-noo) أَسكُنُ	*(ah-ssee-loo)* أَصِلُ
(ah-ra) أَرى	*(ah-qoo-loo)* أَقولُ
(ee-la) *(ahd-ha-boo)* أَذهَبُ إلى	*(ahb-qa)* أَبقى
(aa-koo-loo) آكُلُ	*(ahsh-ra-boo)* أَشرَبُ
(oo-ree-do) أُريدُ	*(ee-la)* *(aH-teh-zhoo)* أَحتاجُ إلى
(ees-me) إسمي . . .	*(lee)* لي

I arrive	I live
I say	I see
I stay	I go to
I drink	I eat
I need	I want
I have . . .	my name is . . .

(oor-see-loo)

أُرسِلُ

(ah-be-roo)

أَبيعُ

(be) (aht-ta-ssee-loo)

أَتَّصِلُ بِـ ...

(ah-naa-moo)

أَنامُ

(ahk-too-boo)

أَكتُبُ

(ah-Tee-nee)

أَعطيني

(theh-men) (ahd-fa-roo)

أَدفَعُ ثَمَن ...

(ah-zhee-oo)

أَجيءُ

(ah-soo-qoo)

أَسوقُ

(ah-ree-foo)

أَعرِفُ

(oo-seh-fee-roo)

أُسافِرُ

(ahq-ra-oo)

أَقرَأُ

I send

I sell

I phone

I sleep

I write

give me . . .

I pay for . . .

I come

I drive

I know

I travel

I read

(ahn) *(ahs-ta-Tee-roo)* أَستَطيعُ أَن	*(oo-raa-dee-roo)* أُغادِرُ
(ahd-hoo-loo) أَدخُلُ	*(hoo-naa-ka)* هُناكَ
(aH-zee-moo) أَحزِمُ	*(rin-dee)* عِندي
(ahf-wahn) عَفواً	*(aH-zhee-zoo)* أَحجِزُ
(ah-droo-soo) أَدرُسُ	*(ar-see-loo)* أَغسِلُ
(ahn) *(yeh-zhee-boo)* يَجِبُ أَن	*(yek-hoo-Doo)* يَأخُذُ

I leave

I can

there is / there are

I enter

I have

I pack

I reserve

you're welcome

I wash

I study

it takes

it must be (that) . . .

(Haa-lahk) (kay-fa)

كَيفَ حالُكَ؟

(Haa-lik) (kay-fa)

كَيفَ حالُكِ؟

(mar-Ha-baa)

مَرحَبا

(fahD-lahk) (min)

مِن فَضلك

(fahD-lik) (min)

مِن فَضلِك

(eh-sif)

اَسِف

(eh-sih-fa)

اَسِفة

(ah-zoo-roo)

أَزورُ

(al-yohm)

اليَوم

(reh-dahn)

غَداً

(ahms)

أَمس

(be-kem)

بِكَم؟

(rin-da-ka) (hel)

هَل عِندَكَ . . . ؟

(rin-da-kee) (hel)

هَل عِندَكِ . . . ؟

(mef-tooH) (moog-lahq)

مُغلَق - مَفتوح

(ka-beer) (ssa-greer)

صَغير - كَبير

hello

How are you?

excuse me / I'm sorry

please

today

I visit

yesterday

tomorrow

Do you have . . .?

How much does this cost?

big/old - small/young

open - closed

(Dy-eef) (zhy-yed)

ضَعيف – جَيّد

(ma-reeD) (sseH-He)

مَريض – صِحّي

(Ta-weel) (qa-sseer)

طَويل – قَصير

(bear-id) (Har)

بارِد – حارّ

(taH-ta) (fao-qa)

تَحتَ – فَوقَ

(ahf-ah-loo)

أَفعَلُ

(ba-Tee') (sa-reer)

بَطيء – سَريع

(ya-meen) (ya-saar)

يَمين – يَسار

(ra-keess) (tha-meen)

رَخيص – ثَمين

(ah-Taa-bahq) (al-rool-we)

الطّابَق العُلوي –

(ah-Taa-bahq) (ah-soo-flee)

الطّابَق السُّفلي

(qa-lee-lahn) (ka-thee-rahn)

قَليلاً – كَثيراً

(fa-qeer) (ruh-nee)

فَقير – غَنِيّ

good - bad

healthy - sick

short - long / tall

hot - cold

over - under

I do

slow - fast

left - right

expensive - inexpensive

upstairs - downstairs

a lot - a little

rich - poor

Now that you've finished...

You've done it!

You've completed all the Steps, stuck your labels, flashed your cards and cut out your menu guide. Do you realize how far you've come and how much you've learned?

You can now confidently

- ask questions,
- understand directions,
- make reservations,
- order food and
- shop anywhere.

And you can do it all in a foreign language! You can now go anywhere — from a large cosmopolitan restaurant to a small, out-of-the-way village where no one speaks English. Your experiences will be much more enjoyable and worry-free now that you speak the language.

Yes, learning a foreign language can be fun.

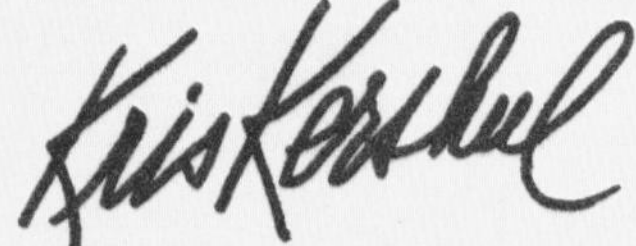

Kristine Kershul

Send us this order form with your check, money order or credit card details. If paying by credit card, you may fax your order to (206) 284-3660 or call us toll-free at (800) 488-5068. All prices are in US dollars and are subject to change without notice.

* What about shipping costs?

STANDARD DELIVERY per address

If your items total	please add
up to $ 20.00	$5.00
$20.01 - $ 40.00	$6.00
$40.01 - $ 60.00	$7.00
$60.01 - $ 80.00	$8.00
$80.01 - $ 100.00	$9.00

If over $100, please call for charges.

For shipping outside the U.S., please call, fax or e-mail us at info@bbks.com for the best-possible shipping rates.

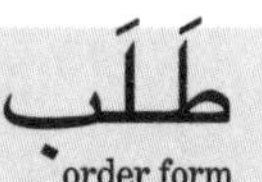

order form

10 minutes a day® Series	QTY.	PRICE	TOTAL
ARABIC *in 10 minutes a day®*		$19.95	
CHINESE *in 10 minutes a day®*		$19.95	
FRENCH *in 10 minutes a day®*		$19.95	
GERMAN *in 10 minutes a day®*		$19.95	
HEBREW *in 10 minutes a day®*		$19.95	
INGLÉS *en 10 minutos al día®*		$19.95	
ITALIAN *in 10 minutes a day®*		$19.95	
JAPANESE *in 10 minutes a day®*		$19.95	
NORWEGIAN *in 10 minutes a day®*		$19.95	
PORTUGUESE *in 10 minutes a day®*		$18.95	
RUSSIAN *in 10 minutes a day®*		$19.95	
SPANISH *in 10 minutes a day®*		$18.95	
***10 minutes a day®* AUDIO**	**QTY.**	**PRICE**	**TOTAL**
FRENCH *in 10 minutes a day®* AUDIO		$59.95	
FRENCH AUDIO CDs only *(no book)*		$42.95	
ITALIAN *in 10 minutes a day®* AUDIO		$59.95	
ITALIAN AUDIO CDs only *(no book)*		$42.95	
SPANISH *in 10 minutes a day®* AUDIO		$59.95	
SPANISH AUDIO CDs only *(no book)*		$42.95	
***Language Map®* Series**	**QTY.**	**PRICE**	**TOTAL**
ARABIC *a language map®*		$7.95	
CHINESE *a language map®*		$7.95	
FRENCH *a language map®*		$7.95	
GERMAN *a language map®*		$7.95	
GREEK *a language map®*		$7.95	
HAWAIIAN *a language map®*		$7.95	
HEBREW *a language map®*		$7.95	
INGLÉS *un mapa del lenguaje®*		$7.95	
ITALIAN *a language map®*		$7.95	
JAPANESE *a language map®*		$7.95	
NORWEGIAN *a language map®*		$7.95	
POLISH *a language map®*		$7.95	
PORTUGUESE *a language map®*		$7.95	
RUSSIAN *a language map®*		$7.95	
SPANISH *a language map®*		$7.95	
VIETNAMESE *a language map®*		$7.95	

Item Total	
* Shipping	+
Total	
† Sales Tax	+
ORDER TOTAL	

† For delivery to individuals in Washington State, you must add 8.8% sales tax on the item total and the shipping costs combined. If your order is being delivered outside Washington State, you do not need to add sales tax.

Name ____________________

Address ____________________

____

City ____________ State _____ Zip __________

Day Phone (_______)____________________

❑ My check or money order for $____________ is enclosed.
Please make checks and money orders payable to Bilingual Books, Inc.

❑ Bill my credit card ❑ VISA ❑ MC ❑ AMEX

No. ____________________ Exp. date ___/___

Signature ____________________

Bilingual Books, Inc. • 1719 West Nickerson Street
Seattle, WA 98119 USA

10 minutes a day® AUDIO

by Kristine K. Kershul

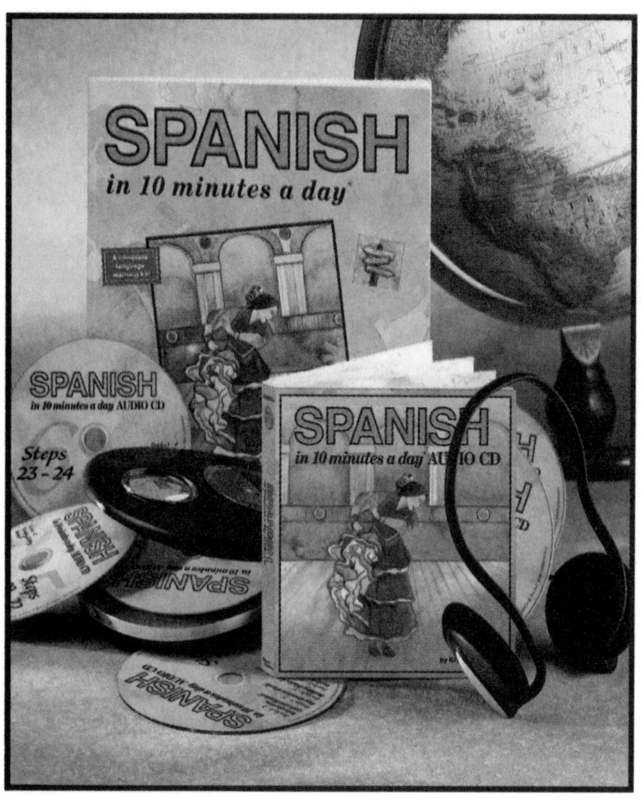

The ***10 minutes a day®*** **AUDIO** is based on the immensely successful ***10 minutes a day®*** Series. Millions of people around the world have used the ***10 minutes a day®*** Series for over two decades.

- Eight hours of personal instruction on six CDs.
- Use the CDs in combination with the companion book, and maximize your progress as you see AND hear the language.
- Listen to native speakers and practice right along with them.
- Suitable for the classroom, the homeschooler, as well as business and leisure travelers.
- The CDs in the ***10 minutes a day®*** **AUDIO** may also be purchased separately from the ***10 minutes a day®*** books.

Language Map® Series

by Kristine K. Kershul

These handy ***Language Maps®*** provide the essential words and phrases to cover the basics for any trip.

- Over 1,000 essential words and phrases divided into convenient categories.
- Laminated , folding design allows for quicker reference while resisting spills, tearing, and damage from frequent use.
- Durable, to hold up to being sat on, dropped, and stuffed into backpacks, pockets, and purses.
- An absolute must for anyone traveling abroad or studying at home.

For a list of available languages and ordering information, please see the order form on the previous page.

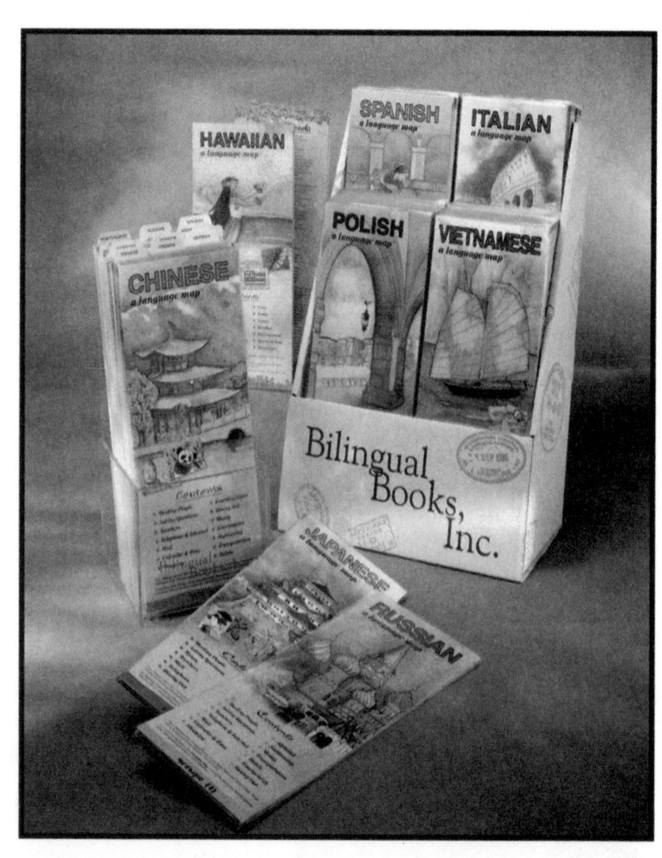